What Is God?

for Margaret Bullitt

Jim Sheridan

What Is God?

Can Religion Be Modeled?

Thomas B. Sheridan

Washington, DC

Copyright © 2014 by Thomas B. Sheridan
New Academia Publishing 2014

All rights reserved. No part of this book may be reproduced or transmitted in any form or by any means, electronic or mechanical, including photocopying, recording, or by any information storage and retrieval system.

Printed in the United States of America

Library of Congress Control Number: 2014944861
ISBN 978-0-9904471-2-2 paperback (alk. paper)

New Academia Publishing
PO Box 27420, Washington, DC 20038-7420
info@newacademia.com - www.newacademia.com

All illustrations and tables are in the public domain, except for those otherwise credited.

CONTENTS

PREFACE   xi
ACKNOWLEDGMENTS   xiii

INTRODUCTION   1
   Purpose of the book
   For whom is the book intended and what is included
   Modeling human belief (in God or anything)
   Objective and subjective models
   Why model? Why make the effort?
   Philosophical perspective

1. KNOWLEDGE, SCIENCE AND MODELING   15
Acquiring knowledge   15
   What is the scientific method?
   Observations on the scientific method
   Logical reasoning
   Private (subjective) and public (objective) knowledge
   Doubt and its relation to doing science
   Using and avoiding evidence
   Metaphysics and its relation to science
   Objectivity, advocacy and bias
   Analogy and metaphor

What is a model? 27
Definition of "model"
A new taxonomy of model attributes
a. Applicability to observables
b. Dimensionality
c. Metricity
d. Robustness
e. Social penetration
f. Conciseness
Examples of models in terms of the attributes
Relevance of the taxonomy to making models useful
Knowledge and social choice
Important distinctions in modeling 44
Simple and complex models
Descriptive and prescriptive (normative) models
Static and dynamic models
Deterministic and probabilistic models
Models that use fuzzy logic

2. SOME PERSPECTIVES ON BELIEVING 47
Variety of belief models 47
Trust 51
Reasons we trust
Trust and faith
Virtual reality 52
What is VR?
Virtual reality technology
Behavior research issues in VR
Philosophical questions: What is presence? What is reality?
Jaynes bicameral theory about hearing gods 60
The basic idea
Poetry, schizophrenia and science

Estimation theory: a model of how belief evolves — 64
The basic idea
Stepping through the model

3. BELIEFS ABOUT GOD — 71
Why is the concept of God important? — 71
Difficulties of discourse about God — 72
History of belief and skepticism about God — 74
Earliest ideas about gods
The first skeptics
Development of different religious traditions
Skepticism in modern times

Traditional "proofs" of God — 85
Anselm's thesis
The cosmological argument (first cause)
Argument from design (teleology)
Argument from morality
Argument from mystical experience
Pascal's wager
So many people believe
It is not possible to disprove the existence of God

More recent theistic arguments — 90
The mind-body dilemma
Another embellishment of the Anselm argument
There is something rather than nothing
No evidence is necessary
Belief in God is simpler than what is required for disbelief
Evolution is no substitute for God's creation
Perfection argument (the second law of thermodynamics)
No cause is necessary; God exists in timeless eternity

    Tillich's ground of being
    The fine-tuning of cosmological parameters (anthropic principle)
    Near-death experiences

The new atheism   96
    Does evolution point to God?
    Is God needed as a basis for morality?
    God of the gaps
    Breaking the spell
    Physicist perspectives

The big bang, the multiverse, and a new discontinuity in our perceived importance   102
    The big bang
    The multiverse
    A fifth discontinuity?

Is science just another religion?   105
Do the magisteria overlap?   106

4. A GOD FOR TOMORROW   109
Current status of belief   109
Demographics and trends   111
Is creationism dead?   113
Is there room for the agnostic? (Or the gnostic?)   114
Metaphor, myth and religious language   116
    Religion as metaphor
    Religion as myth
    The bible as literal truth
    Yes, Virginia, there is a Santa Claus

Spirituality	121
Reverence	123
Opposing perspectives that seem to converge	125

    Karen Armstrong says we need God to grasp the wonder of our existence
    Richard Dawkins argues that evolution leaves God with nothing to do
    Convergence?

Can the nature of God be modeled?	134

    Testing God against the model attributes
    What is there to model about God?

Can religious practice be modeled?	139

    Using science to study religion the same as we would study anything else
    Modeling the acquisition of different kinds of belief
    Prayer: does it work?
    Why do people affiliate with only one religious tribe?
    Does religious practice enhance health?
    Do religious institutions do more good than harm?
    Do church-goers say what they really believe?
    Religious practices are culture, and changing culture is not easy for the brain

Redefining God	149

    Creating God in our own image?
    A liberal Jewish "plausible God"
    A better definition of God (revisiting God-of-the-gaps)

Evolve the church into a secular community organization	152
5. CONCLUSIONS	155

APPENDIX: EXAMPLES OF OBJECTIVE MODELS THAT CHARACTERIZE BELIEF — 159

Examples of models that use different forms of language — 160

- Verbal models
- Graphs, maps and schematic diagrams
- Logic diagrams
- Fuzzy logic
- Statistical inference from evidence

Examples of models of human cognition — 176

- A qualitative model of levels of cognition and action
- Correlational model of human perception
- Human judgment of utility (relative worth)
- Decisions under conditions of certainty
- Decisions under uncertainty
- Information communication
- Information value
- Competitive decisions: game models
- Signal detection
- Feedback control

REFERENCES AND NOTES — 207
BIBLIOGRAPHY — 215
INDEX — 219

PREFACE

Why another book on God? What I am offering is what I think is a different approach, one based on *modeling*. Modeling is effort to characterize a thing or process in language that is specific, unambiguous, denotative and can be understood by interested parties. Modeling is widely employed in science, engineering, medicine, business and government.

Our linguistic difficulty in coping with the idea of God is hardly novel. But abandoning the effort to examine God and religion because of insufficient language seems inexcusable, much as it is inexcusable to abandon effort to cope with the many other "imponderables" of life and love and being for which written language falls short.

Some scientists and some philosophers claim that denotative modeling is a *sine qua non* for asserting what is real, at least real in the sense that a thing or process can be understood publicly, i.e., not confined the private subjective thoughts of one person, and communication is limited to metaphor such that interpretation of meaning is arbitrary.

The question of God has bothered me for many years, both because the idea is so incompatible with science, but also because throughout history God has been the justification for killing and mayhem on a grand scale, and that same tradition is alive and well today. What has also frustrated me is that people, especially those who make a profession of religion, refer to God as though they know what God is, and imply that others know what is meant by the term.

I hope it will be shown to the reader's satisfaction that the abstract concept of God is not amenable to modeling but the human practice of religion is.

Modeling is what I have done in the context of human performance and human-machine interaction for my entire academic career. As with religion, modeling human-machine interaction involves people's beliefs and faith in computers and technical entities that are non-human, though nowadays computers may be called "intelligent", but often are not well understood by the people using them. Traditionally those same properties are attributed to God. There is an interesting parallel relationship between God and "intelligent" machines.

I have not been unchurched. I was raised in a Midwestern Presbyterian church. Since marriage my wife and I have been active in a New England Congregational church, where she has been a deacon and Sunday school teacher. I have also been a deacon as well as serving two stints as moderator, or lay leader of the congregation, and I have lectured to meetings of the World Council of Churches. For several years I convened a monthly discussion group on the subject of God and religious belief, but then we discontinued that group because it seemed that it was becoming uncomfortable for participants to probe their religious beliefs too deeply.

Following an introduction the first chapter of the book reviews the acceptable criteria for denotative modeling as contrasted to expression of an idea in connotative language such as metaphor. The second chapter includes some rather different perspectives on believing anything, but surely perspectives pertinent to the God question. A third chapter reviews what different well-known individuals throughout history have had to say about God: primarily philosophers and theologians, including all sides of the issue. A fourth chapter deals with belief demographics, answers to the question of what can be modeled, and proposes a redefinition of God. Finally, the fifth chapter is a summary and conclusion.

ACKNOWLEDGEMENTS

Several colleagues have contributed to this work in very significant ways. My huge gratitude starts with Neville Moray, a thoughtful critic and longtime friend who read several drafts and provided wise counsel in getting this oddball effort off the ground and challenging many of my assertions along the way. Alex Kirlik, Catherine Alexander, Jack Hunter, Ray Nickerson, Shelly Baron, David Gil, Michael Martin, Luis Fernandez, Victor Stenger and E.O. Wilson are also thanked for reading drafts and providing valuable comments. To Russ Ferrell, my coauthor in a 1974 book, the copyright to which we jointly own, I owe thanks for many of the model explanations in the Appendix here that closely parallel those in that earlier book. And of course my great love and appreciation to Rachel, who tolerated many hours of my head-in-the-computer.

INTRODUCTION

Purpose of the book

Juxtaposing the two terms *God* and *modeling* is jarring for most people. The two words seem not to fit together. As the term model is ordinarily used, it has to do with science, engineering, economics, business, and government. In those activities one strives to describe and explain things and relationships *objectively* in *denotative* language that is clear and concise, that refers to observable evidence, that will be widely accepted and understood, and will be useful. Ideally the logic of a model enables quantification and thus makes it easier to verify predictions.

With respect to *God* the book purposely avoids discussion of religious traditions, and deals with God only as an abstract concept and an entity usually believed to be a supernatural being. In any religious tradition God is an entity that has to do with subjective experience: feelings, faith and worship. The nature of God is normally expressed in *connotative* language such as metaphor, myth, poetry and music. These expressions might be called models, but surely they are of a different kind of model from the way this book uses the term. Connotation allows for personal interpretation as to meaning, which is its strength in a human society. Denotation seeks to be precise and unambiguous in meaning, which is its purpose. I purposely make a distinction, though one can cite examples that lie between the poles.

God language seems to lie as far from the language of denotative models in science, engineering, economics, business, and government as one can get. And surely metaphor, myth, poetry, music and other forms of connotative expression are all very important for enriching our lives. Life would be dull without them.

So does it make any sense at all to try connecting denotative modeling to the subject of God and religion? When it comes to human belief in an entity as something that is real I would contend that it does make sense to examine the challenge. Surely one can try to model the *behavior of people* who profess belief: the activities of worship, prayer, and participation in church activities by giving time, money and creative energies. But it is a different challenge to model God *per se*, to describe and explain what God *is*.

The book will deal with both challenges. Note that I am limiting the discussion to modeling God *per se* and to people's belief in God, so I am avoiding the facts of history and beliefs concerning human prophets such as Jesus and Muhammad.

My approach to these two challenges asks what can be accomplished with respect to God through denotative modeling, which can also be called *scientific modeling*. Scientific modeling means formulating a specific representation of something based on observable evidence and reason. The more of perceived reality that can be lumped together in this formulation the better. Further, It is better if the formulation involves some metric, if the resulting model is robust in its application, if it can find acceptance by many people, and if it is stated concisely to make it unambiguous. The book goes into detail on these modeling attributes.

This approach is clearly in the vein of positivist philosophy. However I do not go so far as to deny acquisition of any knowledge through introspection and intuition, or from metaphorical written or verbal communication (they surely are models of a sort). The important distinction is that metaphorical modeling *intends* to leave interpretation of meaning to the observer, whereas scientific modeling does not.

I believe the modeling approach is different from most writings on the subject of God. On the other hand the emphasis on modeling is consistent with a perspective on reality common in modern physics called *model based realism*. This is emphasized by physicist Stephen Hawking in his recent book *The Grand Design*[1]. This perspective assumes that the only way we know reality is through our models. It says there is no other or any independent test of reality.

Sometimes two or more models are equally predictive of observations, which makes for ambiguity in knowing reality. But that's what we are stuck with.

Reality of course is a subject that has been debated by philosophers through the ages, and there is no intent here to settle the matter of what is "real". Some dictionaries define reality as what actually exists, whether observable or not, as contrasted to what is thought (imagined, felt, dreamed). A different perspective is that we know our world only though our perceptions, which are thoughts. What is clear is that the reality of perceptions and thoughts, though we may try to share them with others, necessarily remain private to a large extent and cannot be observed directly. In contrast, public reality is what is available to be observed by anyone wishing to make the effort. A full discussion of what is real is a matter of semantics and philosophy that cannot be settled here. A later section of the book discusses the question of whether mental function can be modeled. For now we pose as a gold standard of reality what is amenable to denotative or scientific modeling.

Model dependent reality is not a new idea. In 1709 Bishop George Berkeley came close when he asserted that things cannot even exist without being perceived by people.[2] I would prefer to assume that there is some reality "out there", and that we just have a hard time getting at it. (Else what is there to perceive, perception in today's psychology being seen as a cognitive transformation of sensations of *something*?)

So, assuming models are how we know things, and scientific models are more reliably explicit than metaphorical models, the prime questions I am posing are: (1) Can God *per se*, i.e., some common understanding of the *nature* (structure and function) of God, be modeled by anything close to what I call a scientific model? (2) Can different people's acquisition of belief, and their religious practice of belief and worship, be so modeled? Some readers might claim that these two questions are inseparable. However I will conclude this book by arguing no to the first question and yes to the second.

Throughout the centuries theologians have told us that God is a perfect person: all powerful, all knowing and all loving. We are told that God created the universe, that He knows each of us intimately, and He loves us dearly. Accordingly we are expected to accept and believe in Him, love Him, obey Him, glorify Him. But since ancient times there have been skeptics: What is the evidence that He made the universe? How can He know everything about every particle in the universe? Why do bad things happen to good people? In this writer's opinion there have never been satisfying answers to these questions, and clearly I am not alone. Every child asks them outright. And every adult thinks them, often guardedly, not to offend others or reveal ignorance or skepticism.

What is at issue with regard to religion and belief? First and foremost, *what and where is the evidence* of God? And what constitutes *credible* evidence? Second, what is our *obligation with regard to seeking truth*, as contrasted to just believing without regard for truth? Is "truth" simply conditional upon what is emotionally satisfying, what makes one feel good? Third, how has the biggest force in human history since the enlightenment, namely science, changed how these questions can be approached, or should be approached?

The anthropologist T.M. Luhrmann[3] has observed and interviewed many evangelical churchgoers and found that many of them apparently do not consider belief in God to be necessarily central to their faith, which seems a logical contradiction to the usual definition of the word faith. As one woman Luhrmann cited put it, "I don't believe it but I'm sticking to it". Luhrmann claims that many people do not go to church because they believe, but rather they believe because they go to church. Apparently the social participation activity is what fosters "belief", not any logical basis.

This book cannot deal comprehensively with those issues, which necessarily must confront fundamental questions in the vast literature on philosophy and religion. Rather, the engagement here is done from the narrow perspective of trying to capture for the reader only the essence of salient arguments that bear on the questions being asked about God. This author is a scientist whose primary qualifications are in the explicit representation of the natural world in words, graphics and mathematics. Most of my experience in research and teaching has had to do with modeling what humans believe and do. Models provide the means by which scientists, engineers and managers communicate their ideas to one another, make predictions, make progress in scientific discovery, and apply their findings to benefit people in living their daily lives.

So again: does or can modeling have anything to do with God and religion? Is it best to leave modeling to science and engineering and not muddle the theological waters with techno-gibberish? After all, we have more than two thousand years of history of beautiful sacred texts full of myth and metaphor, which many will claim are means quite capable of dealing with God and the human urge to worship a transcendent being. However, insofar as myth and metaphor may fall short as ways of fully knowing reality, and to the extent that scientific modeling of the observable secular world around us has become more rigorous, it poses a grand challenge. The challenges are (1) to model what people believe God *is or might be* (and is that even possible) and (2) to model people's acquisition and practice of belief in God. And to do so with as much scientific rigor as can be brought to bear. I claim the modeling approach makes a sharp distinction between these two challenges that so often are blurred in people's minds.

With respect to God *per se*, i.e., the *nature* of God, what appears to emerge from the considerations discussed in this book is that there is a shortage of substance in the writings of philosophers and theologians sufficient to constitute any kind of scientific model. More bluntly, *there is nothing there to model*. The book will go to some effort to show that the first modeling challenge appears impossible to meet. With respect to people's acquisition and practice of belief in God, there is plenty of substance available. Studies of many kinds have been done and will continue to be done, but there remains a challenge to formulate better models and make predictions.

If we cannot model God in a credible way, does that mean that God cannot be considered real, and therefore is the practice of religion a complete delusion and waste of people's energy? But this is getting ahead of the story.

For whom is the book intended and what is included

This book is aimed at anyone interested in science, philosophy, psychology and religion with academic background sufficient to understand the terminology and patience enough to wade though some complex ideas. It seems necessary for the reader to appreciate the distinction between denotative scientific models on the one hand, and connotative metaphysical and theological explanations and religious myth on the other.

Coping with the above issues will require taking a plunge into the methods of science and modeling, presented in Chapter 1. The latter reviews a number of issues regarding what a model is. I offer a novel taxonomy of model attributes, according to which one might assess the quality of a model. There is a review of different types of models in the Appendix. Mostly Chapter 1 addresses the "science of modeling belief".

Then, in Chapter 2, in order to bridge to the discussion of belief and God, several topics are discussed that imply models of how people come to their beliefs of what is real in the context of ordinary daily activities (as contrasted to religion). This is apart from difficult challenge of formulating a scientific model of God. It is useful to contrast some different perspectives on believing, where potential belief in existence of anything precedes the effort to model (else why model, what would there be to model?). These considerations include trust, virtual reality, a curious historical theory about self-consciousness, and a model of belief formation borrowed from computer science.

Next, Chapter 3 is a review in abbreviated form of what various luminaries throughout history have believed about the existence and nature of God, both pro and con. This review, at least from the writer's perspective, demonstrates the paucity of compelling arguments for the kind of God we are supposed to believe in. The arguments against belief seem to easily outweigh those in favor.

Chapter 4 then pulls together what has been said about models and belief to offer some demographics about belief and answers the two challenges posed above: (1) what can be modeled about what God *is*, and (2) what can be modeled about how God is worshipped. Finally Chapter 5 is a brief concluding summary of the main points.

Through examples, an Appendix illustrates belief models cast in terms of different languages: words, graphics, logic, and mathematics. In each case I suggest how that model might be stretched to be applied to religion. (Keep in mind that these models were never intended for that purpose). Some of the example models, especially those that require mathematics, the reader can ignore if desired

Introduction   7

Modeling human belief (in God or anything)

All models are representations of human belief, in the sense that they are statements about what the human modeler believes to be true about the relevant objects or events. But this allows for several alternative possibilities, as depicted in Figure 1.

A first distinction is whether the focus of the model is on *state* or *process*. A model can focus on the belief as to the *state* of the objects or events, i.e., exactly *what* is the truth about their existence, structure or function (e.g., *what* is God, as mentioned above). Or it can focus on the *process*: the causal logic of *how* that belief is or was arrived at and/or is exercised (e.g., how people practice religion, how ideas of God are handed down and reinforced within communities).

A second distinction is about the hierarchy of beliefs: who is it that believes what about whom or what. If a model is about inanimate objects or events the relationship is indicated by the line labeled A in Figure 1, emanating from the modeler in the diagram. In contrast, the model can be a specification of what the modeler believes some subject human or group of humans believes. In the diagram B1 indicates the modeler's focus on some subject human(s), while B2 indicates the modeled belief of those subject human(s).

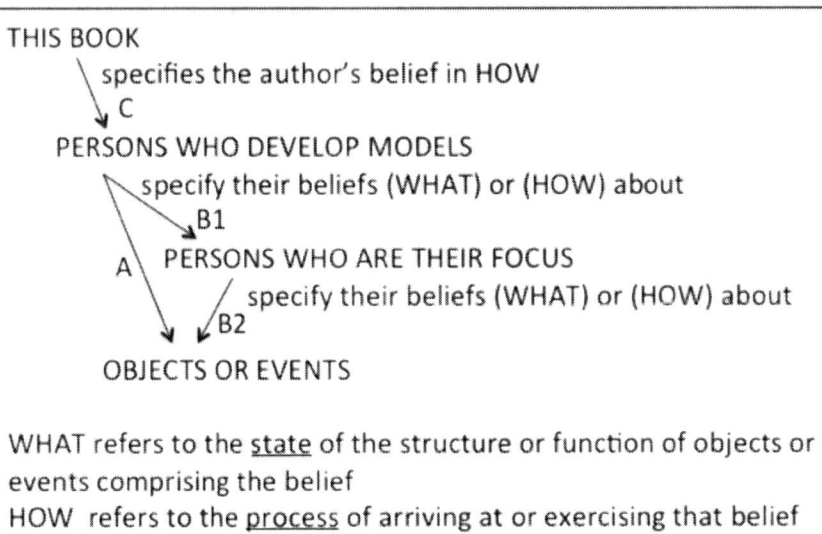

Figure 1. The modeling ladder of beliefs

This book is about modeling human beliefs, so it takes the B1-B2 path. Actually, the book could be said to be a discussion at a still higher level, C, namely what this author believes about hypothetical human modelers who in turn try to model the beliefs of other people.

Objective and subjective models

A model is a representation of very limited aspects of the thing or events being modeled. In that sense all models are wrong with respect to the full reality of the slice of nature being modeled. Consider a global map of the world. The globe is not the same as the real world. The globe is a very different size. The globe has different colors to identify countries. The world is not colored the same as the globe. The globe shows distances between cities, but the distances are not the same as those of the world. What is the same are the *relative distances* between cities and the *proportionate spatial relations* of rivers and country boundaries. That is all. But as such this model is very useful and aids understanding with regard to those particular attributes.

Increasingly, science and technology as well as government and industry are being driven by models.[4] In physics, for example, our understanding of the universe is largely based on model extrapolations well beyond what we can observe directly, and huge experimental efforts are made to verify the models (e.g., the hunt by particle physicists for the Higgs boson). Social science is definitely progressing, and in the future may well be aided by progress in neuroscience, but has not come close to that level of sophistication in quantitative modeling as used in physical science and engineering.

In all fields of science and technology models serve the function of asserting in a public way what the modeler believes to be true, thereby allowing for criticism and refinement by the relevant community. It may be said that to the extent that we can model we have a basis to form consensus and therefore have useful knowledge. In this sense the usefulness of the model is in forming a belief system about the domain of interest.

As noted above, a scientific model is fully denotative and rational, as contrasted to one that is essentially connotative, such as a novel, a poem, a myth, or an artistic statement (abstract or non-realistic painting, music or dance). A scientific model adheres to strictures of the scientific method (explicated further below), such as having a basis in objects or events that are observed by two or more people (and potentially observable by anyone). It is stated concisely. Often it aspires to generality, implying (or explicitly stating) that the model applies not only to the objects or events observed, but also to things other than the ones used as the basis of the model. Such generality is achieved in science by stating that certain dependent (output) variables are specific functions of certain independent (input) variables, where both sets of variables are well defined and observable to anyone equipped with the required means to measure them.

The quality of any model, but especially a scientific model, depends on the number of variables that can be accommodated simultaneously, the rigor of the measurement process that goes with the variables, the robustness or breadth of applicability of the model, and the degree to which the model is understood, accepted, and applied by the peer community.

There are plenty of examples of where scientific models have failed. Failure typically occurs where there is a rush to apply modeling where it has not been previously tried, and the target problem has not been thought through sufficiently, or the modeler expects too much too fast. An outstanding example is the Wall Street debacle of 2008, where the "quants" employed models to take statistical risks that were much greater than what was warranted, and the result was not pretty. More recently the bond rating agency Standard and Poor was sued by the US government for basing ratings on a proprietary model that was known to be faulty, an action that also helped precipitate the financial crisis of the same period. Normally models are published in the open literature and peer reviewed, but it is a right of any institution to maintain privacy. They do so at their own risk.

The term *simulation* is often used in conjunction with modeling. Simulation, today usually referring to simulation by computer, simply means putting the logic and mathematics in computer software form and then running computer trials to test what different inputs to the model produce as outputs. Computer software is a special form of scientific modeling.

Computer scientists like the term *ontology,* which in their domain is defined as meaning "formal representation of knowledge as a set of concepts within a domain, and the relationships between those concepts"[5] (In philosophy ontology means a *theory of being or existence.*) The computer community emphasizes that an ontology is a "specification of a conceptualization", where the stated purpose of designing ontologies is to share knowledge and make intellectual commitments". As a practical matter computer scientists are compelled by these formalities to make the various bits of software (they call them "agents") work together. Thus a common ontology defines the vocabulary with which queries and assertions can be exchanged. Ontological commitments are agreements to use the shared vocabulary in a coherent and consistent manner. The computerized agents sharing a vocabulary need not have the same knowledge (share the same knowledge base). Each may know things the others do not, and is not required to answer all queries that can be formulated in the shared vocabulary. In short, a commitment to a common ontology is a guarantee of consistency, but not a guarantee of completeness. That is a reasonable way to think about models in general, and how people can use models to accomplish useful goals. (In any case the formality makes the computer scientists sound like they know what they are talking about!)

Throughout the book we shall confront the problem of modeling God and modeling people's exercise of religious belief. *The reader is reminded that the purpose of considering the above details of scientific modeling in its explicit denotative rigor is to draw a contrast with how vague are available characterizations of God, lacking in anything close to scientific rigor.*

Why model? Why make the effort?

Modeling takes effort. To find the right words, words that have common meanings, to say what needs to be said and say it succinctly, to get the diagram, graph or other image just right so that it communicates, to do the math correctly if math is appropriate to make the case—all of that takes real effort. Why do it? What's the point?

One instigates a modeling effort for the same reason that one investigates an interesting plant on the hiking trail, makes a note in one's diary of a special personal interaction, or follows up any observation that arouses interest and curiosity. Modeling engenders satisfaction, better ability to share the experience with other people, and the improved likelihood of making some predictions that might be useful later on.

Though individuals can gain insights in various ways, for the scientist modeling is the *sine qua non* for staking public claim to some new insight, or asserting a better way of considering some aspect of the world and communicating it to colleagues. From a crass perspective a model might help get a paper published.

But there is a further, probably more important reason. That is that the very process of modeling forces one to think hard about the slice of nature under consideration, to ask and answer the question of what are the essential features of the structure and function, and to make "If X, then Y" predictions. Committing to a model is tantamount to committing to think hard. It involves putting one's reputation on the line, which surely motivates the thinking process.

So the premise is that by trying to model God and religious belief we can shed light on what we really know about God and religious belief.

Philosophical perspective

In considering the question of God the modeling approach will appear to take the philosophical perspective of positivism. That is the view that all authoritative knowledge is derived from sensory experience and logical (and mathematical if appropriate) analysis of such data. It is tantamount to saying we know reality only through science. In medieval times many philosophers claimed that reality is known through metaphysical contemplation, though both Aristotle and Aquinas seem to have emphasized the role of sensory experience. Philosopher Auguste Comte later proposed that the scientific method replace metaphysics[6].

Recent critics of positivism claim that behavioral/social sciences are distinct from natural science with respect to what exists (ontology) and what is justified belief (epistemology). For example sociologist Max Weber would claim that students of history would have to throw out most information, and that "social facts" don't exist "out there" but are necessarily mediated by human consciousness.[7] This view was even supported by physicist Werner Heisenberg, inventor of quantum mechanics, who commented in 1969.[8]

> The positivists have a simple solution: the world must be divided into that which we can say clearly and the rest, which we had better pass over in silence. But can anyone conceive of a more pointless philosophy, seeing that what we can say clearly amounts to next to nothing. If we omitted all that is unclear, we would probably be left with completely uninteresting and trivial tautologies.

I would acknowledge that this book assumes a positivist perspective in talking or modeling denotatively about people or God (i.e., with as much logic and science as can be brought to bear). At the same time I strongly assert that connotative language such as metaphor plays a key role in human communication and thinking. As the Heisenberg comment suggests, it may be more important than denotation in communicating and experiencing what really matters in life.

These two kinds of knowledge are complementary, and they both are amenable to representation in language. But the kinds of language are very different. The denotative one is objective and couched in elements of language that aspire to unambiguous meanings that discourage free interpretation. The connotative one is subjective and difficult to communicate except through words that tend to be ambiguous and understood by different people to mean different things in different contexts.

The above statement makes the denotative/connotative distinction as though it were a clean one, but in reality it is not. There is always some fuzz between categories. In the Appendix I describe *fuzzy logic*, a relatively new approach that wrestles with the linguistic fuzz in an objective way. Thus the modeler's task of word selection is always a challenge. That is why mathematics and graphics are so useful for scientific models to augment the words.

Ludwig Wittgenstein (1889-1951), the most respected of modern analytical philosophers, is best known for his thoughts on language, and what he called "language games" in expressing belief. He asserted that religious belief is a different sort of belief than belief based on physical evidence. Most theologians prefer to take this position, and avoid talking about God in the language of science, perhaps for the reason that they can point to nothing physical to observe, and therefore nothing to know in a positivist sense. But they nevertheless tend to talk about God as though He is a person with human-like attributes of knowing, forgiving, judging, condemning, and exerting power on people.

For example they frequently talk about a loving God, and knowing God through the sense of feeling reciprocal love. Do I know that I love my wife? I know that I *feel* love, but I cannot say that I understand love (or hate or any other such abstract idea) in the same way that I understand simple laws of physics, on the basis of which I can model and predict. Furthermore, unlike God as well as abstract words like love, I can physically see and touch my wife, so I *can* model and predict her *behavior*, on the basis of which (I would claim) love evolves. But that is still not the same as understanding and denotatively modeling my love for her in an objective sense. Modeling God is doubly elusive: nothing to observe, posing a challenge even to denote God's actions—as well as having to resort to connotative words to describe what God *is*. But though we can't observe God we *can* observe the *people* who claim to believe.

So God is an idea, a powerful one indeed. One can love the idea that God exists, and can imaginatively "expect" love from God and express love in return. No one can deny that such feelings may be genuine. But one can also love the idea that God is a metaphor for human longing to understand the mystery and wonder of the universe. One can know the *feeling* of love in either case (or fear or some other emotion), but that is a private subjective experience. Is there any other way to know God? Is there something to model beyond a subjective feeling, either about God or about the humans who believe? Is the term God better used as a *metaphor for mystery*, and nothing more?

For now let us hold off on taking the easy path to accept that religion is beyond science. We need to look at the God idea and the people who espouse that idea with all the science and modeling that can be brought to bear, and then ask what can be said rationally. That is the issue I will wrestle with in this book.

1

KNOWLEDGE, SCIENCE AND MODELING

The whole of science is nothing more than the refinement of everyday thinking.
—Albert Einstein, *Physics and Reality*, 1936

Physical concepts are free creatures of the human mind and are not, however it may seem, uniquely determined by the external world.
—Albert Einstein, *Evolution of Physics*, 1938

Our belief in any particular natural law cannot have a safer basis than our unsuccessful critical attempts to refute it.
—Karl Popper, *Conjectures and Refutations*, 1963

The great tragedy of science: the slaying of a beautiful hypothesis by an ugly fact.
—Thomas Huxley, *Biogenesis and Abiogenesis*, 1870

You can observe a lot by watching.
—attributed to Yogi Berra

Acquiring knowledge

There are many ways for humans to acquire knowledge. No doubt there are also many ways to classify the means to acquire knowledge, and below are mentioned just a few of them.

Knowledge can be acquired by the brain during the evolutionary process by successive modifications to the genes. That finally results in fertilization of egg by sperm and the gestation process in the mother. Certainly all this depends on the sensory-motor "operating system" software that makes the sense organs and muscles work together. But evolution also plays at the level of higher cognitive function. As Noam Chomsky has shown us, much of the syntactic structure of grammar is evidently built in at birth.[9] What knowledge we acquire after birth is a function of what we attend to, and what we attend to is a function of our motivation for allocating our attention, which ultimately is a function of what we know, so knowledge acquisition after birth is a causal circle.

Learning has to do with what sticks, and how we respond to the stimuli we observe. One theory of learning is the process of Pavlovian (classical) conditioning, where a *conditioned stimulus*, originally neutral in its effect, becomes a signal that an inherently significant (reward or punishment) *unconditioned stimulus* is about to occur. This results only after multiple pairings, and the brain somehow remembers the association. The originally neutral stimulus becomes conditioned, meaning that the person (or animal) responds reflexively to the conditioned stimulus the same as s/he would to the unconditioned stimulus (e.g., the dog salivates with the light or bell).

Somewhat different is Skinnerian or *operant* conditioning.[10] This is where a voluntary random action (called a free operant) is rewarded (reinforced), that association is remembered, and after sufficient repetitions, the voluntary actions occur more often (if previously rewarded)). Operant learning can be maintained even when rewards are infrequently paired with the conditioned action.

But there seems to be much more learning that is not conditioning of either type. Chomsky made clear the lack of evidence that language is all acquired by conditioning.

Knowledge can be public, where two or more people agree on some perception or interpretation and others can access the same information. Or it can be private, where it has not or cannot be shared. The issue is tricky, and that is why modelability is proposed as a criterion for what can be called public knowledge. Two people can look at what we call a red rose, and agree that it is red, because they have been conditioned to respond with the word *red* upon observing that stimulus. But ultimately exactly what they experienced cannot be shared.

We can posit that some learning is simply accepting, unquestioningly, information from some source because that source is trusted or because the learner is compelled in some way to learn. (This is probably how many believers in God acquired their belief.) We finally contrast the above models to learning by means of the scientific method, which is detailed below: Critical observation and hypothesizing are followed by collection of evidence, analysis, logical conclusions, and modeling to serve one's own use or to communicate to others.

WHAT IS THE SCIENTIFIC METHOD?

Science has its own formal model of how to determine the truth. The scientific method is usually stated as consisting of the following nine steps:

1. **Gather information and resources** (informal observation).

2. **Question** the relationships between aspects of some objects or events, based on observation and contemplation. An incipient mental model may already form in the observer's head.

3. **Hypothesize** a conjecture resulting from the act of questioning. This can be either a predictive or an explanatory hypothesis. In either case it should be stated explicitly in terms of independent and dependent variables (causes and effects).

4. **Predict** the logical consequences of the hypothesis. (A model will begin to take shape.)

5. **Test** the hypothesis by doing formal data collection and experiments to determine whether the world behaves according to the prediction. This includes taking pains to design the data-taking and the experiment to minimize risks of experimental error. It is critical that the tests be recorded in enough detail so as to be ob-

servable and repeatable by others. The experimental design will have a large effect on what model might emerge.

6. **Analyze** the results of the experiment and draw tentative conclusions. This often involves a secondary hypothesis step, namely exercising the statistical null hypothesis. The null hypothesis is that some conjecture about a population of related objects or events is false, namely that observed differences have occurred by chance, e.g., that some disease is not affected by some drug. Normally the effort is to show a degree of statistical confidence in the failure and thus rejection of the null hypothesis. In other words, if there is enough confidence that the differences did not occur by chance then the conjectured relationship exists.

7. **Draw formal conclusions** and **model** as appropriate.

8. **Communicate** the results, conclusions and model to colleagues in publication or verbal presentation, rendering the model in a form that best summarizes and communicates the determined relationships.

9. **Retest and refine** the model (frequently done based on review and critique by other scientists).

OBSERVATIONS ON THE SCIENTIFIC METHOD

The above is also called the hypothetico-deductive method. As stated it is an idealization of the way science really works, as the above steps are seldom cleanly separated and the process is typically messy. Often experimentation is done in order to make observations that provoke additional observations, questions, hypotheses, predictions, and rejections or refinements of the starting hypothesis. Especially at the early observation stage the process can be very informal. One of the writer's students used to say that what we did in the lab was "piddling with a purpose." Einstein is said to have remarked that the most important tool of the scientist is the wastebasket.

Francis Bacon (1620)[11] asserted that observations must be collected "without prejudice". But as scientists are real people there is no way they can operate free of some prejudice. They start with some bias as to their initial knowledge and interests, their social status and physical location, and their available tools of observation. They are initially prejudiced as to what is of interest, what observations are made, and what questions are asked. Philosopher Karl Popper (1934)[12] believed that all science begins with a prejudiced hypothesis. He further asserted that actually a theory can never be proven correct by observation, but can only be proven incorrect by disagreement with observation. Scientific method is about falsifiability. That is the basis of the null hypothesis test in statistics. (But of course the falsifiability is itself subject to statistical error; one can only reject the null hypothesis with some small chance of being wrong.) The American Association for the Advancement of Science asserted in a legal brief to the U.S. Supreme Court (1993)[13] that "'Science is not an encyclopedic body of knowledge about the universe. Instead, it represents a *process* for proposing and refining theoretical explanations about the world that are subject to further testing and refinement".

Historian Thomas Kuhn (1970)[14] offered a different perspective on how science works, namely in terms of *paradigm shifts*. Whether in psychology or cosmology, researchers seem to make small and gradual refinements of accepted models, until new evidence and an accompanying model provokes a radical shift in paradigm, to which scientists then adhere for a time. When a new paradigm is in process of emerging the competition between models and their proponents can be fierce, even personal (who discovered X first, who published first, whose model offers the best explanation). We also must admit that search for truth is not the only thing that motivates us as scientists and modelers. We are driven by ambition for recognition from our peers as well as by money.

I emphasize again the relevance of reproducible observability. Having to deal with observables is the most critical factor in an epistemological sense (what we know). This is because it distinguishes what may be called truth based on scientific evidence that is openly observable from experiences that are not observable by others (e.g., personal testimony and anecdotal evidence.) Observability also comes into play for what are called mental models.

Mental models can be called models of a sort, but being private they are not subject to direct observation by other people. Experiments in psychophysics, where subjects make verbal category judgments or button-push responses to physical stimuli of sound, light, etc., are regarded as conforming to scientific method. This is because the human is making a direct mechanical response to a given stimulus, such as pushing a button, not having to articulate in arbitrary words what he or she is thinking. However when subjects are asked to explicate in their own words their mental models of how they believe something works, or what are cognitive steps of a particular task as might be asked of subject matter experts, there is no external physical reference; scientific method here is more challenging. And of course there must be repeatability, or aggregation of the results from many subjects. Observability clearly is a challenge for modeling what God is, though not as much for modeling human behavior in the practice of religion.

While social scientists often point out that humans have a predilection for reaffirming the status quo, science nevertheless is a truth system committed to change, as warranted, rather than preservation. But while science actively pursues possibilities of change, the null hypothesis testing by its very nature demands a significant level of statistical confidence in order to reject the null hypothesis that there is no real change (that there is only random difference between the hypothesized variant and the control).

The scientific method is a method wherein inquiry regards itself as fallible and purposely probes, criticizes, corrects, and improves itself. This universally accepted attribute stands in sharp contrast to religious traditions around the world. Science is the one human endeavor that has proven relatively immune to the passions that otherwise divide us.

LOGICAL REASONING

A model may be derived from logical reasoning or it may be stated out of ignorance or for purposes of deception. It may also be a metaphorical model, where, because of ambiguity in the words or drawings, it is not possible to conclude that it is logical. If it is based on logic and assuming no ambiguity in the words, pictures or symbols, it is relevant to mention three different types of logical reasoning[15]:

Deduction allows deriving *b* from *a* only where *b* is a formal logical consequence of *a*. In other words, deduction is the process of deriving the consequences of what is assumed. Given the truth of the assumptions, a valid deduction guarantees the truth of the conclusion. For example, given that all bachelors are unmarried males, and given that some person is a bachelor, it can be deduced that that person is an unmarried male.

Induction allows inferring *b* from *a*, where *b* does not follow necessarily from *a*. *a* might give us very good reason to accept *b*, but it does not ensure that *b* is true. For example, if all of the swans that we have observed so far are white, we may induce that all swans are white. We have good reason to believe the conclusion from the premise, but the truth of the conclusion is not guaranteed. (Indeed, it turns out that some swans are black.)

Abduction allows inferring *a* as an explanation of *b*. Put another way, abduction allows the precondition *a* to be abduced from the consequence *b*. Deduction and abduction thus differ in the direction in which a rule like "*a entails b*" is used for inference. As such abduction is formally equivalent to a logical fallacy, that a unique *a* occurs where there are multiple possible explanations for *b*. For example, after glancing up and seeing the eight ball moving in some direction we may abduce that it was struck by the cue ball. The cue ball's strike would account for the eight ball's movement. It serves as a hypothesis that explains our observation. There are in fact many possible explanations for the eight ball's movement, and so our abduction does not leave us certain that the cue ball did in fact strike the eight ball, but our abduction is still useful and can serve to orient us in our surroundings. This process of abduction is an instance of the scientific method. Logically there are infinite possible explanations for any of the physical processes we observe, but from our experience we are inclined to abduce a single explanation (or a few explanations) for them in the hopes that we can better orient ourselves in our surroundings and then eliminate some of the possibilities.

PRIVATE (SUBJECTIVE) AND PUBLIC (OBJECTIVE) KNOWLEDGE

Model development necessarily begins in the head of some person, and only later is the model rendered in words, graphics or mathematical language so that it can be communicated to others. The term *mental model* refers broadly to a person's private thoughts, though some psychologists would confine its use to well-formed ideas about the structure or function of some objects or events, such that it is potentially communicable in understandable format to another person.

For many years psychologists have struggled with how to extract a person's mental model. Psychophysical methods of having experimental subjects rank-order stimuli or assign preferential numbers or descriptive categories (as done by political pollsters) is a common approach. With more complex situations, and particularly those that have social implications, a problem is that what people say they believe and what they actually believe may be quite different. People are inclined to say what they think some other person wants to hear; social etiquette reinforces this behavior. (Many church-goers would fall into this category when professing their religious beliefs.)

DOUBT AND ITS RELATION TO DOING SCIENCE

Many philosophers, from Rene Descartes[16] to Charles Sanders Peirce[17], have proposed methodological doubting (also called Cartesian skepticism, methodological skepticism, or hyperbolic doubt) as a means to test the truth of one's beliefs. Descartes applied the method to doubting his own existence, leading to a "proof", namely *Cogito ergo sum* (I think, therefore I am). If he was able to doubt he must be alive and real. I recall attending a "Skeptics Seminar" at MIT at which the famous mathematician and founder of cybernetics Norbert Wiener emphasized the importance of doubting in order to refine one's beliefs.

Doubt is deliberation on error and failure. Together with a graduate student I once offered an experimental graduate course called

"Seminar on Failure" in which historians, psychiatrists, scientists and engineers were invited to reminisce on failures in their own professional experiences. We learned that failure often led to discovery and learning, and that success often led to overconfidence and carelessness and eventually to failure. Failure and success are the Taoist yin and yang of our experience; they are mutually complementary; one could not exist without the other.

Doubt and questioning motivate scientists to think of different hypotheses and try different experiments. Pioneer in cybernetics Ross Ashby (1903-1972) is known for his "law of requisite variety," which asserts that in order for one system to control another it must possess a greater variety of states. This law has been applied to genetic mutations believed to be essential to the evolution of species as per Darwin's theory. There is requisite variety in our own social and environmental encounters in life, from which we can refine our beliefs and models of what works and what does not work. Edwin Hubble's doubt led to the discovery that the brightness of a spot in the Andromeda cluster could not be from our own galaxy, the first proof that there were other galaxies in the universe.[18] Sometimes it is not simply doubt but absolute failure that provokes a wider search for solution and improvement, whether in a computer or a person.

USING AND AVOIDING EVIDENCE

Thus far the discussion has assumed that a rational person accepts a model or a belief because the preponderance of evidence supports that model or belief. People are always free to "choose" a belief because it is what parents or peers say they believe, or what individuals believe they should believe, for whatever reason. Perhaps it is because they think believing will make them feel better, or there will be punishment for professing disbelief. But these are not acts of seeking truth. No one says that truth-seeking is easy, particularly when what appears to be the rational truth is in conflict with claims by authority figures or other trusted sources.

Let's face it. Truth-seeking has its costs. In many ways evolution has designed us not to be rational in every act. Hyper-rational insistence on bare-faced truth clearly gets us into trouble—in interpersonal relations where etiquette is required, in supporting and defending a child from destructive criticism, in winning an argument, etc. The truth may be messy and ugly. Some will surely feel that absolute truth is second to happiness, and who will ever know the ultimate truth anyway? Isn't happiness the real goal? In any case we may want to be careful about flaunting what we believe to be the truth.

METAPHYSICS AND ITS RELATION TO SCIENCE

Metaphysics is a traditional branch of philosophy concerned with being – what things exists and what are their properties. Prior to the 18th century all questions of ultimate reality were addressed by philosophers. Aristotle believed that things have within them their own purpose (a teleology)[19]. He is well known for distinguishing between two essential properties of things: *potentiality* (the possibility of any property a thing can have), and *actuality* (what is actually in evidence). There are modern manifestations of Aristotle's dichotomy, such as the distinction between potential and kinetic energy in physics. Thomas Aquinas called metaphysics the "queen of sciences" and wrote widely on the subject.

Since the Enlightenment the field of metaphysics has evolved into a philosophical pursuit of topics that have not been easy for science to handle, such as religion, being (existence), mind, perception, free will, consciousness and meaning. In later sections of the book we will discuss how science has begun to confront some of these issues. Whether over time they will be clarified, remain as conundrums, or whether the verbal constructs will just fade away remains to be determined. I would guess some of each.

As noted above, Descartes' conclusion that "I think, therefore I am" was proffered as a metaphysical basis for his own existence. He asserted that while all else could be doubted, the fact that he could do the doubting meant that he must exist in order to doubt.[20]. Such thought experiments are common in philosophy. We shall discuss later a thought experiment rationale that to imagine a thing or event is to make it exist, namely the famous "proof of God" offered by Anselm of Canterbury[21]. Surely thoughts exist as neural activity in the brains of people who have the thoughts; they constitute what we have called mental models. But our concern here is for existence of things perceived from observables, other than as one person's imagination.

OBJECTIVITY, ADVOCACY AND BIAS

Ideally the scientist is supposed to be disinterested, completely impartial to how any test of a hypothesis turns out, and what the implications of the results are to the world. But scientists are people, and people do things because they are interested in achieving some objectives. The very act of formulating a hypothesis is a creative act, motivated by the interests of the scientist. But given this unavoidable level of interest, the scientist has an obligation to be as objective as possible, and not favor one aspect of the results while hiding some other aspect.

Nevertheless everyone is subject to bias, including this author. Psychologists have studied human biases extensively. In dealing with value-laden topics like religion biases are especially salient. One most pertinent category of bias is what is called the *confirmation bias*. Nickerson defines the confirmation bias as "the seeking or interpreting of evidence in ways that are partial to existing beliefs, expectations, or a hypothesis in hand". He reviews evidence of such a bias in a variety of guises and gives examples of its operation in several practical contexts.[22] Other biases include overconfidence in one's own predictions, giving more weight to recent events as compared to earlier events in judging probabilities, assessing greater risk to situations one is forced into as compared to those voluntarily selected, and inferring illusory causal relations.

Many democratic societies have judicial systems based on advocacy, where the advocates of the two or more sides of any argument confront one another in a highly procedural venue in front of a jury of peers. The assumption is that the jury can judge the arguments, weigh the evidence presented, and detect efforts to hide something. Because conventional jury selection is not set up to include experts on particular fields of science or technology, there have been various proposals to develop "science courts" that would somehow demand more rigorous objectivity in presenting and judging arguments and evidence. (One can only imagine the difficulty the US Supreme Court has in confronting the evidence in regard to challenges based on religious belief.)

ANALOGY AND METAPHOR

Analogy is a broad class of cognitive process or linguistic expression involving transfer of meaning from one object or event to another because of some similarity. Analogy plays a critical role in creativity, problem solving, memory, perception, explanation and communication.

It can also be said that science depends on metaphor (and simile) in the sense that an active and curious observer is constantly seeing analogies, likenesses between elements of nature. The observed likenesses lead to hypotheses that permit generalization.

For example in the field of physics mechanical force, mechanical pressure, electrical voltage, and temperature are all seen as having the property of force. Mechanical velocity, fluid flow, electrical current, and heat flow are all seen as having the property of flow. Mechanical friction, fluid viscosity, electrical resistance, and thermal insulation all have the property of resistance to flow. Depending on the spatial configuration the differential equations relating the forces, flows, and resistance to flow are identical. These analogies are powerful concepts in physical science that also have counterparts in traffic analysis, economics and other fields. Much academic teaching in the physical sciences and engineering employs analogy.

A metaphor is a figure of speech that makes use of analogy. It is a word or phrase describing a thing or an action that is regarded as representative or symbolic of something else, especially something abstract—even though it is not literally applicable. This is in contrast to a simile, in which something is said to be *like* something else, and the attribute of likeness is spelled out or implied. Joseph Campbell (1904-1987)[23] uses the following examples: The boy *runs like* a deer (simile). The boy *is* a deer (metaphor).

Literature, poetry, music and the arts are full of metaphor; they depend on metaphor. Metaphor can say things more emotionally powerful than simple rational statements. Metaphor provokes the human imagination, as in myths, allegories and parables. It has been said that literature and the arts often realize human truths well before other branches of human endeavor do. Since it is a figure of speech, a metaphor is not a belief (a mental event); rather it is a way to describe a belief. Things are not metaphors, but can be expressed through metaphors. Every metaphor is both metaphorically true (if it is an apt description) and literally false.

An analog representation, whether in words or any other medium, can be a model. This author cut his academic teeth using analog computers as models of human behavior. The point is that certain relationships (e.g., in magnitude and time of the graphical traces output by the analog computer) *denote* magnitude and time relationships of the target thing or events being modeled. It is understood by the user of the analog computer that other properties of the analog computer (physical hardware, electron flow) are irrelevant.

Metaphorical description can be a kind of model, though not a scientific model, as previously noted. This is because the interpretation of the metaphor as a representation of the target object or event is a creative act by the reader or listener, since the connection between the metaphor and the target is not explicit (it is *connotative*). Religious myth fits this category.

What is a model?

In this section we discuss the notion of modeling in very general terms. A definition is offered, a taxonomy of attributes of models is proposed by which to evaluate models, and some important distinctions in modeling are made

What do a verbal treatise on how some aspect of the economy works, a miniature replica of an airplane, a mathematical equation characterizing driver steering behavior, and a girl posing before a camera or a painter have in common? We call each of them a model. There are other entities that normally we do not call models, such as a myth or a poem, but by a broad definition they too are models, though not the kind this book focuses on.

DEFINITION OF "MODEL"

For purposes of this book a model is defined as *a concise, denotative representation of the structure or function of some selected aspects of our world to one or more observers for the purposes of communicating a belief about some relationships, expressing a conjecture, making a prediction, or specifying a design of a thing or a set of events.*

Obviously the term *model* as defined above is quite general. Beyond the idea of *representation* are synonyms such as *specification, rendering, map, or characterization* of the relations between elements or variables of the defined set of objects or events. There are semantic overlaps with related terms such as *abstraction, construction, explanation, portrayal, depiction, theory, idea, concept, paradigm, pattern,* etc.

An important word in the above definition is *selected*. No model purports to include all of the factors (variables) relating to the target object or set of events. Much (indeed most) will be left out. It is obligatory that the modeler specify which variables are included, and by implication everything else is omitted. The idea is to capture the independent variables that have the greatest effect on the dependent variables of interest.

A model can be said to be a description of a concept. Models can be described using words, graphics (e.g. graphs, diagrams, pictures), mathematical equations, physical things or some combination of these (e.g., computer simulations that run equations and output numbers, graphs, dynamic animations, etc.). The word *concise* is added to the above definition to emphasize that a model states the intended relationships briefly but completely and unambiguously, eliminating redundancy and extraneous words or symbols. This excludes longwinded, wordy statements or graphics with elaboration that are unnecessary to the message. There unfortunately is no clean distinction as to when a particular statement qualifies as a model or not.

Semiotics is the theory of signs, which includes syntax (grammar, structural constraints of words or symbols), semantics (their meaning) and pragmatics (effects of their use on people). Semiotics makes an important distinction between *denotation* and *connotation*. Denotation refers to the explicit literal meaning of the words, symbols or signs. Connotation refers to the implied or suggested meaning, as with metaphor. A photo of or a verbal statement about a red rose with a green stem *denotes* nothing more than a red rose with a green stem, but it *connotes* affection or celebration. In this book we mostly restrict the word *model* to denotative representation. This accords with the use of models in all fields of science.

Modern society makes ever-greater use of denotative models, particularly in science and technology. Dating from early Greek civilization we have had verbal models, but more and more since the Enlightenment we have seen the development of mathematical, graphical and other symbolic models. Our ability to run fast-time computer simulations on large databases for weather, physics, engineering, economics, genomics, transportation, etc. has made huge strides in recent years.

A model typically states explicitly, or at least strongly implies, an "IF X, THEN Y" relationship. For example if you look at a particular location X on a map or within the human body you will find Y. Or if X is the input or independent variable to a given system or process then Y will be the result. The latter is common to a scientific model that is intended to generalize about and predict observations.

Mostly scientific models are intended to be predictive so as to be useful in some application. It can be said that models without application are useless (essentially by definition if *application* is interpreted broadly). It should be noted that basic science routinely develops models that are used only to communicate understanding of how the world works, which only much later may find practical application.

Some people distinguish a model from a theory, where a model is a rendering of specific relationships relevant to a theory, a theory being a statement that circumscribes some relationships within the larger, more complex reality. The theory can be just a hypothesis or it can be an accepted statement of some reality. Ideally the theory includes statements of constraints on application: where, when and how the theory or the derived model applies or does not apply. So models and theories of application naturally go together, and unfortunately the terms are often used to mean the same thing.

A cross section of denotative models in different applications might be:

- Business model: a framework of the business logic of a firm
- Computer model: a computer program that simulates abstractions about a particular system
- Ecosystem model: a representation of components and flows through an ecosystem
- Physiological response model: description of a neural process that simulates the response of the motor system in order to estimate the outcome of a neural command
- Macroeconomic model: a representation of some aspect of a national or regional economy
- Map: used for navigation by air, sea or land
- Mechanism model: a description of a system in terms of its constituent parts and mechanisms
- Molecular model: a physicochemical or mathematical description that describes the behavior of molecules
- Pension model: a description of a pension system including simulations and projections of assets
- Standard model of physics: the theory in particle physics that describes certain fundamental forces and particles
- Statistical model: in applied statistics, a parameterized set of probability distributions
- Wiring diagram: as used by an electrician

For the reader interested in examples of objective (scientific or denotative models) the Appendix of this book provides examples in two categories. First are examples of general models that use different forms of language. Included are sections on: Verbal models; Graphs, maps and schematic diagrams; Logic diagrams; Fuzzy logic; and Mathematics: statistical inference from evidence. Next are examples of modeling human cognition (religious belief is a form of cognition). Included sections are: Qualitative levels of human cognition; Correlational model of human perception; Human judgment of utility (relative worth); Decisions under conditions of certainty; Decisions under uncertainty; Information communication; Information value; Competitive decisions such as game models; Signal detection; and Feedback control. In some cases relevant mathematical formulations are included.

It is important to note that the above-listed models of cognition, what people think and believe, are generated from observable data of what human subjects say or do in controlled laboratory experiments, where subject responses are not expressed in free form but are highly constrained so that credible averages and statistics may be calculated by aggregating subject responses. *A premise of this book is that thoughts about what God is, while expressible in connotative language, cannot be sufficiently constrained to objective categories or metrics such that by aggregation an experimenter can calculate and make much sense of averages or other statistics.*

A NEW TAXONOMY OF MODEL ATTRIBUTES

We need tools to assist in model evaluation. To that end Table 1 illustrates a proposed general taxonomy of models, with six attributes shown as rows and relative levels as column headings. For

	ATTRIBUTE	1 (LEAST)	2 (MODERATE)	3 (MOST)
A	APPLICABILITY TO OBSERVABLES	Not based on observables	Describes past observables	Predicts future observables
B	DIMENSIONALITY	Single input, single output	Multi input, single output	Multi input, multi output
C	METRICITY	Limited to nominal relationships	Primarily ordinal relationships	Entirely cardinal relationships
D	ROBUSTNESS	Unique focus on limited objects or events	Moderate focus to a variety of objects or events	Comprehensive of a wide slice of nature
E	SOCIAL PENETRATION	Confined to a mental model	Communicated to the relevant community	Accepted and used by the relevant community
F	CONCISENESS	Wordy, redundant, unclear, ambiguous expression	Minor wordiness, redundancy, or ambiguity	Concise and clear, no redundancy, no ambiguity

Table 1. A taxonomy of model attributes

each attribute there are three level descriptors, marked 1, 2 and 3, where level 1 is the least of the given attribute, level 3 is the most of that attribute, and level 2 is in between those limits. If each of the six attributes were considered to have only three discrete levels (1,2,3) there would be 3x3x3x3x3x3=729 combinations. However, for each attribute the three levels can also be considered rough descriptors of values along a continuum, yielding what scientists would call a continuous six-dimensional state space. The meaning of the attributes is explained below. This taxonomy will be used later to evaluate what we can or cannot model about God and religious practice.

A. Applicability to observables

The first attribute, and the one most coupled to what the modeler intends the model to be, is *applicability to observables*. *Observables* here refers to objects or events that can be sensed directly by humans or measured using some repeatable physical means. And it is important to note that the objects or events must potentially be observable by *any* human; personal experiences that cannot be shared with others do not count as observables, a criterion well established in the philosophy of science.[24]

Level 1 of this attribute characterizes statements or renderings that fail or where there is no intention to explicitly describe or predict the real world in terms of observable data, past or present. Evidence in a scientific sense is non-existant at this level. Such a statement, might be an original metaphorical construct: fiction, poetry, music, abstract art, or dance. In this regard it must be emphasized that metaphorical statements need not be of low quality in the sense of value. Life would not be the same without metaphor. Feelings and spirituality are represented in abstract words and music, surely connecting to people, but the meaning or essence of the rendering need not represent explicit observable events external to the rendering itself.

Note that for level 1 the rendering *per se* surely consists of observable and measurable events: music has continuous pitch; painting is done in a spectrum of color; and dance is continuous in motion and time. But in this case it is up to the observer to make a connection (or not) between these intrinsic data and any external data. The mapping to the real world is not explicit. Such representations are very different kinds of statements from what are published in scientific papers. We could call them models at a "low" level, because it is not necessarily clear to observers what they are models of. That allows ample room for arbitrary interpretation. Level 1 of the Applicability to Observables category necessarily precludes any such model from being called objective or scientific.

At the other extreme a level 3 model seeks to predict with precision some future events based on some well-defined independent observable and measurable variables. It represents how they interact to produce a result, whether static or dynamic. Level 3 epitomizes what we mean by a model in this book.

Somewhere in between is a description of existing events or objects, a representation of some aspect of the world as it is. It may lack an explicitly stated "IF X THEN Y" rule to predict new data output from given data input. A photograph is an example, or a desktop model of the Eiffel Tower. Succinct explications of historical events, where there is no effort to generalize regarding lessons for the future, would also fit this intermediate level.

B. Dimensionality

The attribute of dimensionality refers to the number of dimensions of the independent (input) and dependent (output) variable state spaces: how many input and output variables in the model. A model can be single-input-single-output, multi-input-single-output, or multi-input-multi-output. (Single-input-multi-output makes no sense since the outputs would be 100 percent correlated if the model was deterministic.) The world is complicated, and in general a complex of many outputs (a vector) is a complex function of many inputs (another vector).

The real world can be said to have an infinite number of variables. To include all inputs and outputs in one gigantic model is totally unrealistic, even for a narrow slice of reality, so the modeler must always put up with variability in the real world that is unaccounted for in the model, presumably caused by input variables not included in the model. Some such input variables may be known, but their effects unknown. And then there are the unknown-unknowns, variables that that the modeler is not even aware of (so-called "unk-unks"). One might hope that a single output is mostly related to a single input, but that is seldom the case. So if one can find several inputs that relate in combination to a single output, that usually accounts for most of the variability, i.e., most of what accounts for changes in the output variable. Even better (more useful) is to model a relation between a group of inputs and a group of outputs (multiple models in one, so to speak).

Thus science now can only model bits and pieces of reality, but a "model of everything" is not conceivable (though physicists dream of it). A literal model of everything would have to predict the behavior of all elementary particles in the universe and thus every object or event that they constitute.

However, a word about causality is in order. Unfortunately there is no way to firmly establish independence between variables or causality between inputs and outputs (as distinguished from correlation) without encompassing the totality of possible variables and their interactions. For example, all output variables could all be caused by one factor (God's will?!). Furthermore, when there are closed feedback loops what is considered as input and what as output may be arbitrary. For example, when you push down on a spring you feel a force – or when you apply a force to a spring it deflects. Which is the cause, the force or the displacement? Obviously either force or displacement can be assumed to be the cause, with the other as the effect.

C. Metricity

The attribute of *metricity* (the quality of measurement) has to do with the meaning of the variables of the model in the sense of the well-known psychophysical scales of S.S. Stevens [25]: nominal, ordinal, interval and ratio scales (see below). At one extreme the relationships are expressed in variables that are only nominal (name) categories. At the other limit of metricity are relationships expressed in variables that have a cardinal property of continuous quantitative values (one can consider equal ratio relations as the very limit with equal intervals close behind). In between are ordinal, expressions that X is greater (e.g., better) or lesser (worse) than Y. More specific definitions are:

A *nominal scale* is a naming process. The object or event is assigned a unique number. For a given set of such operations on different objects or events, any change of number assignments to the items is permissible so long as every object or event has its own unique number. Examples are: social security numbers, numbers on football player shirts.

An *ordinal scale* assigns numbers to order the objects or events. A greater number means a greater value of some attribute. Any new number assignments are permissible so long as monotonicity (the same ordering) is preserved. Examples are: quality ratings of hotels or films, Brinell hardness of surfaces. Sometimes the order ratings are done by appointed human judges (e.g., professional food tasters), and sometimes by scientific instruments.

An *interval scale* assigns numbers to the objects or events in such a way that equality of numerical intervals is preserved. Any change in number assignments is permissible if it maintains the equality of intervals between any set of objects or events. For example, if A and B are 2 feet apart and B and C are 2 feet apart, one can transform to inches or meters and the A-B and B-C intervals are still the same number (as each other) apart. Note that an arbitrary number can be added to each of A, B and C and the intervals between them would not change. Temperature measured in degrees Fahrenheit would be an example of an interval scale; zero degrees on this scale has no particular meaning.

A *ratio scale* is an even stricter cardinal scale that assigns numbers to objects or events relative to some absolute zero reference, which means that under any reassignment of numbers to the items the ratios are preserved. Note that if A = 4 and B =2, then A=2B. Transformation to a scale with half-size units would make A=8 and B=4, so A is still 2B. Note that in this case an arbitrary number cannot be added to each of A and B, for the ratio property would not then be preserved. Temperature measured in degrees Kelvin would be an example of a ratio scale. On the Kelvin scale the zero has a physical meaning (the molecules stop moving), and a number twice as large as another number is truly twice as hot. On the

Centigrade or Fahrenheit scales that would not make sense, since a number twice as large as another number (say 40 degrees C or F) does not mean twice as hot as 20 degrees C or F) in any physically meaningful way.

Note further that each successive scale (in the order given above) retains the properties of the one preceding it. I have lumped the interval and ratio scales into the level three metricity category for convenience, though the ratio scale is more extreme than the interval scale.

D. Robustness

The attribute of *robustness* refers to the breadth of applicability. The least robust model is one that has only one purpose, a unique application, and is otherwise useless. An example might be an instruction for how to operate a particular home appliance or item of software. At the other extreme is a model that has extremely wide applicability, say Newton's law, F=MA, i.e., Force equals Mass times Acceleration. We can assert that in the limit a model that applies to everything from atomic scale to galactic scale does not exist, though, as noted with the Observables attribute, physicists are thinking hard about what it would take for a "theory of everything".[26]

E. Social penetration

The attribute of *social penetration* has to do with the degree to which a model is known, understood, accepted, and used by the appropriate community of people. The scale goes from purely mental models that are confined to internal thoughts of some one person[27] to models that are widely understood, accepted and applied by a large and diverse community of people. In between are models that are described to others or published in the literature, perhaps in competition with other models for the same application, and perhaps used by only a few practitioners.

Social penetration is perhaps the most difficult attribute to achieve, or at least the most time-consuming aspect of modeling.

Any new model, particularly if it threatens the old, will be challenged (not a bad thing, science depends on it). Opponents will question the observations, as well as its relevance in terms of addressing a salient question. In a sense a new model must be actively marketed by its advocates, else it may never be accepted. However success in marketing a model (having more people believe it and use it) does not by itself mean it is more useful and reliable. The model can be fraudulent, in which case its legitimacy will eventually be questioned as more evidence is gathered. The earth was flat for a very long time. If a model is marketed as answering some question, one can also challenge whether the question is meaningful.

F. Conciseness

The attribute of conciseness is added to provide a metric on brevity of presentation, along with adherence to denotation, clarity and reason. Adherence to brevity, denotation, clarity and reason is the principle that has come to be called *Ockham's razor*. This principle was originally attributed to philosopher William of Ockham (1288-1347), according to his pronouncement *Numquam ponenda est pluralitas sine necessitate* (plurality must never be posited without necessity).[28] The idea is that one should use the simplest statement that does not compromise explanatory power. Of course too few words may reduce explanatory power.

A hundred-page exposition of an argument, theory, premise or relationship would not normally be considered as a model. This book is not a model, though this taxonomy of model attributes is a model.

EXAMPLES OF MODELS IN TERMS OF THE ATTRIBUTES

Now let us consider examples of models that combine different levels of the attributes. Note that any one model can have different levels of any given attribute, referring to the lettered rows and numbered columns of Figure 1. We assume that all the examples below qualify on the conciseness attribute at least at the moderate level. We assume that more of the attribute of conciseness always makes a better scientific model, other things equal, so for simplicity that attribute is excluded from the various combinations compared below.

[A1,B1,C1,D1,E1] is a mental model (a musing) assigning some hypothetical simple relation between hypothetical entities, e.g., a particular imagined unicorn is green.

[A1,B1,C3,D3,E1] is a mental model on a provided numerical or category scale. By itself it cannot be called an objective or scientific model. Only when it is aggregated with other such responses, all of which can be said to be responses on the same scale to a common stimulus can it begin to have the makings of such a model.

[A2,B2,C2,D2,E2] is a hypothetical framework of relationships with moderate focus communicated to an interested community. The present taxonomy of models might be an example. By itself it is only an expression of my idea in my language, but can become accepted as an objective (though qualitative) model if others agree.

[A2,B2,C2,D1,E1] is a mental model (contemplation) by an experimenter to rank order particular experimental data for later analysis (and an eventual model).

[A2,B2,C3,D1,E1] is a mental model based on numerical relationships between known data that are broadly applicable within some special industrial context. This might be considered of a way to analyze cardinal data (from observations) in a given experiment, and lead to a model.

[A2,B1,C3,D2,E3] is a widely accepted quantitative depiction of past or present facts such as a graphical plot of past stock prices.

[A3,B3,C2,D2,E3] is a predictive, ordinal, well accepted model with moderate applicability. This might be an experimentally-based qualitative or best-practices design guideline that is standard within a given industry.

[A3,B2,C3,D3,E3] is typical of widely accepted and applied models in science and engineering such as the physical laws of Newton, Ohm, Bernoulli, Faraday, etc.

At the ultimate limit [A3,B3,C3,D3,E3] is a fully predictive, quantitative model that applies to and explains all of nature and is accepted without hesitation. It is a presentation of relationships between well defined variables pertaining to all objects or events, communicated to others in a combination of written words, symbols or graphic images that conveys quantitative structure including explicit cardinal relationships and is demonstrably communicated widely and understood and accepted for use. It is based on data that are empirically observable by anyone, has a demonstrable record of being predictive within a wide set of circumstances and with high statistical confidence, does not conflict with other models of relationships between the same variables, and applies at all magnitude levels of nature from subatomic to intergalactic. This is what physicists aspire to as the previously mentioned "theory of everything" but have not yet reached, and surely never will.

RELEVANCE OF THE TAXONOMY TO MAKING MODELS USEFUL

Useful models, broadly defined, span the full range of the taxonomy, short of the physicist's "theory of everything". The impression must not be given that useful models are easy to come by, that they always tell the truth (complete truth is never known), and indeed that more of each attribute *necessarily* makes for a more useful model (too much math will make it incomprehensible to most people). For those reasons it is important to add some caveats.

With regard to **applicability to observables** a model builder at first may consider verbal propositions or hypothetical "framework" models that are not bound by any specific past observations (e.g., hypotheses and conjecture about the problem at hand, how to bound it in terms of what independent and dependent variables to include, what is known and what is unknown, and what is important) at the A1 level. As the model develops, explicit data from completed experiments and experience should be applied at the A2 level. The goal is to predict success in terms of future observable data or physical system measurements (A3).

However, in an effort to "sell" the model to colleagues, modelers have been known to fudge the data, or fake it completely, or select those observables that support the desired conclusion and ignore the others. We see that in political campaigns, where protagonists for one side or the other point to models based on carefully selected observables that support their position, and carefully avoid including observables that support the other side. Alternatively, once the model is complete and makes a projection, there is a tendency to interpret the result in a manner to support the modeler's bias.

High levels of the *dimensionality* attribute are common in models that are inherently complex with many variables (such as those in social, economic and medical fields). When quantitative measures are available modelers may tend toward factorial experimental designs such as analysis of variance. But more often multi-input-multi-output relationships tend to be those used in more qualitative (low level of metricity) modeling. Such models are employed by clinicians (e.g., a particular pattern of maladies is associated with a given pattern of symptoms) where the intent is to check for obvious effects of a drug or some policy intervention.

One pitfall of modeling is encountered when building a descriptive model based on a given set of data by using a large number of model parameters. The model may then result in a good fit to the particular data. But then if the same set of input variables has slightly different values the model may not fit at all, in other words have no predictive capability. A standard joke is that with enough parameters one can concoct a model that will draw an elephant or whistle Dixie. This problem is characteristic of models based on a large set of rules, e.g., one rule for each variable, where each rule is more or less tailored to the specific value of the variables in the original data set. It is against this problem that Occam's razor is relevant.

The *metricity* attribute is mostly a matter of the modeler's intent. Human behavior can be represented in words (C1), and much social science literature does that and no more. Human performance modeling mostly implies at least ordinality (C2): that something is bigger, faster, or better by some criterion. Models that predict in cardinal relationships (C3) are most desirable, because cardinal (continuous numerical) relations subsume order relations but offer greater precision.

But again there are dangers. Models that predict numbers and involve complex equations may appear to be more sophisticated (and get published in a scientific journal), but for many applications they may be of less use than a very simple model in the nominal or ordinal category that is easier for users to understand.

The *robustness* attribute is partially a matter of intent. Any reasonable modeler knows that the applicability of any human performance model is initially quite limited (D1), though he or she might hope that it can gain wider applicability with time and revision to include other variables and wider use. Being human, the modeler is naturally a protagonist, and may easily get caught up in marketing the model beyond what is warranted.

In the development of any model, the *social penetration* evolution begins with the initiator's mental model (E1) and possibly evolves over time to full acceptance (E3) by the community of experts and practitioners in the field. Usually this does not occur in a linear, one-directional process. Typically a scientific model becomes open to review and criticism by peers in the submission/publication process by any reputable journal. It may be rejected at first, but with suggestions to the author and rethinking the model may then be refined. There will always be a delay in publication. And after initial application it may be subjected to further active feedback and refinement to make it more understandable and useful.

Finally, adhering to the *conciseness* attribute requires effort on the part of the model developer. That effort pays off in making the model more easily reproducible (it saves space) and transferable. That makes it more useful.

One of the highest quality (in the sense of this taxonomy) human performance models ever developed is the McRuer and Jex[29] model that specifies the explicit transfer function (as a first-order differential equation plus time delay) to characterize the combined human operator and controlled element in a target tracking feedback system. It is elegant because it has a fixed form and comes with a table of (relatively few) parameters with specified dependence on the input bandwidth and controlled element dynamics. In that sense it conforms well to the edict of Occam's Razor (simpler is better). This is a [A3, B2,C3,D2,E3] model. It evolved after many years of government funding to many investigators (including this author) interested in pilots flying high performance fighter aircraft and maintaining control stability. However, even though the McRuer-Jex model set a high standard for human performance models, it is of relatively little interest today because now aircraft are mostly flown on autopilot or fly-by-wire software that provides automated compensation to prevent instability accidents.

In a different vein, a modeling approach called ACT-R (Adaptive Character of Thought)[30] represents procedural knowledge in units called *production rules*, interacting with declarative knowledge called *chunks* – all implemented in computer software. This approach is now widely used by other behavioral modelers, e.g. for car driving.[31] The general approach aspires to the [A3,B3,C3,D2,E3] category. However one problem with such complex simulator models is that they contain many parameters that are adjusted to provide fit to the available data for the given application, so that predictability is limited and adherence to Occam's Razor is a stretch.

Models are now being used in an astonishing new way. A model of some technical function couched in computer logic (e.g. for an aircraft control system) can be made to directly specify the software code without a programmer ever having to write specific and detailed lines of code. The danger herein is that no human may ever know exactly what instructions the computer has been given. This is the sort of problem that the "father of cybernetics" Norbert Wiener warned about in his 1964 Pulitzer Prize-winning *God and Golem Inc.*[32] that computers may do things they were programmed to do but those actions were never really intended by the human programmer.

One final caveat regarding usefulness of models. While it may seem that the explicit prediction (for a given input what is the output) is the most useful property of a model, that is often of only secondary importance. The most useful aspect may well be that the conception, development and publication of the model caused people to think hard about the problem—what are the variables that count the most, how best to formulate the problem, and so on. A model requires the model-builder to think, and it should also require the model reader/user to think, and more thinking is usually a good thing.

MODELS AND SOCIAL CHOICE

The totality of our publicly accepted models forms our store of what we reasonably assume we know. Individual mental models encapsulate individual subjective beliefs, whether based on evidence or based on faith, but they do not contribute to the general store of knowledge—they are private. Unfortunately at this point in our evolution we mostly lack objective means to capture individual mental models and somehow compare them or combine them where they agree. Of course people can share mental models by verbal expression or by acting on their beliefs, as in coordinated athletic team sports, where individuals infer each other's mental models as they interact.

One objective means to discover a mental model is using voting to capture the mental preferences or beliefs of a group. Pollsters work hard in posing simple questions to get valid answers about what people really believe. The problem here is that the simple questions are posed in words that often have ambiguous interpretation: Do you believe in X? What kind of X?. Do people all mean the same thing by what is being called X? What does "believe" mean? Do I believe X or not believe X because that is my tradition, that is what is comfortable to say I believe? Did I really ever question my belief in X? For religious belief, especially because of such subtleties, it is difficult to pin down by polling what people actually believe.

We tend to make key decisions in groups and communities by voting. Group decision-making is called *social choice*. Economists who have studied the issues of social choice reveal certain difficulties in finding the preferences of a group. Kenneth Arrow[33] won a Nobel Prize for, among other things, showing that it is logically impossible for people offered choice among at least three alternatives to always come up with a clear choice by majority vote. Of course there can be tie votes. If you allow people to rank order preferences among A, B and C, one person can prefer A to B to C, another can prefer B to C to A, and still another C to A to B. There is then no group preference. The latter is called *preference intransitivity*. It can get much more complicated. It is probably just as well, because, while one might like to establish public policies such as those that impinge on religious belief according to majority voting, tyrannizing the minority opinion on religious belief seems particularly inappropriate.

Important distinctions in modeling

Beyond the six model attributes detailed above there are several other distinctions that are important to consider.

SIMPLE AND COMPLEX MODELS

A simplest model is a statement that X is Y, where X is a thing or event and Y is a descriptor (adjective, number, etc.). A very complex model might be the complete engineering specification of a jumbo jet aircraft or the voluminous US Code of Federal Regulations.[34] In the simplest model case the independent variables have to do with what qualifies as X. In the case of the jumbo jet the independent variables have to do with what exact part of the airplane and what function of that part we are talking about. For the Code of Federal Regulations the independent variables would provide information enabling a user to go to a specific chapter and rule and determine what the regulation stated. Some readers might complain that I am using the term model too broadly here, but there is really no way to restrict the term to a narrower range.

DESCRIPTIVE AND PRESCRIPTIVE (NORMATIVE) MODELS

A *descriptive* model serves to tell how some specific thing is structured or provide detail on some set of events. It looks back in time in the sense that it refers to objects or events that exist or have existed in the past. If the model describes an object yet to be built or a plan yet to be implemented, the descriptive model is based on the already completed design or plan. A *prescriptive* model tells what *should* happen in the future according to specified or assumed norms. They can be social/cultural norms or they can be physical norms (e.g., how some aspect of the world works: that a (given) input should produce a stated output.

STATIC AND DYNAMIC MODELS

In a static model neither the input nor the output variables change with time, while in a dynamic model either input or output or both vary with time. For example when you press down with force F on a spring having stiffness parameter K it will deflect a certain distance X. That is a static model; nothing changes with time. If a clock pendulum is initially displaced from a resting position to an angle A and then released, a simple dynamic model will predict the trajectory of how it will swing back and forth with time as a function of initial angle A, the pendulum length and the force of gravity. An economic dynamic model might have as input the continually changing price of gasoline over a one-year period and output the modeled effect of those changes on vehicle use over the same period. Static models require only algebraic equations, whereas dynamic models make use of differential equations with time as the argument. Thus the output of a dynamic model is a curve that plots one or more variables against time.

DETERMINISTIC AND PROBABILISTIC MODELS

A *deterministic* model says that if X is the input then Y is the output—for certain. A *probabilistic* model says that if X is the input then Y is the output with some probability less than one. More generally for input X the probabilistic model will specify a set of outputs each with a different probability (possibly a probability distribution). A common type of probabilistic model (called a Markov model) is a tree graph that branches from one or more nodes representing initial states, where the branches to downstream or peripheral nodes are tagged with probabilities. Starting from any initial node the probabilities of ending in any downstream node is thus calculable.

Whether the model is deterministic or probabilistic, a computer can be programmed to try a large number of different inputs to test the resulting outputs. The inputs can systematically proceed

46   *What Is God?*

by intervals through a given range of values, or can be selected randomly from a given distribution. The latter is called a Monte Carlo model after the casino gambling reputation of the Principality of Monaco.

MODELS THAT USE FUZZY LOGIC

In recent years a new analytical tool has found increasing acceptance as a way to represent the "soft associations" exhibited by the overlaps of meaning between words. It is called *fuzzy logic* or *fuzzy set theory*.[35] It has applicability to making decisions involving a large number of variables where the many rules available for deciding on an action in any specific context are only available as verbal statements (which is the case for the explication of most real knowledge in this world). An example of fuzzy logic is found in the Appendix.

Fuzzy logic has a fascinating history of rejection by computer scientists in the West, whose *crisp* mathematical ways of thinking have proven ineffectual in dealing with soft, overlapping ideas, and by technology managers who are put off by the term *fuzzy* as being unscientific. At the same time theorists in Asia have pushed ahead not only with fuzzy theory but also with applications. Systems based on fuzzy logic are now in digital cameras, washing machines, subway speed controls, and automobile transmissions.

2

SOME PERSPECTIVES ON BELIEVING

Nothing is easier than self deceit. For what each man wishes, that he also believes to be true.
—Demosthenes, 384 BC

There are no whole truths; all the truths are half truths. It is by trying to treat them as whole truths that plays the devil.
—Alfred North Whitehead, *Dialogs*, 1923

Tell all the truth, but tell it slant
Success in circuit lies
Too bright for our infirm delight
The truth's superb surprise
As lightning to the children eased
With explanation kind
The truth must dazzle gradually
Or every man be blind
—Emily Dickinson, *Complete Poems*, 1955

Variety of belief models

In the preceding chapter we discussed models: concise, hard-edged logical representations of belief that could be called scientific, many adaptable to quantification. This chapter moves to some diverse perspectives on what it means to believe, why we believe, the history of believing, and the linguistic factors we must consider in such discussions. These are modeling perspectives with a softer edge, that tend to be qualitative, are more debatable and without consensus among scholars.

There admittedly is no intended coherence between the topics in this chapter. They are topics that somehow seemed relevant to the more focused discussion of belief in God that follows in succeeding chapters.

Trust is an included topic that has been left outside of science until fairly recently when economists and psychologists picked it up. A new Journal called *Trust Research* appeared in 2011.[36] System engineers concerned with safety have especially become interested in trust.[37]

The topic of virtual reality is included because it offers means to conduct experiments on human subjects who can be shown to experience (and believe in) phenomena that physically do not exist.

This is followed by a review of a curious and very controversial psychological theory called the "bicameral mind" alleging that ancient peoples believed that God (or gods) were directing them – much as they might have been hypnotized (another type of "virtual reality"). Finally I include a model I particularly like that suggests how belief evolves. It is a model commonly used by engineers to make computers learn.

Consider Emily Dickinson's famous phrase "Tell all the truth but tell it slant". Initially the user of a model generated by someone else cannot understand the full implications of what the modeler intended. The truth cannot be absorbed in one bite. Belief evolves. Nor can the modeler appreciate where that reader is coming from, what life experience that reader has that will affect their initial interpretation. Further, no matter how sophisticated, how elaborate the model, the whole truth will never be told: there is just too much to tell, there are just too many variables to the reality of the whole truth. Finally, the modeler will never know the whole truth of whatever the model is about. Much as any modeler would aspire to tell "all the truth," that is clearly not possible: it ends up being "slant".

There is a common expression that all models are wrong. Modelers who are wedded to a particular model and are overly aggressive in marketing it are sometimes disparaged as claiming that they "Have model, will travel." The "gradual dazzling" of the truth requires feedback, clarification, further communication, and mental soaking time for both modeler and reader. An established model, one with a high level of social penetration, represents a convergence based on gradual refinement and necessarily the passing of time.

Philosophers, logicians, economists and others too numerous to review have been proffering theories of belief for decades. From the ancient Greek philosophers until today there have been lively philosophical arguments about whether we believe based on rationality or on emotion. For example philosopher David Hume (1711-1776)[38] claimed that "Reason is, and ought only to be the slave of the passions." Allegedly he was referring to one's innate sense of morality, that in dealing with moral issues one cannot reason independently of one's passions. We know that emotion plays a large role in belief, whether in a moral context or not.

Charles Sanders Peirce (1839–1914) characterized inquiry not so much as an effort to gain truth but as a means to avoid doubts, social disagreement and irritation, so as to reach a belief on the basis of which one is prepared to act. He distinguished several approaches to inquiry such as sticking to some original belief in order to bring comfort and decisiveness (he called this *tenacity*), being brutally authoritarian and trying to dominate others who offer contrary evidence (he called this *authority*), and conformity with current paradigms, taste and fashion, i.e., what is more respectable (he called this *congruity*), and finally the method of science, which seeks to criticize, correct and improve upon itself. I suppose real human inquiry is a blend of all of these modes.

G.E. Moore (1873-1958) posed the following paradox, namely that people are inclined to say things such as "It is raining but I can't believe it is raining" which is patently absurd but nevertheless logically consistent. This led Moore to assert that one cannot believe falsely, though one can speak of someone else that they believed falsely.

Modern economic and cognitive science has worked hard to formalize models of belief. It continues to be recognized that belief is not simply a matter of being rational and having a straightforward way to draw conclusions about what is true and what is not. If one knows the probabilities associated with various kinds of observable evidence (probability of a particular observation given that a particular hypothesis is true) there is a well-known mathematical model called Bayes' theorem that works well to estimate the truth or falsity of premises (see Appendix). But the problem is that those contingent probabilities are subjective and are only vaguely held in mind. This goes for both the mental formulation of the hypothesis and the estimation of probability contingent on each hypothesis. Further, some hypotheses may be well formed mentally along with some basis for estimating their probabilities, while some other plausible hypothesis may be overlooked or offer no hint of its probability. In using a Bayesian approach a "don't know" category is often treated as indifference with 50-50 probability belief. But some belief analysts rebel against interpreting "don't know" as a 50-50 probability estimation, and regard that judgment as very different from making a probability assessment.

There has been recent formal (logical, mathematical) work on belief called *Dempster-Shafer belief theory*[39]. In some sense it is a generalization of Bayes' theorem cited above as one of the example models concerning statistical inference from evidence. It differs from Bayes' theorem in that the procedure is not limited to subjective probability judgments directly on the proposition. Rather, it is based on deriving degrees on belief for a given proposition from subjective judgments for both *strength of belief* and *judgment of plausibility* regarding various other questions (sets of *possibilities*) that contain the proposition. For example, a set of four possibilities might be: (1) X is true, (2) X is false (3) X is neither true nor false, and (4) X is either true or false. There is a rule in Dempster-Shafer theory for combining multiple such degrees of belief when they are based on elements of evidence that are mutually independent. The degree of belief in the main proposition depends on the answers to related questions and the subjective probability of each answer.

There is the further problem of *unknown unknowns* (unk-unks) mentioned earlier. Some relevant properties are known as credible variables, i.e., previously observed and identified as variables, their values unknown. Other properties have never been known or considered: the unk-unks. The believer or modeler simply has no thought of their existence or their relation to the issue at hand. This suggests that formal belief models should include two components: (1) the current state of belief, and (2) a rule for how current belief would be updated in light of new variables and new evidence. Unfortunately the second component is missing in most cases.

Trust

REASONS WE TRUST

There are multiple factors that engender trust. Most obvious is reliability, whether a person or system has consistently performed well or as expected, and did not fail. Immediately following a failure we are inclined not to trust. This can be irrational in the case where otherwise reliable systems have rare chance failures and there is evidence that the person or institution takes pains to acknowledge the failure and makes serious efforts to prevent such failures in the future. If the failure was in the long past and recent performance has been successful we are inclined to trust.

We tend to trust people and things that are familiar, events that we think we understand, and have experienced. For this reason we adhere to beliefs and cultural norms held by our parents and friends growing up—in short, our tribe. Unfamiliar people, systems and situations provide insufficient statistical evidence on which to base trust. We also tend to trust people and systems that we depend on, perhaps because we must (we may have no choice), but also because those entities are familiar. Commercial advertising is a greater determiner of what we trust than we are willing to admit.

Trust may be based on evidence that is not direct but is second hand. Having initial trust in a person or institution, we are inclined to trust something that person or institution says.

Experiments and models of trust are now becoming more popular in various fields of science and technology, especially in psychology (interpersonal trust), in computer science (cyber security, and operation of complex systems such as air traffic control) and in political science.[40]

TRUST AND FAITH

Religious belief is said to be based not on physical evidence but rather on faith. But what is faith, and is it really any different than trust? Religious faith emanates from trust we have in believing persons or institutions that appear to warrant trust themselves and have actively taught us to trust. And those people and institutions acquired their trust in the same manner, and so on *ad infinitum* back in time. We call it religious tradition.

When is faith (or trust) based on nothing more than tradition? Is the only justification for faith a lack of evidence? How much of faith is simply hope regarding preferences in some future events?

One can certainly contend that science is a matter of faith: faith that use of scientific method based on evidence will reveal the truth. Put more broadly, one must have faith in a value system to underpin any interpretation.

Philosopher Daniel Dennett likens religious faith to falling in love. He claims that the language of romantic love and the language of religious devotion are all but indistinguishable.[41] Neither faith nor romantic love is rational. Neither is a matter of comparing plusses and minuses to determine a best policy. Irrational faith is an empirical fact, and we must deal with it. In one sense it may be rational if it makes one feel better—we return to that argument later.

Virtual reality

WHAT IS VR?

Now we take up a very current topic that impinges on the question of what we perceive to be reality. The reader may be well aware of the term *virtual reality* (VR), meaning the art of producing the experience of seeing, hearing and feeling what is not really there. We refer to the new technology of computerized animation in TV ads, movies and computer games. How does that topic relate to modeling our beliefs about real objects and events? The answer is that there is a rich vein of research and understanding of how people perceive reality emanating from so-called virtual reality technology. This writer has been involved in VR research, and it is for that reason that I see a connection to the question of modeling God.

First let us admit that the term virtual reality is an oxymoron, a self-contradiction from the normal use of English words. If something is virtual it is not real, and if it is real it is not virtual. But the term has caught on, is in the current vernacular, so we will use it. However it might be noted that "virtual environment" is perhaps a more precise phrase for what is meant.

Let us also reflect on the fact that in some primitive forms the art of eliciting a virtual reality experience has been around for a very long time. Verbal story-telling probably dates back to primitive peoples who lived in caves. One can easily imagine that good story telling, whether to groups huddled around a campfire or to children by parents at bed-time, has always stirred the listeners and conjured up active and *realistic* mental images. After the invention of writing there were depictions of battles and other events that actively provoked the reader's imagination. Later came the theatre. Much more recently came radio, and who of us oldsters can forget radio serials such as the Lone Ranger, the Shadow and other serial radio programs that kept listeners glued to the set, filling in for visual images that were not there. All of these communication media can be said to have elicited a virtual reality experience.

VIRTUAL REALITY TECHNOLOGY

To appreciate virtual reality let's consider the dramatic technological advances that have come about in only a few years. Virtual reality (VR) technology has resulted from the fact that computers can be programmed to generate dynamic displays that are highly realistic: of people, animals, plants, vehicles, buildings—anything at all, in full color and with accurate motion. We are so accustomed to seeing such virtual computer-graphic images in TV advertisements that we are numb to the wonder of it all. But what makes for a far more compelling experience is new technology that lets the viewer *immerse* himself in a virtual environment. This is achieved by the participant wearing a head-mounted display, a helmet or eye glasses that present to the viewer a computer-generated image. Since the helmet or eyeglasses have sensors that detect which way the head is pointing (up or down, left or right) the computer can sense this and make the computer-generated image be what the viewer would see if the head were turned in the same way while viewing the real environment. This is very compelling and produces the striking sensation that VR researchers call "immersion" in the virtual environment.[42]

Auditory VR technology is such an old story that we do not recognize it as virtual reality. Apart from story telling on the radio we have electronically recorded music, enhanced to produce a stereo effect by using earphones or strategically placed loudspeakers corresponding to placement of microphones at the recording site. More recently a scientific understanding of how the shape of the ear enables us to distinguish sound behind or above the head has resulted in added electronics to replicate this effect. For example a listener can be made to experience a virtual buzzing insect swirling around the head at easily identifiable locations, where the insect is produced electronically.

New technology also permits haptic immersion in a virtual environment, where the participant can experience the sense of touching objects in the environment that are not really there. How can this possibly be? It is achieved by having the participant wear a specially made glove that stimulates the tactile nerve endings on the skin in correspondence to whether the computer software indicates contact with an object at any particular location.

In addition to entertainment from TV and computer games there are many practical applications of virtual vision, hearing, touch and force feedback. An earlier application was the flight simulator, used in pilot training. By suspending the pilot and whole cockpit on a six-legged computer-moveable base, flight trainers are able to produce realistic roll, pitch and yaw motion simulation (e.g., of mid-air turbulence). The resulting virtual reality can be made so true to that of flying the actual aircraft that in many cases no training in the actual aircraft is required before the pilot flies the actual aircraft with a load of passengers. Similar devices are now used for highway vehicle driver training. Another application is in the domain or design of machines or buildings, where the designer can view a computer-graphic representation of his design from any viewpoint at any angle, or the architect or his prospective customer can "walk through" a virtual building, look in any direction and see what the designer put there – before any actual machine or building exists.

Using similar technology the participant's hand can be placed within a mechanism that causes a remote hand/arm arbitrarily far away to touch or handle real objects. The human hand can receive force feedback corresponding precisely to the forces the remote hand encounters in its (remote) environment. This technology for remote handling was originally applied to enable a human operator to peer through a leaded glass (shielded) window to manipulate objects in a nearby radioactively hot environment.[43] Without the virtual touch and force feedback it would be impossible to perform such telemanipulation safely and reliably.

Figure 2 illustrates the operation. The dashed line around the remote manipulator arm suggests that the remote arm can be either real or virtual, and that if the visual and/or tactile feedback is good enough there will be no difference in the human operator's perception (mental model, shown in the cloud) of the (real or virtual) reality.

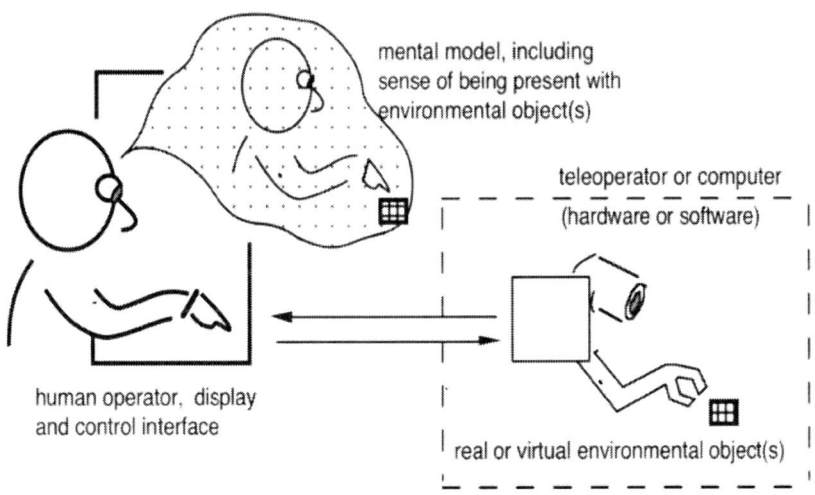

Figure 2. Human operator controlling a remote hand to grasp objects in a real or virtual environment.

Developments in remote telemanipulation have led to robotic surgery, where the surgeon views a TV image and performs the surgical manipulations by placing his hands in force and touch feedback devices.[44] By the latter he positions the miniature TV camera and steers the surgical tools inside the patient's body. For some very delicate operations movements can be "scaled down" so that movements in comfortable range for the human (e.g., inches) correspond to movements of a small fraction of an inch inside the patient. Manipulation control can similarly be "scaled up" for control of remote vehicles maneuvering in space, undersea or on land.

BEHAVIOR RESEARCH ISSUES IN VR

The review of virtual technology research above is provided to help the reader understand how modern technology has truly enabled us to manipulate the perception of what is real.

This enables a new kind of behavior research into how humans perceive "where" they are present and what they perceive as reality. The research helps us understand how easily we can be made to experience what is not really there.

In any of the above-cited cases of telemanipulation the remote hand or vehicle or objects being manipulated can be virtual (simply computer generated) or can be real. This suggests that a paradigm such as that shown in Figure 2 can be generalized to an experimental apparatus to explore virtual reality perception.

There are several "quality" measures that can be applied to virtual environments. One type of measure is the sense of reality—how "immersed" does the human subject feel, measured on a subjective scale. That is important in entertainment applications. However it may or may not be important in more practical applications such as simulation (e.g., flying the flight simulator, performing virtual surgery, checking to make sure the components fit together in a virtual instantiation of a mechanical design or building). In the practical applications cited above one is concerned with learning, so both performance in the virtual environment and transfer of that learning to the real environment are what is important.

With respect to sense of reality there are three factors that contribute to the experience of reality, the "immersion":[45]

(1) The *display information rate*, consisting in turn of:
a) spatial resolution (defined in *pixels* for vision, *taxels* for touch);
b) temporal resolution (frame refresh rate in images per second); and
c) magnitude resolution (binary bits per pixel embodied in color or gray scale).

Note that the mathematical product of the above three quantities (pixels per image, images per second, and bits per pixel is equal to bits per second, the key metric for rate of information transfer.

(2) The *ability to move about* and orient in the sensory space (e.g., to scan a visual display with the eyes, to actively move the hand across a tactile display, to move the body within a virtual room).

(3) The *ability of the subject to effect changes* in the virtual environment (e.g., as in telemanipulation).

If what is seen, heard or touched does not correspond realistically to scanning or viewpoint or bodily changes, the sense of presence is lost. This loss can occur if there is sufficient delay between movement and display response (more than 0.1 second), which can occur if too much computing is necessary to effect timely and accurate movement-display transformation.

We have ample evidence that the sense of presence ("immersion") in the virtual environment is enhanced when multiple senses are employed (e.g., vision plus hearing, vision plus touch, all three sensory modes). This is in contrast to the subject perceiving simply that he/she is physically located in a laboratory and simply being asked to play an artificial game. With regard to religion, these same lessons apply to worship rituals. Immersion is amplified by involving all the senses: hearing music or the spoken word, singing, dancing—all while actively imagining.

One trick used to enhance the sense of presence is to have the human control, through bodily motions, a human-like avatar (which in turn may perform some task in the virtual environment). This is essentially a form of telemanipulation, but the virtual teleoperator is given human-like bodily form. The actual human operator then tends to empathize with the teleoperated avatar.

Finally, there is a mental exercise that has been shown to make a big difference in perception of presence in the virtual environment, and that is for participants to mentally try to *suppress disbelief* (actively resist any tendency to perceive that they are engaging a simulation and not the real thing).[46] Suppression of disbelief is not difficult when you are compelled by your senses, where there is feedback consistent with the virtual world, and the humans around you play along with the game. This author has participated in such experiments.

We speak of divine presence in religious ceremonies. *One has to wonder what there is in common between perception of virtual presence and perception of divine presence.*[47] The reason for wading through the technology and the behavioral research aspects of virtual reality is the suggested connection to understanding and modeling belief in the supernatural, and the question of whether religious practice can be modeled. Experience with virtual reality suggests that it is not so difficult to produce a compelling belief in what is not really there.

PHILOSOPHICAL QUESTIONS: WHAT IS PRESENCE? WHAT IS REALITY?

We conclude from the active development and ready market for virtual reality technology that there is a strong interest by people to engage in virtual reality experiences, perhaps to get away from the somber realities of the real world. VR is enjoyable. Also we note two attributes of human behavior that have been shown to enhance the VR experience. The first is that active bodily participation helps to make the virtual seem real. Second, we note that active voluntary suppression of disbelief (that the VR is not real) has a strong effect on enabling psychological "immersion" in the experience. We will have more to say about this later when we discuss the tendency toward religious belief.

Let us now contrast two ontologies of reality, two philosophical perspectives regarding what is real. One is what is commonly called Cartesian or mind-body dualism – that the brain processes perceptions of the outside world and these are passed to an immaterial "mind". The latter is attributed to French philosopher Rene Descartes because he postulated himself as a *res cogitans*, usually translated as a "thinking substance": he was conscious and existed because he could doubt. However there is controversy as to what he meant was located in the "mind".[48]

Modern science mostly assumes that there is a true material reality "out there" and by means of the scientific method we struggle to bring our scientific and our mental models to be ever closer approximations to the external truths. The brain is surely material and exists. Most scientists do not consider the "mind" to exist apart from the functioning of the brain. There are objective measures of the external environment and subjective measures of what we are thinking. This is called the rationalistic tradition, or realism.

The German philosopher Martin Heidegger (1889-1976) rejected the Cartesian view and asserted that all meaning, hence all reality, is conditioned by interpretation, including the beliefs, language and practices of the interpreter.[49] According to Heidegger[50] we are thrown into situations where action is unavoidable (*throwness* in Heidegger terminology), the result of such action is unpredictable, and stable representation of the situation is not possible. In normal use of a tool or other object (e.g., in hammering) the tool becomes transparent to the user, who then cannot conceive of the tool independently (it *is ready-to-hand* in Heidegger-speak). However, if some abnormality occurs (e.g., the hammer slips) there *is breakdown*, and the tool can then be conceived in the "mind" (it becomes *present-at-hand*). Normal "being", in Heidegger's view, means complete involvement in a dynamic interaction in which subject and object are inseparable. Only by stepping back and disconnecting from the involvement can a person perceive the separate elements of the situation.

Seemingly related to the Heidegger view are ideas put forth by American psychologist J.J. Gibson. According to Gibson, perception is the acquisition of information that supports action, especially with regard to overcoming constraints on action[51] Gibson calls this constraint-conformance *affordance*. Actions affect the environment, and the environment in turn affects the action in complete reciprocity. Perceptions are true, as Gibson sees it, to the extent that they support action in the environment.

I find the Heidegger and Gibson views both compatible with one another and credible in a certain sense. The Heidegger-Gibson perspective is credible in the sense that all perception is based on the result of previous action and learning (with exception of instinctual perception and response). At the same time there is a credible view that there must be some reality "out there" that forever must be unknown in many (most) respects—no chance to unravel it no matter how much science is brought to bear for any finite time into the future. In a later section I suggest an "estimation" model that helps mediate between these views of reality and how we can come to know it, or at least improve our knowledge of it.

Jaynes bicameral theory about hearing gods

Now we turn to a fascinating but very controversial theory about how the voice of God (or gods) impacted ancient man. In 1976 psychologist Julian Jaynes authored a book that posited a theory suggesting how it is that mankind came to be religious. The book is titled The *Origin of Consciousness in the Breakdown of the Bicameral Mind*[52]. The term *bicameral* (literally, two chambers) refers to the two distinct hemispheres of the cerebrum connected through the corpus callosum. In addition to the left hemisphere receiving from and sending neural signals to the right side of the body, and the right hemisphere receiving signals from and sending them to the left side of the body, there is further specialization. The left hemisphere is known to control audible speech and writing, whereas the right hemisphere excels at spatial and nonverbal tasks. It is said that the left side is "analytic" and "logical", whereas the right side is "holistic" and "intuitive". Obviously many functions, if not most, involve both sides.

THE BASIC IDEA

The gist of Jaynes' radical idea is that consciousness, subjectivity, awareness of self, the ego, the ability to introspect, autobiographical memory, all originated in mankind only 3000 years ago. Prior to that people were driven by auditory hallucinations, what they considered to be the gods talking to them and telling them what to do, particularly in situations of stress. The voices of kings (they were gods too) were also heard, even after their deaths. The voice hallucinations were not imagination but were the manifestation of man's volitions. Experiences originating in the right hemisphere were transmitted to the language centers in the left hemisphere, namely Wernicke's and Broca's areas.

Jaynes is no slouch when it comes to ancient history. He reviews in great detail what we know about these hallucinations from ancient writings such as the Iliad and the Hebrew Bible, and other relics from Mesopotamia, ancient Greece, Peru, etc.

So Jaynes' theory is that early man believed that the second voice that he was hearing, that directed him in times of stress, was the voice of a god. But around 1000 BC he became aware that the voice was his own: he became self-conscious. Consciousness is not an easy topic. Philosophers have pondered the subject for a very long time and have as yet no simple answers. One can say consciousness is a process rather than a thing, but that seems not to help much. We do observe that much of our behavior is automatic, not driven by conscious will. When we do think consciously we tend to think and understand in metaphors. An example is time. The particular metaphor we use is space. Time goes from left to right. We also tend to use narrative, a mental description of a sequence of events to make sense to ourselves. Jaynes' claim is that prior to 1000 BC this kind or processing either did not exist or existed in a form much more primitive than what we experience today by introspection.

Primitive peoples had speech, but writing came later. Speech was converted to writing only 3000 years ago. The earliest writing was to keep inventory for food, arms, etc. But, Jaynes asserts, certain ideas we now take for granted were originally missing. For instance a word for "mental will" is absent in Homer's Iliad (eighth century BC). But they surely had words for gods. Gradually writing included narratives of god-related events, descriptions of when and where voices of gods were heard. Then, along with writing and story telling, there came a weakening of the importance of the gods appearing in auditory form. And there was recognition of the chaos and suffering of the period (Trojan wars, earthquakes around the whole Mediterranean area about 1200BC). Earlier there had been no need for prayer and supplication to the gods since the gods were obviously in control, but now all the chaos made the gods seem missing. Various rituals and intermediaries (angels and demons) were invented to help counteract the confusing violence and apparent malevolence of the gods and gain access to them. Human prophets were recognized. There were new efforts to divine the speech of the now silent gods. Words for spirit, soul and mind appeared (e.g., *psyche* from the Greek).

While originally there were only words relating to external events, new words relating to internal sensations appeared, then mental processes, then introspection. For example in Amos, which some scholars claim is the oldest chapter of the Hebrew Bible originally written about 800 BC, there were no such words, and similarly for Jeremiah and Ezekiel. Ecclesiastes, the newest chapter (200 BC), does have words for pondering and spatialization of time, and seeks wisdom, not just the authoritarian Yahweh. Sacred texts in India changed over a similar period, from the *Veda* (*sruti*, or directly revealed, "what is heard") to the much more subjective *Upanishads* (consisting of human commentary). Jaynes refers often to the rise, at the time of the bicameral shift, of what he calls the "analog I". By this he distinguishes the linguistic term of self-reference from the actual person, and claims that prior to the bicameral shift no such terminology was in use, i.e., the concept of "I" was not available.

Jaynes recounts numerous connections of modern religions to the ancient bicameral absolutes (and away from the somewhat more difficult *agape*). There is a seeming desire to make contact with the lost authority in the unsubjective bicameral past. For example, the ancient oracle priestesses (sibyls) who operated under influence of the gods are found on the ceiling of Michelangelo's Sistine Chapel. Even today statues and paintings of the Virgin Mary are claimed to shed tears. There are cults that speak in tongues, hold training sessions to bring on trances so as to become possessed, all in submission to an authoritarian God that can talk through them. Modern religious rituals invoke procedures that incorporate other compelling attributes of expectancy and authority.

POETRY, SCHIZOPHRENIA AND SCIENCE

Jaynes devotes considerable discussion to poetry.[53] It is interesting that in bicameral times the gods supposedly spoke in poetry rather than prose: the Oracle of Delphi, the Indian Veda, the prophets of Yahweh. The Iliad is written in poetry, and the trend simply continued as the bicameral mind broke down. The Bhagavad Gita and other writings of the later period are in poetry. Speech is primarily in the left hemisphere, but poetry, which is much closer to song (music), is in the right. Jaynes suggests that music may have been invented "as a neural expectant to the hallucination of the gods" in the absence of self-consciousness. His idea is that the continuance of poetry and music resulted from the "change from a divine given" to a human activity based on nostalgia for the absolute. There is no question but that sacred music still inspires and conjures feelings of awe.

Because of the obvious connections to his notions of the bicameral mind, Jaynes cannot avoid the topics of hypnosis and schizophrenia. The history of hypnosis is littered with bizarre accounts, including Anton Messner's claim that hypnosis is a human-to-human gravitational attraction that accords with Newton's gravity. Accordingly he fed subjects iron to see if they became attracted to one another, but mostly got convulsive behavior. But we know that teaching of expectations (prior statements of how subjects would behave) and focusing of attention (by having subjects stare at a light, or voluntarily attend to only the voice of the authority figure) can bring on a hypnotic state. Jaynes suggests that this activates right brain domination over left brain ego control.

Schizophrenia is claimed to be uniquely consistent with the bicameral mind—a partial relapse to that primitive state. It is said to be accompanied by a failure of coherent narrative ability, hallucination, erosion of the ego, and in certain cases fading of a body image (or connection between self and environment).

Jaynes concludes his treatise by asserting that science itself can be read as a breakdown of the bicameral mind in a search for a hidden divinity: "God is right out there under the stars to be talked about and heard brilliantly in all the grandeur of reason, rather than behind the rood screen of ignorance in the murky mutterings of costumed priests." Poetically put!

Jaynes' book provoked much controversy when it was first published, and remains a theory for psychologists, psychiatrists and neuroscientists to contend with. One picking point is that a story called Gilgamesh Epic, reported to predate all the Hebrew Bible, does exhibit features of introspection. But Jaynes has countered that a more complete version of the story that was discovered in post bicameral times does not really contain significant introspection.

Recent neuroimaging studies tend to support Jaynes by providing new evidence of hallucinations that arise in the right temporal-parietal lobe and are transmitted through the corpus callosum to the left temporal lobe[54]. Modern brain imaging techniques, particularly PET (positron emission tomography) and functional MRI (magnetic resonance imaging) that reveal local brain activity will no doubt have much more to say about bicameralism in the future.

Philosopher Daniel Dennett comments that this *divination* was primitive man's way to avoid self-control and to pass the buck to something that can be held responsible if things don't go well.

We have seen that, assuming the Jaynes theory has credibility, that primitive peoples experienced a kind of virtual reality, a virtual authoritarian presence that was ascribed to divinity (there being no other evident reason for the inner voices). Further, according to Jaynes, mankind has retained vestiges of that virtual reality right up to modern times.

Estimation theory: a model of how belief evolves

Now we jump to the present day and a very non-controversial model being employed today to make computers learn. Hopefully it will provide some idea to the layman about how computers acquire belief by interacting with their environments (and by analogy how people do the same). I believe it bridges the Cartesian and Heidegger-Gibson viewpoints mentioned previously in conjunction with virtual reality. It is a procedure that pervades the world of control engineering. Complex computer-controlled machines and systems all over the world are based on this idea. In essence it is a way to discover the essential features of a physical environment one wishes to control, and to embody the properties of that environment (the external reality) in a computer-based "internal model". In its engineering instantiation the idea is attributed to Rudolf Kalman (1960)[55] though the basic idea surely dates back much earlier. We spare the reader all the mathematics, but trust me that it is well and widely documented and works well in computers. One could easily regard it as analogous to how people come to their beliefs, though surely with people the process is not so neat.

THE BASIC IDEA

I ask the reader to tolerate a block diagram, in hopes that this will make the explanation of the estimation procedure more clear than otherwise. We start with the notion that in the external physical environment "out there" lies a true reality that that can never be known fully (the PHYSICAL REALITY blob on the right) of Figure 3. It is important to understand that by a "reality" is meant

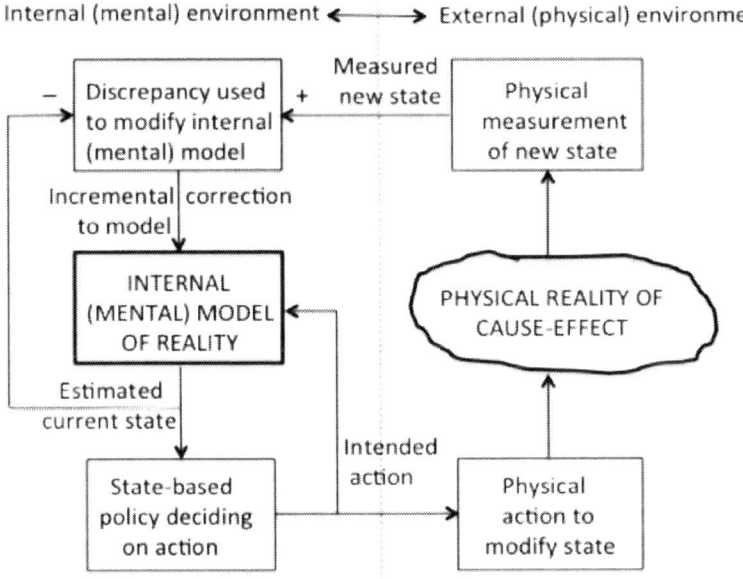

Figure 3. Estimation model of perceiving external events

the full set of physical cause-effect relationships in the slice of the world that is being considered, how any action results in a new state. This is more than simply a measurement (a single snapshot) of the state of the world in one time or place. By itself such a snapshot cannot tell the computer much of how the world "out there" really works. But by test actions on the world one can see how it responds. And by enough such actions one can derive a good model of the world's action-response characteristics, which after all is what is of interest in "believing".

The true physical reality, or course, consists of an infinite amount of cause-effect information (potential-action-to-new-state transformations). The intention is to construct an "internal model" of some subset of that reality (a clear instantiation of model dependent reality as mentioned in the Introduction). The internal model can at best represent only a minute fraction of the cause-effect information in the true reality, cast in terms of only a few dimensions of interest (i.e., of interest to the engineer designing the control system or to the person whose perception we represent). In the engineering version the internal model of the environment is within a computer, whereas in our diagram we suggest that the internal model can be mental, in the head of the person confronting the considered slice of physical reality. The internal model is the key component within our larger model of a person's belief acquisition.

STEPPING THROUGH THE MODEL

At the center left on the Figure 3 is a rectangular block in bold outline labeled INTERNAL (MENTAL) MODEL OF REALITY. Thus at the heart of our overall model of perceiving reality lies another model (a model within a model). The internal (mental) model is where the above-mentioned small slice (of the full set of cause-effect relations) is represented. This corresponds to a person's mental perception. The current state of the mental model (its output) is a momentary value of a small set of variables that specify the best estimate of the properties of the reality (in the engineering version a mathematical vector). It is represented by an arrow from the bottom of the block. This triggers a policy decision, namely an intention of what action to take to modify the external environment in a desirable direction. In engineering this STATE-BASED POLICY DECIDING ON ACTION is called a *control law*. It says if X is the case then take action Y.

Following the arrows, the resulting intention signal is sent to the physical environment (through what corresponds to motor neurons) to the PHYSICAL ACTION TO MODIFY STATE block (which in a person is muscle). Note that this same signal of intended change is sent back up to the internal model, so that the internal model can be updated to a state corresponding to what state it thinks the physical reality will take when the intention is realized in the external world.

Thus the (human or mechanical) muscle produces an actual change in the PHYSICAL REALITY OF CAUSE-EFFECT. This is usually a small incremental change, only enough to make a small change in the PHYSICAL MEASUREMENT OF STATE (performed by physical sensors in the engineered system or human sensors). Now we begin to see the Heidegger-Gibson notions appear: the key involvement of both the muscle actions and the sensors in the process that eventually determines perception.

Now the question is whether the internal (mental) model really has a true perception of what is going on with the physical reality (at least that very small segment of reality that the internal model is concerned with). It did update itself based in the intention resulting from the change policy—a kind of dead reckoning. But this update was blind to what *really* might have happened when the intention was transformed by the muscle to make a real impact on the physical reality. To set the record straight another bit of ingenuity is involved, and that is to compare what actually happened (MEASURED NEW STATE) to what was thought would happen. The two are compared by the block at the upper left labeled DISCREPANCY USED TO MODIFY INTERNAL (MENTAL) MODEL. Then that discrepancy result is used to tweak the model to better conform to what actually happened.

This is the raw outline of the estimation process. The process continues in small increments, thus enabling the internal (mental) model of reality to hone in, or to evolve through successive interactions, to an ever more valid perception of reality, at least in terms

68   *What Is God?*

of the variables of concern. It combines open-loop dead-reckoning with feedback control. Realize that simple feedback control amounts to blind error-nulling (described later in the Appendix) without any effort to build an internal model of the external reality.

In control engineering practice the logic of what goes on inside the two blocks above and below the internal model block are somewhat complex and the subject of ongoing research. Further, because the physical action and physical measurement blocks above and below the physical reality may be less than perfect (time delays, noise, etc.), there are additional elements that help, such as a computer model of the measurement process. But the above description should provide sufficient explanation for the reader to appreciate how perception can be modeled as an interactive "bootstrap" improvement process. In this process perception is clearly contingent on what actions are taken to modify the external reality, and what measurement is made on same. In control engineering this estimation technique is also called an *observation* process. Sounds like cognitive perception, doesn't it?

The estimation model can be used further to reflect on what we humans do when we "behave". Suppose a person could sense the external environment perfectly and continuously in time. This would necessitate accurate sensing for vision, hearing, touch, and muscle position and velocity. But suppose that person was unable to relate what was sensed to any internal model of the environment, any map, any procedure. The person would be reduced to simple error-nulling, much as a thermostat. He/she could be programmed (or motivated) with a goal set-point, and then could take action in proportion to the perceived instantaneous error between the goal set-point and the sensed current position or state. This is the way simple feedback control devices do work, and that seems to be close to how much autonomic (automatic, unconscious) behavior of animals works – simple reflex responses that comprise much of our low-level behavior.

Now suppose at another extreme our person had no sensors that look outside to see or measure the external environment, but he/she had a perfect internal model of the environment at some initial point in time. Suppose also that there was perfect muscle control, so that he/she could calculate what would result from any and all responses that were made. Thus, starting from an initial position, by perfect dead-reckoning our person could know the resulting location exactly no matter what action was taken, even though being blind to the actual environment. But if something in the outside world changed the internal model would no longer be valid. The person would have no way of knowing about new obstacles and thus any dead reckoning calculations would not provide an accurate prediction of location.

Both the feedback control and the dead reckoning paradigms outlined above assumed that either exteroceptors (that measure the outside world) or interoceptors (that measure and control the actions of the muscles or motors) were perfect. However in the estimation model of perception the sensory mechanisms can be imperfect and noisy and the system will still hone in on an accurate model of cause-effect relations. A real person makes many movements open-loop for short periods of time, but intermittent feedback comes to the rescue and the internal model eventually provides a decent estimation of the external reality.

This paradigm of estimation clearly seems to fit the Heidegger-Gibson theory as well as the general notion of model-dependent reality. It also fits the oft stated view that perception is conditioned by culture, which itself is clearly a function of what one does and what one sees and hears over an extended period of time. And it represents a means to continually cope with an external environment that is always changing. It is fully analogous to the process of science itself in the sense that science must gradually chip away *through interaction* to refine any model of what is being investigated. The interaction is what enables the perception and the resulting belief.

Which suggests the question we now want to deal with: Can God be perceived and believed through such interaction? What does it mean to interact with God?

3

BELIEFS ABOUT GOD

> There is only one God, knowledge, and one evil, ignorance.
> —Diogenes Laertius, *Lives of Eminent Philosophers*, I-5, around 400 BC

> What is it: Is man only a blunder of God, or is God only a blunder of man?
> —Freidrich Wilhelm Nietzsche, *The Twilight of the Idols*, 1889

> Without this playing with fantasy no creative work has ever come to birth. The debt one owes to the play of imagination is incalculable.
> —Carl Gustav Jung, *Psychological Types*, 1923

Having considered the subject of modeling in some depth and having offered several quite different perspectives on believing, we now turn to the subject of God, because that is the theme of the book and because that subject for the writer poses the greatest challenge with respect to believing and modeling. We can try to model God per se, namely *what is* God. Or we can try to model the *process* by which people arrive at a belief in God or practice that belief in religious pursuits. Those are different things.

Why is the concept of God important?

The concept of God is important simply because many people think it is. And that has been true since the beginning of recorded history.

In Judeo-Christian religions one day of the week is set aside to worship, and in Islam prayer is required several times every day. Further, God is traditionally viewed as the creator of everything, the basis of morality, the supreme authority. God is the ultimate *raison d'etre.* God figures prominently in literature, music and the arts.

God-expressions figure often in our lives:

God is great (Allah Akbar)
God almighty
God the father
God the son
God the holy spirit (holy ghost)
God's will
God willing
Creator God
Loving God
In God we trust
So help me God
One nation under God
God damn
God everlasting
All God's children, and at the end of every American presidential speech:
God bless you and God bless America

Throughout history wars have been fought in the name of God and over only slightly different interpretations of the concept. Or who has the right to make pronoucements on behalf of God. Many people have devoted their working lives to God and/or died as martyrs to their beliefs about God.

Difficulties of discourse about God

In much of today's culture the subject of God is a conversation stopper. These days one can talk sex, politics, or just about anything else, but in polite company, and *especially* among educated persons, it is uncomfortable, impolite or even threatening to bring up the subject of God. In some cultures only the trained religious authorities (theologians) are entitled to discuss the nature of God. I would remind the reader that the term *theology* is derived from Greek *theos* (God) and *logos* (reasoned discourse, according to Aristotle). We will be looking hard at the reasoning aspect of theology.

The topic of God does not accommodate easily to rational discourse in words that have commonly understood meanings. Philosopher Michael Martin points out that "God" has many meanings.[56] At one extreme we have a *theistic* God: an omniscient, omnipotent, omni-benevolent personal God who loves and cares about all creatures and hears their prayers. At the other extreme is a *deistic* God, an abstract entity that created the universe but then retreated to letting the universe run on its own, never intervening in human affairs or altering the laws of nature. Deism, which first appeared in the 17th century during the Enlightenment period, rejects the supernatural (except for a Designer of the initial creation) and any need for revelation.[57]

Accordingly atheism also must have many meanings—which version of God is not believable. Martin suggests that based on the Greek roots of the term (*a* meaning without, and *theos* meaning God), the term *negative atheism* be used, i.e., having no belief in God. For the more common meaning, a belief that there is no God or gods, he suggests the term *positive atheism*. Both terms are to be distinguished from *agnosticism*, the position of neither believing nor disbelieving (from the Greek: "without knowledge").[58]

Spirituality is a term that means something different to just about everyone. It can refer to churchgoing, prayer or other religious practice. Or it can refer to private meditation or contemplation, quiet reflection on nature, yoga, absorption in music, etc., completely exclusive and apart from worship of God or any organized religion. As the term is normally used there is clear evidence for spirituality in humans. In addition there are reports of out-of-body experiences (associated with illness and near death as well as ingestion of drugs) that are sometimes called spiritual.

In the first chapter of the book the distinction was made between a model that focused on (belief about) the *state* of the object or event that is being modeled (the "what") on the one hand, and the *process* of arriving at or exercising that belief (the "how") on the other hand. In modeling God what are we talking about?

God has been defined as not being a thing (unless a spirit or a force is a thing) and being timeless. Being thingless and timeless makes modeling the *state* (what God is) difficult for us creatures who live in a world of things and time. That very difficulty will be evident in the discussion to come, and is one reason to investigate whether God is modelable. And then, can we know God if we cannot model God? In ancient times the gods were modeled as special people and animals. However most of what has been written about God in more recent times are arguments about the *process* of coming to a belief, coming to faith, and exercising that belief and faith.

The historical fact is that the existence of God, in whatever form and understanding, is a tacit belief in Western and much of world culture. Right up to the present time discussions of God tend to start with that existence assumption and go on from there. The question of whether God can be modeled, namely "what is God?", as contrasted to how people behave in worship after God has been assumed, demands questioning of that tacit existence assumption.

History of belief and skepticism about God

In this chapter we review a few bits of the history of gods and God, along with some history of the skepticism that grew alongside. After dealing briefly with the ancients of Egypt, Greece and Rome the discussion is mostly about western religions.

EARLIEST IDEAS ABOUT GODS

According to mythology and drawings that have been found, ancient Egypt had 60-100 gods and goddesses who were believed to be present in, and in control of, the forces and elements of nature (between 3000 BC and 100 AD).[59] The myths about these gods explained the origins and behavior of various elements in nature. The practices of Egyptian religion were efforts to provide for the gods and gain their favor.

Egyptian religious practice centered on the pharaoh, the king. Although he was a human, he was believed to be descended from the gods and acted as the intermediary between his people and the gods. There was an obligation to please the gods through rituals and offerings in order to keep order in the universe.

In one charming myth:

> At first there was only Nun, Nun was the dark waters of chaos. One day a hill rose out of the waters. This hill was called Ben-Ben. On this hill stood Atum, the first god. Atum coughed and spat out Shu, the god of the air, and Tefnut, the goddess of moisture. Shu and Tefnut had two children. First, there was Geb, the god of the earth. Then, there was Nut, the goddess of the sky. Shu lifted Nut up so that she became a canopy over Geb. Nut and Geb had four children named Osiris, Isis, Seth and Nephthys. Osiris was the king of the earth and Isis was the queen. Osiris was a good king, and he ruled over the earth for many years. However, everything was not well. Seth was jealous of Osiris because he wanted to be the ruler of the earth. He grew angrier and angrier until one day he killed Osiris. Osiris went down into the underworld and Seth remained on earth and became king. Osiris and Isis had one son called Horus. Horus battled against Seth and regained the throne. After that, Horus was the king of the earth and Osiris was the king of the underworld.[60]

With succeeding pharaohs many other gods came into prominence. Ra, the sun god, became the most important. From a purely rational perspective, one might assert that worship of the sun made a lot of sense since the sun provides heat and light, energy to grow crops, etc. The sun is essential to our survival. It was obvious, consistent and satisfying that the sun god traveled across the sky by day, and traversed hades by night, to reappear reliably the next day. Ra is pictured in Figure 4.

76   *What Is God?*

Figure 4. Ra, the sun god.

Both the Greek empire (dating from roughly 800 BC) and the Roman empire (dating from the founding of Rome by Romulus in 753 BC) had their panoply of gods as listed in Table 2[61]. The Roman equivalent is shown in parentheses. Starting with the ancient Egyptians through to the Greek and Roman gods—all were anthropomorphic (human-like), though some also had features of animals. That was well ingrained in the notion of what a god was. To be other than creature-like was not imaginable.

Zeus (Jupiter) - Lord of the sky and supreme ruler of the gods. Known for throwing lightening bolts.
Poseidon (Neptune) - **Ruler of the sea.** Brother of Zeus. Carried a three-pronged spear known as a trident.
Hades (Pluto) - **Ruler of the underworld** and the dead. Brother of Zeus. Had a helmet which rendered its wearer invisible.
Hestia (Vesta) - A virgin goddess and sister of Zeus. No distinct personality or part in myths. Goddess of the hearth, the symbol of the home.
Hera (Juno) - Zeus's wife and sister. Protector of marriage, spent most of her time punishing the many women Zeus fell in love with. Likes cows and peacocks.
Ares (Mars) - God of war and son of Zeus and Hera. Likes vultures and dogs.
Athena (Minerva) - Daughter of Zeus alone. Having no mother, she sprang from his head full-grown and in full armor. The protector of civilized life, handicrafts, and agriculture. Invented the bridle, and was first to tame the horse.
Apollo (Apollo) - Son of Zeus. Master musician, archer god, healer, god of light, god of truth, sun god. A busy god who likes the laurel tree, dolphins, and crows.
Aphrodite (Venus) - Daughter of Zeus. Goddess of Love and Beauty. Likes the myrtle tree, doves, sparrows, and swans.
Hermes (Mercury) - Son of Zeus. Wore wings on his sandals and his hat, thus was graceful and swift.
Artemis (Diana) - Apollo's twin sister and daughter of Zeus. Lady of wild things and huntsman to the gods. As Apollo is the Sun, Artemis is the moon.
Hephaestus (Vulcan) - Son of Hera, god of Fire. The only ugly and deformed god. Makes armor and weapons forged under volcanoes.
Gaea (Terra) - Mother Earth.
Asclepius (Aesculapius) - God of medicine.
Cronus (Saturn) - God of the sky; Ruler of the Titans (Roman mythology: God of agriculture)
Demeter (Ceres) - Goddess of grain.
Dionysus (Bacchus) - God of wine and vegetation.
Eros (Cupid) - God of love.
Hypnos (Somnus) - God of sleep.
Rhea (Ops) - Wife of Cronus/Saturn. Mother goddess.
Uranus (Uranus) - God of the sky. Father of the Titans.
Nike (Victoria) - Goddess of Victory.

Table 2. The Greek and Roman gods

The early Persian empire (550-330BC) also had its large cadre of gods.[62] Every worldly object had a counterpart in the complex sacred world. In Arabic al-Lah, the supreme being, is masculine. The divine and inscrutable essence of God al-Dhat is feminine. Babylonians and Aryans were aware that their myths were not facts but expressed a mystery. Reason was not denied but was transcended. The ancient Persian philosopher Zoroaster (also known as Zarathustra, approx. 630-650BC), who helped unite the Persian Empire, rejected the old multiplicity of gods. He also promoted the idea a single wise God, Ahura-Mazda, who ruled the entire world. Zoroaster taught that Ahura-Mazda was constantly fighting Ahriman, the spirit of darkness and evil. If you lived a virtuous life you would go to heaven after death, otherwise be punished in hell. Eventually the world would see eternal goodness and peace. Zoroaster's teaching became the basis of the Persian Bible, the Avesta.

In Greece Pythagoras (570-495BC), aside from his great mathematical achievements, believed that the soul was a fallen god in human body, and that the body was reincarnated again and again into humans, animals, or vegetables, ultimately to become immortal again.[63] Plato (428-348 BC), and his teacher Socrates both were influenced by Pythagoras, and often spoke about the nature of wisdom and beauty (which they called eternal "forms"), attributes which later became close to how God was defined.[64]

According to Aristotle (384-322 BC) the eternal forms had reality insofar as they existed in concrete objects in the world.[65] There was a hierarchy of forms at the top of which was the unmoved mover God, which consisted of pure thought. This god could have little impact on individual lives.

The Jews had already been uniting around the idea of a single personal God, Yahweh. The Mabite stone dated to 840BC first mentions Yahweh (abbreviated YHWH). Yahweh was a contrast to the gods of the Greeks, Romans and Hindus that had human attributes but were otherwise distant and impersonal.[66]

Jesus (7-2 BC to 30-36 AD) was a Jewish carpenter/teacher in Roman Judea. A number of overlapping attributes were that he was a rabbi, a healer, a social reformer, a rabble-rouser, a sage and philosopher, and a self-described messiah (a savior/liberator). Because of his political protests and success in generating social unrest he became a thorn in the side of the local Roman administration and was crucified on orders from the Roman prelate Pontius Pilate. History supports these statements as fact.[67]

However, that he was born of a virgin, was the son of God, rose from the dead, ascended into heaven and will return, and fulfilled the messianic prophecies of the Hebrew Bible are matters of dispute, certainly among Jews and Muslims, but even among modern Christian scholars.

Within the early Christian community there was controversy over whether Jesus was divine or not. Since Jesus was an obedient human it was said he could not be God. Emperor Constantine called the synod of bishops to Nicea on May 20, 325 to settle the controversy. Though the decision was not unanimous, the resulting Nicene creed made Jesus one in substance with God (as part of the Trinity).[68]

The Hindus already had a kind of trinity in the form of Brahman, Shiva and Vishnu who were three aspects of a single God. Today, of course, Muslims take Christians to task for having three gods and assert "There is no god but God".

THE FIRST SKEPTICS

Protagoras (CA. 490-420 B.C.) was the first Greek philosopher known to have explicitly implied agnosticism. In his work *Concerning the Gods* he asserted that "I am unable to discover whether they exist or not, or what they are like in form." In the tragic play Bellerophon, possibly performed in the fifth century BC, there are the words "Does someone say there are indeed gods in heaven? There are not, there are not, if a man is willing not to rely foolishly on the antiquated reasoning." In the play *On Piety* by playwright Cretius the principal actor tells how "someone first persuaded mortals to believe that there exists a race of gods."[69]

We know that Socrates (469-399 BC) left no written works; however his questioning about the gods is known through his students. For example Plato (428-347BC) in his *Apology* says of Socrates' accusers "Those who hear them suppose that anyone who inquires into such matters must be an atheist".[70] In 399BC the Athenians formally charged Socrates: "Socrates does wrong by not acknowledging the gods the city acknowledges, and introducing other, new powers. He also does wrong by corrupting the young." Socrates was eventually sentenced to death by drinking the hemlock, and there followed a period when not only the Greek philosophers but also the Romans, Jews and Christians avoided openly doubting that the gods existed and referred to any doubters as atheists.

Siddhartha Gautama, the Buddha, (around 450BC) taught that

80   *What Is God?*

one's sense of transcendence in meditation is not contact with a god but with oneself.[71] It was agreed that asking a Buddhist about life after death is simply improper, since the answer was beyond any human understanding.

In early Christianity Mark's gospel was the earliest and therefore probably the most reliable. [72] He implied that Jesus was a normal person growing up. Jesus never claimed to be God, but spoke of God in seemingly personal terms as a loving father. Plotinus (205-270) in contrast described God as everything and nothing, beyond all human categories.[73] Already there were very opposite descriptions of what/who God was.

DEVELOPMENT OF DIFFERENT RELIGIOUS TRADITIONS

Augustine of Hippo (354-430) is one of the greatest Christian thinkers and profoundly influenced the medieval world view, particularly the Catholic church.[74] He defined Trinity for the Latin church, and is also considered to be a father of the reformation due to his teaching on salvation and divine grace. Augustine believed that humanity was damned because of Adam's and Eve's sin (guilt passed on through their sexual encounter) but has been redeemed by the death and resurrection of Jesus. Where Christianity originally regarded women positively, Augustine believed their only function was childbearing. It is recorded that he prayed "Lord, give me chastity, but not yet".

Around 610 an Arab merchant named Muhammad is said to have had a vision of the angel Gabriel on a mountain, receiving over time all the words in what we now know to be the Quran.[75] Allegedly he remembered it perfectly and later recited it so that scribes could record it. By the time of his death in 632 he had united almost all tribes of Arabia into a united community (an *ummah*). The first official compilation of the Quran was 20 years after Muhammad died. The Quran emphasized surrender (Islam) to al-Lah, a moral imperative. It dismissed theological speculation about ideas of Trinity and incarnation as self-indulgence and guesswork.

Most of the Prophet Muhammad's followers wanted the community of Muslims to determine who would succeed him. A group called the Shia thought that someone from his family should take up his mantle. They favored Ali, who was married to Muhammad's daughter, Fatimah. Sunnis believed that leadership should fall to the person who was deemed by the elite of the community to be best able to lead the community. And it was fundamentally that political division that began the Sunni-Shia split. The Sunnis prevailed and chose a successor to be the first caliph. Eventually, Ali was chosen as the fourth caliph, but not before violent conflict broke out. Two of the earliest caliphs were murdered. War erupted when Ali became caliph, and he too was killed in fighting in the year 661.[76]

Later, in the ninth century, a new type of Islam emerged (Falsafah), agreeing with the Greeks in emphasizing a continuous search for wisdom through reason, since God was said to be the same as reason. They began to accept the monotheistic God of the ancients as the same God as al-Lah. But the Muslim sects continue to disagree with one another. The Shia caliphate in Tunis (later Cairo), was opposed to the Sunni caliphate in Baghdad. Shii believed Imams were special in their perfect surrender to God, much as were Jesus and Moses.

The period 1096-1099 saw the first Christian crusade against the infidel Jews and Muslims.[77] Soldiers fought under the banner of St George, seeing Jesus as a feudal lord. They sought to recover Jesus' patrimony and honor.

The Greeks had always distrusted Augustine's Trinity. Greek theology was contemplation of the mystery of Trinity and incarnation. The Latins made it too comprehensible and rational. Christians started adopting falsafah just when Greeks were losing faith in it. Rabbi Moses ibn Maimon (Maimonides, 1135-1204) believed that the highest knowledge of God derived more from imagination than from intellect.[78]

Thomas Aquinas (1225-74) in his Summa Theologica tried to combine the ideas of Augustine and Greek philosophy.[79] Namely, the exact nature of God is inaccessible, but certain premises must hold, including that God is a superior and perfect being whose existence is necessary, and who was creator of the cosmos at the beginning of time. He argued five ways to "prove" the existence of God. They boil down to God being (1) the essential first mover that (2) cannot have a prior mover and (3) that is not contingent on another being and (4) is maximally causative and (5) is maximally knowledgeable. He articulated what is now the common description of God as omniscient, omnipotent and omnibenevolent.

Isaac Luria Ashkenazi (1534-1572)[80] was a foremost rabbi and Jewish mystic in the community of Safed in the Galilee region of Ottoman Palestine, and was a hero and saint of Kabbalism. He dwelt on the old question of how could a perfect God create an imperfect world. His answer was that God abandoned part of himself. Luria preached a doctrine of good works, and so helped European Jews be positive in their hard times. This was in contrast to Luther and Calvin who in the same period said salvation was only by grace.

Martin Luther (1483-1546) believed that life was a battle against Satan.[81] God can only be found in suffering as symbolized by the cross. Faith was a trusting leap in the dark, not any human assent to certain propositions. Luther was a strong anti-semite and misogynist, who had a loathing and horror of sexuality.

John Calvin (1509-64)[82] inspired the puritan revolutions in England under Cromwell and colonization of New England. God was believed to be the absolute ruler. But Calvin also believed in predestination, which limited the interactions of a personal God with the people.

Rene Descartes (1596-1650)[83] reworked Anselm's ontological proof (that God exists because one can think no greater thought). He most famously asserted that the very experience of doubt tells us that the doubter must exist. "I think, therefore I am" was his way of putting it. His proof of God involved a number of premises, which will not be reviewed in detail here. But key among these was that one's grasp of the infinite must be prior to one's grasp of the finite, and that the idea of God is completely clear and distinct and contains more objective reality than any other idea.

Blaise Pascal (1623-62)[84] thought belief in God had to be a matter of subjective choice among alternatives rather than a conclusion from rational deduction. He went along with Luther, that belief in God requires a leap of faith.

The Dutch Jew Baruch Spinoza (1632-1677)[85] was excommunicated from his synagogue at Amsterdam. He believed that God amounted to the sum of all the physical laws. Therefore to say that God must be separated from everything makes no sense, for in that case it would be impossible to say that he exists.

Isaac Newton (1642-1727)[86] was anxious to rid Christianity of mystery. During the seventeenth century as the ideas of the Enlightenment became popular, defining God in terms of mystery, myth, and mysticism was seen as a problem that had to be cleared up. At the same time people started calling out those who acted as though God did not exist as "atheists." But literal atheism (disbelief) was unimaginable for most people since religion dominated everyday life.

SKEPTICISM IN MODERN TIMES

Aquinas and the Roman church had encouraged the idea that human reason was limited and therefore must be subjected to divine revelation. In contrast, Descartes believed that theological knowledge is not special but must pass the same empirical rationality criteria as used in worldly matters. But as noted above he tried to prove the existence of God by using the traditional argument of St. Anselm of Canterbury (1033-1109) that God must exist because by definition "no greater being can be conceived" — a position that left him open to criticism on rational grounds.[87]

The arguments of rational empiricism versus mystical reflection went back and forth. John Locke (1632-1704)[88] criticized Descartes' efforts at theological rationality, asserting that the concept of God can only be derived from "ideas received from sensation and reflection".

Henry More (1614-1687)[89] defined God not as a transcendent mystery but rather as an infinitely extensible spiritual body, to be distinguished from a solid body. He saw God as the harmonious sum of everything.

David Hume (1711-1776)[90] confronted the question of God head-on. He made plain that theism is incompatible with empiricism, and that if one reasoned from known phenomena one would have to drop supposition and conjecture about God.

Immanuel Kant (1724-1804) in *Critique of Pure Reason* provides an erudite and detailed discussion of causality and time precedence. Those issues were not novel, for Aquinas and others earlier had discussed causality. In fact the awareness of causality seems to date to pre-Socratic times when people realized that they themselves were at least immediate causes of events and not the gods. Today we appreciate that temporal precedence is more complex than what Kant understood, time precedence depending on arbitrary assignment of what is the cause (e.g., when you push on a spring does the motion cause the force or the force cause the motion?) Today we also appreciate the distinction between necessity (B occurs only if A occurs first, or both A1 and A2 occur) and sufficiency (B can occur if either A1 or A2 occurs first). With respect to God, Kant asserted that God would have to be regarded as beyond the limits of human knowledge.[91] That meant that one would either have to dispense with God altogether or alternatively believe in a transcendental God. Kant chose the latter. He was getting closer to a theme of this book, though in a later section I criticize the notion of a transcendental God.

Denis Diderot (1713-1784) was an openly self-professed and explicit atheist.[92] He rejected theism in favor of a completely materialistic view of the universe. He had intellectual stature and so could not be dismissed out of hand as a fool or a malcontent.

Ludwig Feuerbach (1804-1872)[93] claimed that the prevailing notion of God was an "incoherent amalgam of personal, quasi-anthropological attributes and impersonal attributes of perfection". He had no use for Christianity.

It is to Friedrich Nietzsche (1844-1900)[94] that we owe the phrase "God is Dead" (first used in his book *The Gay Science)*. Nietzsche claims that eliminating God will lead to the rejection of a belief of cosmic or physical order, and also to a rejection of absolute values. This would also be a rejection of belief in an objective and universal moral law binding upon all individuals. This rejection is called *nihilism*. Nietzsche worked to find a solution for nihilism by re-thinking the foundations of human values, foundations that went deeper than Christian values.

The above very abbreviated recitation of names and beliefs provides a thumbnail historical picture of the struggle of prominent thinkers to resist convention in coping with the question of God's existence.

Traditional "proofs" of God

Many of the arguments for the existence of God can be categorized under the philosophy term *ontology*, which, as was said earlier, deals with questions concerning what entities exist or can be said to exist. It is closely related to *epistemology*, which deals with knowing and the methods of obtaining knowledge (like the scientific method).

There is a rich and growing literature on arguments about the existence of God, pro and con. The brief summary below is not meant to be comprehensive but to provide the gist, in layman terms, of the main arguments. Each argument for existence is stated succinctly, followed by the popular rebuttal. Some of these arguments are referred to in later discussion about belief.[95]

ANSELM'S THESIS

Probably the earliest argument explicitly offered as "proof" of God's existence was that mentioned earlier, offered by Anselm of Canterbury (1033-1109), a Benedictine monk, philosopher and theologian.[96] It was accepted for hundreds of years by the Roman church. In his *Proslogion* Anselm defined God as "that than which nothing greater can be conceived". In other words, and as stated by Anselm's defenders, if something is so great that it is at the limit of what can be "conceived" (imagined I assume), then it cannot exist only in thought but must exist in reality because existence in reality is greater than existence in thought. Anselm claimed that "only a fool would think otherwise".

Anselm's argument continues to garner attention and be discussed to this day. I have many issues with it and find it contorted logic. Comparing what exists in reality and what exists in thought as to "greatness" seems a strange exercise with no means to validate a judgment. "Greatest " could mean all-inclusive, but that would have to include all that is bad as well as all that is good. If Anselm meant only all that is good one would have to ask by whose criteria. God's criteria? But many theologians have implied that we are not party to understanding God's criteria. Further, there are lots of things that we readily admit are beyond human understanding (perhaps most things!). Does that prove the existence of an omnipotent, omniscient, loving God?

On the other hand I believe Anselm suggests a way to *redefine* God—simply as a way to express what is beyond human understanding—with no need for anything supernatural. This is a very different meaning for God than what is normally assumed. In fact later I suggest that the term God be used in exactly that way. But to define God as the sum of *all* that is beyond human understanding and *nothing more* (i.e., NOT a supernatural being) seems a very far cry from the way the term God has been used throughout history.

THE COSMOLOGICAL ARGUMENT (FIRST CAUSE)

The cosmological argument is also known as the argument from universal causation or the argument from first cause. It was used by Aristotle in ancient Greece, more with a slant toward physics than theology. In his *Metaphysics* Aristotle claimed that there must be something to explain why the Universe exists: causality is linear, so something had to exist first before anything else could exist.[97] He called this an unmoved mover, an uncaused cause. Aquinas picked up on the Aristotle argument, denying that that there can be an infinite causal chain; there must be a stopping point. He stated that even if the universe has always existed, it still owes its existence to an uncaused cause...and this we understand to be God.

The usual retort to the first cause argument for God is to ask "What caused God?" British philosopher Samuel Clark (1675-1729) argued that even if an infinite regressive chain existed there would have to be a transcendental cause for the entire succession. Hume declared that each step in a causal chain would need a cause, and there is no need to go outside the chain.[98]

ARGUMENT FROM DESIGN (TELEOLOGY)

Teleology means having a purpose. The idea of this argument is that the universe was created for a purpose. The analogy is made to the organs of the human body, each of which has an apparent purpose. So too all the parts of the universe must have a purpose as part of a grand design by God. This argument was put forth by William Paley (1743-1805)[99]. He pointed out by analogy that a wristwatch has to be designed by a human designer who understands its purpose. The wristwatch design argument for God has been a favorite to rebut by modern Darwinians (we cite them later).

Critics of this argument raise the question of the gratuitous evil and suffering in the world, which is incompatible with what might be assumed to be actions of a loving God. The counter argument regarding evil in the world devolves with the theist claiming that (1) we are not privy to God's purpose, (2) that God must have His reasons, and that the purpose of life is not necessarily universal happiness, (3) that evil in the world is because mankind has misused the moral freedom God has provided, and (4) that God's purpose carries into eternity and does not end with this transient life.

ARGUMENT FROM MORALITY

The argument here is that God's revealed laws for living set the basis for morality, and without the revelations and worship of God we would have no basis for morality. But then one must ask about so much of what appears immoral in sacred texts, especially the Hebrew Bible. We do not accept worship practices such as sacrifices of children and punishment by death for what today we would regard as minor infractions (examples of this are offered later). Contemporary writer Sam Harris argues that religion is a questionable basis for morality, and suggests that morality has actually evolved over time from what works for the betterment of society.[100]

ARGUMENT FROM MYSTICAL EXPERIENCE

It is common for people to report mystical experiences that seem to have no explanation based on reason or experience, and these can be attributed to God. The counterargument is that there are many reasons for such experiences, such as hallucinations (e.g., the bicameral mind hypothesis of Julian Jaynes cited earlier, as well as dreams, disease, drugs, etc.). Proof of attribution to God would be difficult in any case.

PASCAL'S WAGER

French philosopher-mathematician Blaise Pascal (1623-1662) made fundamental contributions to probability theory as well as to physics. In his "wager" (also known as Pascal's gambit) he asserted that everyone, like it or not, was subject to a wager about belief in God's existence: If you believe in God, and God actually exists, Pascal wrote in his *Pensees*, you radically improve your chance of going to heaven, and that is for an infinite time (therefore infinite gain).[101] If God exists but you are an atheist your chances (gain) will be much less, maybe go negative. If God does not exist, whether you believe or not would make no difference (zero gain). Therefore a rational person will believe in God.

The counter to this argument is that "belief" based on such a wager with one's self would be dishonest for many people who saw no other basis for believing, and that a loving God would always wish for one to be intellectually honest. There are also issues with the existence of heaven, who gets to go, and on what terms.

SO MANY PEOPLE BELIEVE

It has been argued that because so many people over a very long time have believed that God exists there must be something to it. It's as though history has taken a poll and God wins hands down. The rebuttal, of course, is that there are many things that most people believed over a long period that turn out not to be true, e.g., that the earth is flat.

IT IS NOT POSSIBLE TO DISPROVE THE EXISTENCE OF GOD

It is common for believers to assert that one cannot disprove the existence of God. That is correct. However, such an argument means nothing, since the obligation on anyone asserting God's existence is to prove or otherwise demonstrate the existence. One cannot disprove the existence of anything at some point in space and time; the possibilities are infinite. Bertrand Russell has an interesting commentary on this argument as quoted below and depicted in Figure 5.[102]

If I were to suggest that between the Earth and Mars there is a china teapot revolving about the sun in an elliptical orbit, nobody would be able to disprove my assertion provided I were careful to add that the teapot is too small to be revealed even by our most powerful telescopes. But if I were to go on to say that, since my assertion cannot be disproved, it is an intolerable assumption on the part of human reason to doubt it, I should be rightly be thought to be talking nonsense. If, however, the existence of such a teapot were affirmed in ancient books, taught as the sacred truth every Sunday, and instilled in the minds of children at school, hesitation to believe in its existence would become a mark of eccentricity and entitle the doubter to the attentions of a psychiatrist in an enlightened age or of the inquisitor at an earlier time.

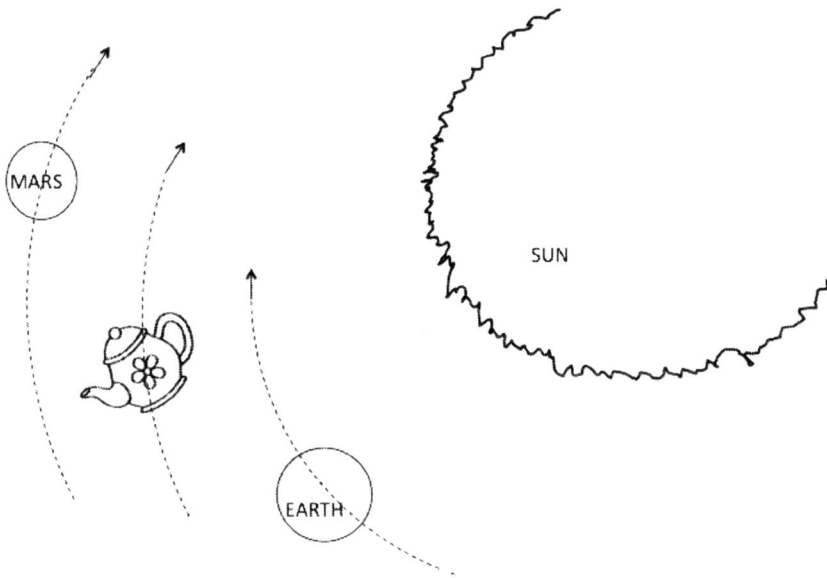

Figure 5. Bertrand Russell's tea pot encircling the sun

Ludwig Wittgenstein and others have argued for what has been called *epistemic responsibility*, that people have a responsibility to seek evidence for what they believe, and that what we cannot speak about (rationally) "we must pass over in silence".[103]

More recent theistic arguments

THE MIND-BODY DILEMMA

This argument by the theists is close to (maybe the reverse of) the Anselm argument that inability to imagine the "greatest" something makes it exist. Surely one can say that any imagined thing does exist — in the "mind". Translated into neuroscience that would have to mean that God surely does exist — in the form of nerve impulses and subtle chemical changes in the brain. But then so does any imagined thing exist, a pink unicorn for example.

The philosophical claim that minds are not distinct from matter (that mental events are experienced counterparts of physical events) is called *physicalism*. Some theists counter-argue that God has mental properties but no material properties, and so His existence is incompatible with physicalism. But insofar as mental activity is physical, that argument cannot stand.

So most cognitive and neuroscientists subscribe to physicalism to the extent that so-called "mind" is just a way of talking (loosely) about what we experience with our brains. Of course a person may imagine or hallucinate an object that does not exist outside the brain.

Scientists shy away from scientific investigations that do not have attributes of space and time. Some scientists declare that supernatural phenomena, if they were to exist, necessarily lie beyond the scope of what is knowable to science. So again, science cannot disprove such phenomena, but neither can the theist offer any proof.

Some theists, however, will continue to maintain that physicalism is inherently accepted by the atheist on faith, and so this puts it on an equal footing with accepting God on faith (and maybe also accepting miracles and paranormal phenomena on faith?). And so the mind-body arguments go back and forth, with the scientists and theists talking past one another.

ANOTHER EMBELISHMENT OF THE ANSELM ARGUMENT

Both theist and atheist philosophers like to make erudite verbal statements that at first blush seem to be compelling. For example theologian William Lane Craig, in reference to God, states that

> A person S is omnipotent at a time t if and only if S can at t actualize any state of affairs that is not described by counterfactuals about the free acts of others and that is broadly logically possible for someone to actualize given the same hard past at t and the same true counterfactuals about free acts of others.[104]

That is philosopher-talk that seems to say that if a being can do anything possible that someone else cannot demonstrate then that person is omnipotent. The rub of course comes in showing that those remarkable feats (e.g, creating life) were in fact done by that supposed being rather than by some other means.

THERE IS SOMETHING RATHER THAN NOTHING

A question often posed in discussing the origin of the cosmos is why is there is something rather than nothing. This apparent fact suggests to some people that only an omnipotent God could create something from nothing. Theist philosopher Richard Swinburne (1934-)[105] asserts that, while science will never to able to solve some problems of science like why the universe exists, by aggregating many such probabilistic contingencies the existence of God becomes more and more probable.

However, in discussing the origin of the universe physicist Victor Stenger (1935-) notes that no laws of physics are violated in going from nothing to something.[106] (The proof of that statement will not be attempted here!)

NO EVIDENCE IS NECESSARY

Theologist Alvin Plantinga (1932-) argues that no evidence for God is necessary beyond what is self-evident, and calls this *foundationalism*.[107] Plantinga claims that the demand for evidential proof is an idea peculiar to Western culture. He believes that some beliefs are primary and self-evident and need not be derived from prior beliefs. As self-evidence he cites the tendency of believers to feel guilty about being skeptical, and then feel forgiven when they repent. Inspiration through reading scripture and support of a community of religious persons also provide self-evidence of God, he claims.

The atheistic response is that accepting these conditions for such basic belief is a bit too easy and that the argument is circular: "I believe in God, therefore it is self-evident that God exists".

BELIEF IN GOD IS SIMPLER THAN WHAT IS REQUIRED FOR DISBELIEF

A slightly different argument by Swinburne is that the hypothesis of theism is much simpler than the hypothesis that a complex physical universe exists as an "uncaused brute fact". He justifies the latter based on the Ockham razor principle (after the 14th century Franciscan monk William of Ockham[108]). The principle states that when competing hypotheses are equal in other respects, the hypothesis that introduces the fewest assumptions and postulates the fewest entities while still sufficiently answering the question is recommended. However the claim that the explanation is God, and that this is much simpler than alternative explanations, necessarily involves very complex contingencies.

The sentence "God did it" may be simple, but that's the only thing that is simple. The Creationists' assertion that God is the simplest alternative explanation is not simple, but it is simplistic, as "God" is totally undefined—merely a substitute term for what is unknown. In science, Occam's razor is a heuristic (a rule of thumb) to guide scientists in the development of theoretical models rather than as an arbiter between published models. Occam's razor is not an irrefutable principle. Nor is it a scientific result. Further, one may question whether Swinburne's assertions meet the criteria of competing hypotheses equal in other respects.

EVOLUTION IS NO SUBSTITUTE FOR GOD'S CREATION

Robert Mackenzie Beverley (1798-1868)[109] accused Darwin of believing that

> Absolute ignorance is the artificer, so that we may enunciate as the fundamental principle of the whole system, that, in order to make a perfect and beautiful machine, it is not requisite to know how to make it. By strange inversion of meaning (Darwin) seems to think absolute ignorance is fully qualified to take the place of absolute wisdom in all the creative achievements of creative skill.

The implication is that Darwin's theory cannot possibly substitute for God's creations.

This completely misses the essence of Darwin's great idea, where "beautiful machines" emerge from a very lengthy evolutionary process in which reproductive capability plus natural environmental forces combine to substitute for the mind of an immediate inventor.

PERFECTION ARGUMENT (THE SECOND LAW OF THERMODYNAMICS)

The French biophysicist Pierre LeCompte duNouy (1883-1947) argued that life, especially the ability to create new life, to continually improve health and age span, etc. defy the Second Law of Thermodynamics. That law of physics says that everything, if left to its own devices, tends toward chaos and degeneration.[110] In other words life itself defies the Second Law. So God must be behind life.

Indeed from a closed system (in space and time) perspective, that might appear to be true. But the counter is that when the totality of the universe and time are considered, the slow succession of stages of evolutionary development, combined with the energy put into the process by the sun, makes life consistent with the Second Law. One cannot isolate the earth from the sun in terms of physical interactions.

NO CAUSE NECESSARY, GOD EXISTS IN TIMELESS ETERNITY

A theist answer to the challenge of what caused God is simply that God was always there, and that the very idea of causality in time is a man-made idea. God is timeless and not subject to having been caused.

A counter-argument is that man is incapable of rational thought about natural phenomena that do not include time and causality. I say "include" because some physical phenomena involve no temporal dynamics: for example a force applied to a spring, as noted earlier. Whether the force is the cause resulting in displacement of the spring, or the other way around, is an arbitrary choice. But in either case there must be a cause and an initiating time for any action. Thus the idea of timelessness and there being no cause at all makes no sense in human language and cannot be understood as an argument for God.

TILLICH'S GROUND OF BEING

Theologian Paul Tillich (1880-1920) was concerned with human existence, and in his *Systematic Theology* discussed the "being" of human existence. He defined God as the transcendent "ground of being", i.e., being itself, rather than a being per se (an object).[111] Others, for example Kant, had tilted in the same direction, warning against an anthropological view of God. This is a difficult concept, for it can be taken to mean a creationist perspective that God made everything without himself/itself being any thing. Tillich emphasized absolute faith. He used phrases like "God above God" to characterize his perspective, and disparaged "theological theism" of literal interpretation of the Bible. His critics assert that he was a pantheist or an atheist but not a Christian. The notion of a transcendent God is currently popular and has been celebrated by writers such as Karen Armstrong (see later *Opposing Perspectives* section). I further wrestle with "transcendent" in a later section of the book.

THE FINE TUNING OF COSMOLOGICAL PARAMETERS (ANTHROPIC PRINCIPLE)

From a scientist's perspective this is perhaps the most credible argument for God's existence. The argument is that the parameters (physical constants) of the universe are fine-tuned, and that if they varied from what they are by even some small percentage we would not exist. Are they really fine-tuned by God or are we just lucky? That all of the parameters would be as they are would seem highly improbable given all the other possibilities. Physicist Martin Rees formulates the fine-tuning in terms of six dimensionless constants[112], namely:

- N = ratio of the strength of gravity to that of electromagnetism;
- *Epsilon* (ε) = strength of the force binding nucleons into nuclei;
- *Omega* (ω) = relative importance of gravity and expansion energy in the Universe;
- *Lambda* (λ) = cosmological constant that appears in Einstein's theory of General relativity;
- Q = ratio of the gravitational energy required to pull a large galaxy apart to the energy equivalent of its mass;
- D = number of spatial dimensions in space-time.

Until recently this was a tough one for physics to explain. But recent theories of the universe shed light on this conundrum There are many notions afloat that might provide answers, such as the statistical chance that our universe is simply one among many existing universes (and we happen to be lucky), or the notion that the big bang is just one stage of an infinitely long oscillation of new universes with differing parameters. A later chapter of the book discusses the emerging multiverse theory further.

NEAR-DEATH EXPERIENCES

A large number of persons have written about their near-death experiences. After being in a coma and recovering they describe seeing marvelous lights and colors, idyllic scenery, heavenly music, angels, even communicating with Jesus or God. For example, one recent best-seller written by a brain surgeon[113] offers what he considers to be scientific proof that his vivid experience of being in heaven was not just a neurological artifact from his illness but the real thing. However the reader comes to the distinct impression that the author has taken considerable poetic license. Further, his description of his illness differs significantly from the reports in the press offered independently by the doctors who treated him. While most reports of near-death experiences have been debunked by investigators, as discussed in the introduction, there is no way to prove that these writers have not had the experiences they describe. These are private events not observable by others and cannot constitute reality based on the requirements of science or model-based reality.

The new atheism

During the last few years there has been a surge of books and magazine articles advocating atheism. Among the most celebrated authors are Oxford University evolutionist Richard Dawkins[114], Tufts University philosopher Daniel Dennett[115], University of California neurologist Sam Harris[116], prolific journalist Christopher Hitchins[117], physicist Victor Stenger[118], SUNY Buffalo philosopher Paul Kurtz[119] and many others. Of course there have long been proponents of atheism within the academic philosophy community such as Michael Martin[120]. What characterizes all of these newer authors is their outspoken urge to bring religion into the spotlight of rational observation and critique, and the feeling that for too long religion has been accepted and tolerated as a social practice that has been assumed to be off limits from investigation. What is especially interesting is that the challenges are coming from diverse academic disciplines, including biology and physics, as well as philosophy.

Of course much of what the "new atheists" are saying is not new. Many of the arguments were made by those in the previous section as well as by others. Perhaps the new atheists are simply adding a contemporary slant and helping atheism gain momentum.

DOES EVOLUTION POINT TO GOD?

The theory of evolution, ever since Charles Darwin (1809-1882), has raised serious questions about the existence of God. Darwin, of course, held off publishing *The Origin of Species* for years after returning from the voyage of the Beagle (mid 1830s). He published in 1859, still conflicted in his own mind about the implications of what he had discovered. Darwin had studied at Cambridge to become an Anglican minister, though his family were Unitarian freethinkers. The theory of natural selection emerged in 1838 from his studies of the evidence he had gathered.[121] He was writing up his theory in 1858 when Alfred Russel Wallace sent Darwin an essay in which he posited a similar theory[122]. Some claim that Wallace should get more credit for the theory of evolution than he has received. The implications for theology of Darwin's book were fairly obvious almost immediately.

Many scholars of evolution have since suggested that evolution does not point to any God. Richard Dawkins (1941-) of Oxford has been the most vocal of these and has published and spoken widely in recent years. In his book *The Blind Watchmaker* he takes issue with the 1802 argument propounded by theist William Paley (1743-1805) that design (e.g. of a wristwatch) implies the existence of an intelligent designer, and therefore design of living forms implies existence of a God.[123] Dawkins details how through natural selection evolution allows complex living organisms to come into being, requiring nothing but chance (and time for evolution to play out). In *The God Delusion*[124] he argues that religious faith is a delusion. The latter book, published in 2006, sold several million copies by 2010.

As might be expected, Dawkins' book elicited a strong protest from theist philosophers such as Notre Dame's Alvin Plantinga (1932-). He has stated "You really can't sensibly claim theistic belief is irrational without showing it isn't true." And that, he argues, is simply beyond what science can do. Plantinga says he accepts the scientific theory of evolution, as all Christians should. The new atheists, he argues, are the ones who are misreading Darwin. Their belief that evolution rules out the existence of God — including a God who purposely created human beings through a process of guided evolution — is not a scientific claim, he writes, but "a metaphysical or theological addition."[125]

Francis Collins (1950-), the former US government head of the Genome Project, is a deeply religious man. He expresses the view in the *Language of God* that faith in science and faith in God are not inconsistent.[126] Being a genetic biologist he cannot run away from evolution, but he repudiates the atheistic view held by many scholars of evolution. He starts from the assumption of God, and assumes that evolution was created by God. In the process he admits that belief in God requires a leap in faith in a God that is outside of nature.

The point made by the atheistic evolutionists to counter theists such as Plantinga and Collins is that the hypothesis of God is simply not necessary to explain the facts of evolution. Darwin explained the mechanism, and there is no need to invoke God. The God construct has no explanatory value. Mathematician Pierre Simon Laplace (1749-1827) said it many years earlier in response to a query from Napoleon: "I have no need for that hypothesis".

IS GOD NEEDED AS A BASIS FOR MORALITY?

Philosophers have long argued about whether there is a basis for morality other than religion. Michael Martin (1932-), in *Theism, Morality and Meaning*[127], offers numerous arguments, stated as syllogisms, to assert that secular reasons can easily provide motivation for atheists to be moral. The most plausible theory to explain the meaning of ethical expressions, he claims, is what is called *ideal observer theory* (originally put forth by Roderick Firth in 1970), where a human observer who is fully informed and impartial, makes judgments of approval or disapproval. This however, seems to beg the question, for who among us can ever be fully informed and impartial?

Sam Harris (1967-), a philosopher and neuroscientist, has authored several books supporting atheism, including *The End of Faith*[128] and *Letter to a Christian Nation*.[129] His third book, *The Moral Landscape*[130], is motivated by the fact that most people, whether believers or not, feel that science has little to say about moral values, and that this failure explains in large part why people turn to religion. Harris confronts this issue directly, claiming that human (and animal and plant) well-being is the only legitimate basis for moral values and that science has a lot to say about this relationship. It will take time to overcome the cultural inertia, but Harris believes that in due time science will be able to tell us right from wrong, and how we *ought* to behave, in addition to telling us how we do behave. He points out, as every scientist already understands, that there is no such thing as Christian or Muslim mathematics, and that science can eventually bring us together regarding morality.

GOD OF THE GAPS

The 2008 National Academy of Sciences report on creationism[131] steers clear of answering whether science disproves religion, noting that many theologians oppose a "God of the gaps" approach (that everything not explainable by science can be left for a supernatural God) because that notion undermines faith.

Actually the God of the gaps idea has been around since 1904, when Scottish evangelist, writer, and lecturer Henry Drummond (1851-1897) developed the concept in his *Lowell Lectures on the Ascent of Man*.[132] He chastised Christians who emphasize things that science cannot yet explain — "gaps which they will fill up with God." He urged them to embrace all nature as the work of "...the God of Evolution, [who] is infinitely grander than the occasional wonder-worker."

God-of-the-gaps has become a popular term for bashing skeptics of God. However, later I will attempt to resurrect the term as a very reasonable way to redefine what we mean by God. It simply changes the definition of God: *not a supernatural person, but rather the total set of phenomena that we simply do not understand!*

BREAKING THE SPELL

Another major figure in the so-called new atheist movement is philosopher Daniel Dennett (1942-) of Tufts University. In his book *Breaking the Spell*,[133] Dennett refers to the "spell" that religion has on peoples everywhere, and the prevalent inhibition from undertaking scientific investigation of the practice of religion – that religion is somehow off limits. He discusses *memes*, ideas that are handed down and evolve in the community in a manner analogous to genes (as described in Dawkins' *The Selfish Gene*.[134]). The implication is that religious ideas are memes handed down from ancient folklore.

Dennett has popularized the interesting term "belief in belief." In other words people feel they are expected (by friends, family, community, other social associations) to believe (or act as though they believe), and so "believing" would be to their social advantage.

Certainly religious affiliation and belief have been polled, doctrines of various religious institutions have been studied and compared, and thousands of books critical of religion have been written. But Dennett focuses on scientific inquiry of religion, involving well-designed experiments, experimental controls, etc.

Leon Wieseltier (1952-) accuses Dennett of believing "in the grossest biologism or in the grossest theism, in a purely naturalistic understanding of religion or in intelligent design, in the omniscience of a white man with a long beard in 19th-century England" and that "Not all aspects of human life can or should be illuminated by science."[135]

Harvard biologist/evolutionist E.O. Wilson (1929-) believes that notions of God and rituals of religion are a result of human evolution. He agrees with Dennett that religion should be studied using scientific methodology. He argues that religious practices do confer biological advantage, through the reduction of reality to images and definitions that are easily understood and difficult to refute. He sees commitment through faith as a kind of tribalism enacted through self-surrender. He claims that myth is used to assert the tribe's favored position on the earth, with supernatural forces providing control and promising apocalypse. He doubts that religion can be easily replaced by scientific materialism, and argues that, because science and religion are two of the most potent forces on earth, theists and scientists should work toward an alliance.[136]

Neuroscientists, including Sam Harris, have suggested that study of the brain will eventually have much to say about religion. Geneticist Dean Hamer (1951-) authored a book *The God Gene: How Faith is Hardwired into our Genes.*[137] He refers to a gene called VMAT2 that has been associated with mystical experiences. Hamer proposes that spirituality and "self transcendence" can be measured by psychometric experiments, and that the tendency to be spiritual can be inherited.

Critics of Hamer have complained that his conclusions are premature and irresponsible, and that no single gene can account for religion, that it is tied to culture and many other factors. Theists such as the Anglican priest John Polkinghorne (1930-) complain that Hamer's contentions "reveal the poverty in reductionist thinking".[138] But clearly there is a suggestion that neurological research will eventually shed light on religious experience.

PHYSICIST PERSPECTIVES

Victor Stenger (1935-), an American particle physicist, has played an active role in the new atheist movement, with several books, the most popular of which is *God, the Failed Hypothesis.*[139] The premise is that if God created the universe there must be some evidence for that, and none has been found. However if a properly controlled experiment revealed hard scientific evidence for God were to appear that would change science in very fundamental ways. He discusses reports of mystical experiences, experiments on intercessory prayer and near death experiences, etc. but there is no evidence that passes muster in terms of what is credible according to the consensual criteria of science outlined earlier. In the preface of his book *The New Atheism*[140] Stenger comments that "the very ideal of religious tolerance — born of the notion that every human being should be free to believe whatever he wants about God —is one of the principle forces driving us toward the abyss" (acceptance that belief should be arbitrary). His point is that truth is not arbitrary, and that people are obliged to consider the prevailing evidence and the rationality of competing models of what is true—and discard those that are evidently false.

The big bang, the multiverse, and a new discontinuity in our perceived importance

In view of our consideration of God and the cosmos, it seems appropriate to present a very brief update on what many physicists are now agreeing to in regard to the origins of everything. Ancient peoples were afraid to venture outside their own universe, the tribal village, not knowing what existed there or what harm would befall them if they searched. Many years later it seemed obvious to most everyone that the earth was flat, and if explorers sailed off too far they might fall off the edge. There were a few (like Aristarchus and Euclid around 300BC) who spoke of a round earth. Eventually explorers figured out that the world was indeed round, but it appeared that the round world was all that existed, save some twinkling things in the heavens where the Gods dwelt. Then astronomers pieced together notions that there are other planets like our own out there, all in orbits around our common sun. Later it was revealed that those twinkling things, the stars, were really suns, around which there were other planets, all in a common galaxy that we now call the Milky Way. Then our telescopes became powerful enough to see other galaxies. Typical galaxies range from dwarfs with as few as ten million (10^7) stars, up to giants with a hundred trillion (10^{14}) stars, all orbiting the galaxy's center of mass. At each stage of discovery the perception of the role of humanity was diminished both physically and psychologically relative to the rest of the known universe.

Let's examine some specifics of our universe. The Big Bang is a good place to start (allegedly that actually *was* the start!).

THE BIG BANG

Physicists estimate that the so-called "big bang", the sudden expansion and cooling of matter that physicists regard as the beginning of our universe, occurred 13.7 billion years ago. This number is based in part on thermal measurements of cosmic radiation and cooling by the 2001 NASA spacecraft called the Wilkinson Microwave Anisotropy Probe. It is also based on Edwin Hubble's 1920 observation that the farther out in the universe we look the redder the light. That means, according to the Doppler effect, that the longer the wavelength (i.e., the redder) the faster the velocity of the galactic light sources moving away from us, which in turn enables a backward calculation to the big bang.[141]

Contemporary theories indicate further that space as we know it is itself expanding, i.e., the universe is not expanding "into" anything outside of itself. The three Nobel laureates who were announced in 2012 solidified the evidence and attributed the cause to the repulsive force of dark energy (whatever that is!) that is continually accelerating the expansion.

The expansion of space is presumably pushing back on the photons as they travel toward us, thus impeding their apparent velocity. As one account on the web puts it "In effect, the light reaching us has to fight its way upstream against expanding space." An analogy would be an ant crawling along a rubber band toward us (at the speed of light relative to the rubber band) at the same time as the rubber band (space) is being stretched. While Einstein's special relativity constrains objects in the universe from moving faster than the speed of light with respect to each other, there is no such theoretical constraint when space itself is expanding. Therefore those most distant galaxies we can see with the Hubble telescope, at the edge of our observable universe, are much more distant than the 13.7 light years away that would be the case were space stable. The current estimate is that the "edge" of the observable universe is roughly 42 billion light years away.[142] The universe could be bigger. Light from the most distant stars may still not have had time to reach us since the big bang.

THE MULTIVERSE

As if the expansion of space were not strange enough, in the last decade cosmologists have been proposing a seemingly much more bizarre idea, published in reputable journals and books and extrapolated from already established theories of physics, that there are multiple universes out there.[143] That is to say, where our own universe is normally defined by all that exists that obeys laws of physics as we know them, there are other universes that exist and follow very different physical laws. *Scientific American* has undertaken a series of articles on the subject. Allegedly these theories are largely based on what is regarded as the most comprehensive theory of nature: string theory, which allows up to eleven dimensions (well beyond our intuitive notions of three dimensions of space and one of time). There is nothing intuitive about string theory!

The multiverses the physicists describe are not empirically observable and would seem never to be. They are theoretical extrapolations of the known physics. The only operable criterion of these theories is internal mathematical consistency extrapolated from where we do have real data. Different individual theorists are coming up with different multiverse theories. Any one can be discredited if some logical inconsistency is found starting from known data.

Some believe that there is great diversity of universes, the laws of physics being quite different from one such universe to another. That would help explain the remarkable fact mentioned earlier that the physical constants of our particular universe have just the right values for complex molecules to sustain life—a chance occurrence within the large random distribution of multiple universes. (Reminder: the improbable set of constants that permit life is a principal reason some modern theologians give for the existence of God.) But the problem is that the idea of "God" has no explanatory value, while a mathematically plausible notion is that by chance we are lucky to live in a universe with friendly physical constants, one among a large random set of universes having different constants. It would almost appear that string theory, which many physicists accept, seems to allow almost anything to be true.

Cosmology scientists are working hard to find a grand unifying explanation to replace the current hodge-podge of separate arguments for the same cosmic phenomena.

A FIFTH DISCONTINUITY?

In a 1995 book *The Fourth Discontinuity* MIT historian Bruce Mazlish (1923-) portrays four breaks or "discontinuities" in man's perceived importance in our physical environment.[144] The first discontinuity was spatial, that being Copernicus' revelation that we humans are not at the geometric center of things. Mazlish's second discontinuity came with Darwin's discovery of evolution: that we are descended from lower creatures. The third discontinuity was Freud's construct of the superego and the id posing on both sides of the conscious ego: that we are not consciously in control of our own behavior. Mazlish's fourth discontinuity is the thesis that machines are gradually overtaking people in ability to sense, respond with speed and power, and think.

With regard to the latter there is no question about the machine's ability to sense well beyond human capability and to move with greater speed and power. While there are plenty of arguments about what "thinking" means, the superiority of the computer has been amply demonstrated, certainly by IBM's Big Blue computer beating the world's best human chess champion, and then by their computer named Watson beating the world's best players of the game show *Jeopardy*.

With new theories from cosmologists about multiple universes, maybe infinite in number, and machines' abilities to outdo mankind in intellectual pursuits, we are confronted with a further decline in our status. That trend suggests that humankind is experiencing (at least) a fifth discontinuity and concomitant decline in how important we humans are in the grander scheme of things. Maybe this is comeuppance for our hubris in thinking that we humans are special, and have any basis for knowing anything about God.

Is science just another religion?

This question is often asked and answered in the affirmative by theists. Since what one accepts as a starting premise determines to a large extent what one concludes is true downstream, I suppose science *is* a kind of religion. And it is a religion that since the 18th century enlightenment has gradually been winning out. However its starting premises are very different from those of any other religion.

Totally unlike any other religion the methods of science include a built-in effort to disprove that any particular hypothesis is true, and that effort is exercised seriously and continuously. Those hypotheses and premises that withstand this test are regarded as *provisional* truth, always *conditional* upon new evidence that forces modification. Scientists around the world, from all different cultural backgrounds, readily participate and respect this process. For those who participate, the religion of science knows no cultural boundaries.

Effort by other "religions" is just the opposite: to reinforce belief in whatever is the professed doctrine. Thus religious doctrine perpetuates itself from generation to generation, resisting new evidence and criticism. In stark contrast, the approach of science is open to new evidence, self-criticism, and refinement. The approach of religion is based on defense of faith. In science the faith is in the method of being skeptical. In this critical sense science and religion are not compatible.

Do the magisteria overlap?

Evolutionary biologist Stephen Jay Gould (1941-2002) in his book *Rock of Ages*[145] spoke of science and religion as "non-overlapping magisteria," where he defined *magisterium* as "a domain where one form of teaching holds the appropriate tools for meaningful discourse and resolution." The idea was that science uses empiricism to specify facts about the physical universe and scientific theory to say why it is made as it is, whereas religion deals with questions of ultimate meaning and moral value."

In an earlier (1997) speech to the American Institute of Biological Science Gould stated that

> Religion is too important to too many people for any dismissal or denigration of the comfort still sought by many folks from theology. I may, for example, privately suspect that papal insistence on divine infusion of the soul represents a sop to our fears, a device for maintaining a belief in human superiority within an evolutionary world offering no privileged position to any creature. But I also know that souls represent a subject outside the magisterium of science.

My world cannot prove or disprove such a notion, and the concept of souls cannot threaten or impact my domain. Moreover, while I cannot personally accept the Catholic view of souls, I surely honor the metaphorical value of such a concept both for grounding moral discussion and for expressing what we most value about human potentiality: our decency, care, and all the ethical and intellectual struggles that the evolution of consciousness imposed upon us.

This view has come in for heavy criticism from Dawkins, who contends, as does Harris, that the divide between science and religion is not so simple. He disagrees with the premise that science has little meaningful to say about ethics and values. Dawkins has stated

It is completely unrealistic to claim, as Gould and many others do, that religion keeps itself away from science's turf, restricting itself to morals and values. A universe with a supernatural presence would be a fundamentally and qualitatively different kind of universe from one without. The difference is, inescapably, a scientific difference. Religions make existence claims, and this means scientific claims.[146]

Clearly the divide was more credible in an earlier culture and way of thinking, when science and rationality held lesser sway in philosophy. Dawkins makes the additional interesting point that not all grammatically correct questions deserve an answer, giving as an example a question "What does the color red smell like?" He goes on to assert that if DNA evidence suggested that Jesus had an earthly father then Gould's claim of non-overlapping magisteria would have to be dropped[147].

This writer's opinion is that Gould was influenced by wanting to be diplomatic, recognizing as I do, that many people have deeply held religious beliefs, and offending them may not be a productive way to persuade. They are comfortable respecting science and striving for rationality in their weekday pursuits, while respecting religion on weekends as a different category of belief. But some of us find it difficult to entertain two different belief systems that are in conflict.

4

A GOD FOR TOMORROW

I myself believe that the evidence for the existence of God lies primarily in inner personal experience.
—William James, *Pragmatism*, 1907

God is a verb.
—R. Buckminster Fuller, *No More Second Hand God*, 1963

Religion is an illusion and it derives its strength from its readiness to fit with our instinctual wishes.
—Sigmund Freud, *Lecture 35*

Current status of belief

Today unquestionably the norm is professed belief in God, with a variety of justifications. Some form of William James' (1842-1910) "inner personal experience" is most often cited, or the Bible or Quran, as tradition or revelation, with tacit agreement that material observable evidence of God is rather sparse. Many clergy emphasize with Fuller that God is a verb, that belief is verified only by active seeking, faith and acceptance. However many others, probably a gradually increasing number, will agree with Freud, that the "instinctual wish" for help from above, for a loving and all-powerful father figure, is the primary driving force. A religious person might claim that this is how God makes Himself manifest.

Michel Shermer (1954-), founder of the Skeptics Society and Editor of its magazine *Skeptic*, recites the following conversation as typical of many that he has experienced:[148]

"What triggered the Big Bang?"
"God did it."
"Who created God?"
"God is He who needs not be created."
"Why can't the universe be that which needs not be created?"
"The universe is a thing or event, whereas God is an agent or being, and things and events have to be created by something, but an agent or being does not."
"Isn't God a thing or being if he is part of the universe?"
"God is not a thing, God is an agent or being."
"Don't agents or beings have to be created as well? We're an agent or being—a human being in fact. We agree that human beings need an explanation for our origin.
So why does this causal reasoning not apply to God as an agent or being?"
"God is outside of time, space and matter, and thus needs no explanation."
"In that case it is not possible for any of us to know if there is a God or not because, by definition, as finite beings operating exclusively within the world we can only know other natural and finite beings and objects. It is not possible for a finite natural being to know a supernatural infinite being."

At this point in the conversation my erstwhile theological opponents typically turn to ancillary argument such as personal revelation, which by definition is personal and thus cannot serve as evidence to others who have not shared that relevatory experience.

As Shermer goes on to point out, as have many others over time,

> The burden of proof is on believers to prove the existence of God, not on nonbelievers to disprove it, and to date theists have failed to prove God's existence, at least by the high evidentiary standards of science and reason.

Demographics and trends

We all know that in surveys about anything the way any question is posed has a great effect on the answer. Professional pollsters take great pains to sample as randomly as they can, and to offer percentages from a large enough sample that there is credible statistical significance. With those caveats here are some data from various sources taken in recent years.

Starting with some older (and quainter) data, in a March 24, 1997 Yankelovich survey of 1018 participants reported in *Time Magazine*, 91% of those surveyed believe in heaven, 67% in hell. 34% believe that they get to heaven because of faith in God, 6% because of good things that they do, and 57% both. 67% believe heaven is "up there." 91% believe they will go to heaven, 1% to hell. 5% believe in reincarnation, 4% in end of all existence. 93% believe angels are in heaven, 79% believe that there they will encounter St. Peter, 43% think they will find harps in heaven, and 36% think there will be halos. 88% believe they will meet friends and family members in heaven. A more recent AP-GFK poll in 2011 claimed that the belief in angels was down to 77%.[149]

According to ARIS (American Religious Identification Survey) in 2001[150] the largest gain in church membership since 1990 were "evangelical born-again" (42%), while self-proclaimed non-denominationals were (37%). The others had no religion (23%).

A 2012 Gallup poll indicated that 46% believed that God created man in his current form, while 32% of the respondents held the belief that humans evolved through the guidance of God.[151]

According to a new national poll by the Pew Research Center for the People and the Press[152] a sharply rising percentage of young people under 30, from the so-called "Millennial Generation," are coming to doubt the existence of God and Judgment Day.

A 2012 Pew survey[153] found that belief in the existence of God has dropped 15 points in the last five years among Americans thirty and under. Pew, which has been studying that trend for 25 years, finds that just 68 percent of millennials in 2012 agree with the statement "I never doubt the existence of God." That is down from 76 percent in 2009 and 83 percent in 2007. Among other generations, belief in God is high and has seen few changes in recent decades.

Between 81 and 89 percent of older generations say they never doubt the existence of God. The older the generation, the more likely they are to believe in God.

A 2011 study by the Pew Forum on Religion and Public Life[154] provided interesting data differentiating religious groups in the US with respect to both college education and annual income (see Figure 6). This is not meant to suggest that we should all become Hindus or reformed Jews; one might suspect that the data are conditioned on where the sample was taken, and the circumstances that led to certain ethnic groups doing well.

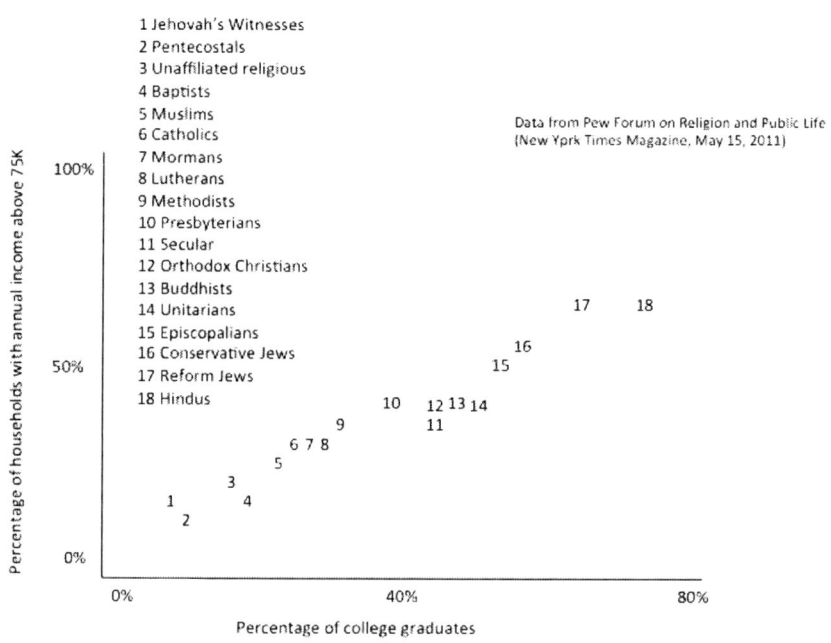

Figure 6. Comparison of US religious groups with respect to college graduation and annual income.

According to a recent (2012) European study[155], 47% of Frenchmen declared themselves to be agnostic. European countries in general have experienced a decline in church membership and church attendance. A relevant example is that of Sweden where the Church of Sweden, previously the state-church until 2000, claimed to have 82.9% of the Swedish population as its flock in 2000. But surveys there showed this had dropped to 72.9% by 2008. However in the 2005 Eurobarometer poll[156] only 23% of the Swedish population said they believed in a personal God. The Eurobarometer Poll found that, on average, 52% of the citizens of EU member states stated that they "believe in God", 27% believe there is some sort of spirit or life force, while 18% do not believe there is any sort of spirit, God or life force. Among other categories 3% declined to answer.

A 2012 survey by Ipsos Social Research Institute[157] shows that only 51 percent of people across the world now believe in God. 18 percent don't believe and 17 percent are undecided. More than 18,000 people participated in the London-based poll in 23 countries conducted by that global research company. The Ipsos poll also found that 51 percent believe that there is an afterlife, while 23 percent believe they will just "cease to exist." Around a quarter (26 percent) simply don't know what will happen after death.

Clearly the US has more believers, at least those who tell pollsters they are believers, than the average of the rest of the world. I suspect that the trend of disbelief will continue world-wide.

Is creationism dead?

Many school districts, particularly in the US "Bible-belt" states, have voted to teach creationism alongside evolution, based on the premise that both are "just theories". The retort of course, is that the evidence for the theory of Darwinian evolution is overwhelming and becoming ever more so, whereas the evidence for creationism is nil by scientific standards. Theories have no meaning without evidence to support them, presumably codified in terms of understandable models.

In 1999 the US National Academy of Sciences published a report *Science and Creationism*[158], criticizing creationism as posing an alternative to evolution. The report stated that "Scientists, like many others, are touched with awe at the order and complexity of nature. Indeed, many scientists are deeply religious." They noted that many believe (with Gould) that science and religion are two separate realms of human experience, and that "Demanding that they be combined detracts from the glory of each." I would certainly agree that they are commonly regarded as two separate realms of human *experience*. But whether they should be two separate realms of human *thought* is a different question.

In 2008 the National Academy of Sciences had become further alarmed by the propensity of some states and communities to pass laws that creationism should be taught to school children alongside evolution. They gathered a broad spectrum of scientists and educators and published a second report, *Science, Evolution and Creationism*.[159] The main conclusion of the report is that evolution is accepted fact based on overwhelming evidence and broadly accepted by the science community, very different from religion, which is based on faith. They concluded that creationism has no place in science education.

Is there room for the agnostic (or the gnostic)?

Agnosticism is defined as belief that the truth or falsity of the existence of God, as well as that of other religious claims, are unknown and indeed unknowable. While Thomas Huxley (1825-1895) is sometimes credited with coining the term *agnostic* in 1869[160], there were agnostics since the early Greeks. This included, for example, the fifth century BC philosopher Protagoras and some early Indian philosophers, including Sanjaya Belatthaputta from the same period, and early scriptures of Vedic Hinduism.

If one chooses to make a philosophical distinction between degrees of what one believes (on a scale from extreme atheist to extreme theist) on the one hand, and degree of being sure about it, from extreme agnostic to absolute conviction (gnostic), one can come up with a two-dimensional chart such as in Figure 7.[161]

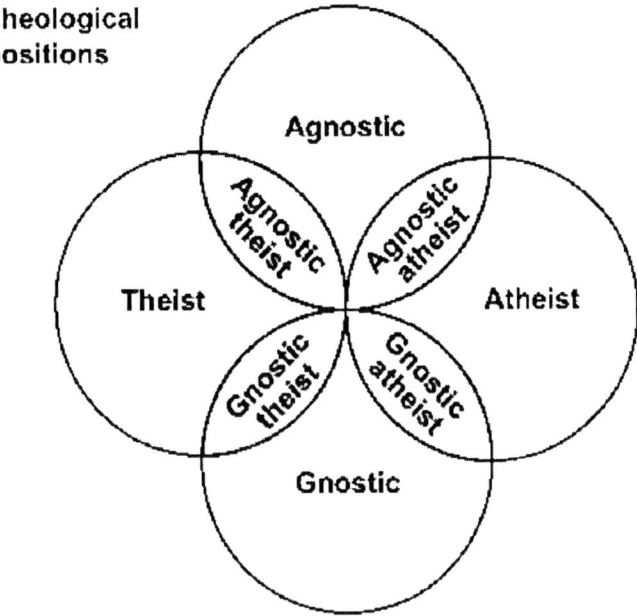

Figure 7. Shades of belief

Gnosticism is primarily associated with pre-Christian and early Christian thought originating in Mesopotamia. They believed that matter is evil and belief is the only way to emancipation. From early writings of their prophet Mani (215-276) we have the original ideas of Manichaeism, the struggle between good and evil, the spiritual world of light versus the material world of darkness. [162]Manichaeism was widespread in the Roman empire and rivaled early Christianity to do battle against paganism and the devil of nature. Saint Augustine (354-439), born in North Africa, initially subscribed to Manichaeism, but later came to revere the Hebrew Bible and saw Manichaeism as assuming unwarranted freedom to criticize the scriptures.[163] From those early Gnostics we have the precedent for the battle between good and evil which today takes the form of agnostic science and rationality versus religion, that nature is something to be explored, not something off limits to rationality.

There have been many more distinctions made between various flavors of agnosticism, including agnostic atheism, agnostic theism, pragmatic agnosticism, ignosticism, strong agnosticism, weak agnosticism, and spiritual agnosticism, with subtleties and shades of meaning that we will have to leave to the philosophers.

Perhaps the most meaningful way to distinguish between atheist and agnostic is in terms of the subjective probability assigned to the existence of God. One might say that harboring even a minute subjective probability that God exists makes one an agnostic. But how small can this probability go before one is an atheist? I firmly believe that I will not be struck by lightning during the next hour, but can I say the probability is zero? For practical purposes if one puts the subjective probability of God to be very very small one can be said to be an atheist.

Metaphor, myth and religious language

RELIGION AS METAPHOR

As stated earlier, metaphor is speech that requires the reader or listener to conjure up in his own mind the meaning, i.e., the implied relationship, between the metaphor and a target object or event. A metaphor always has two meanings: a literal one and an implied one.

Read any religious document and you will probably find lots of metaphor. You will find many words and terms that are not explicitly defined. You will have seen many of them from earlier encounters, and will allow them to pass based on familiarity, having only an imprecise understanding of what the writer really means. It has been said that religious models do not explain, but merely evoke a response from the listener. Nietzsche cynically commented that metaphors become accepted and are then regarded as truth.[164]

Is "God" a metaphor? Janet Soskice, a British theologian, writes

> We may justly claim to speak of God without claiming to define Him, and to do so by means of metaphor. Realism accommodates figurative speech which is reality depicting without claiming to be directly descriptive."[165]

Joseph Campbell (1904-1987) claimed that

God is a metaphor for a mystery that absolutely transcends all human categories of thought, even the categories of being and non-being. Those too are categories of thought. I mean it's as simple as that. So it depends on how much you want to think about it, and whether it's doing you any good. And whether it is putting you in touch with the mystery that's the ground of your own being. If it isn't, well, it's a lie. So half the people in the world are religious people who think that their metaphors are facts. Those are what we call theists. The other half are people who know that the metaphors are not facts. And so, they're lies. Those are the atheists."[166]

RELIGION AS MYTH

A myth is a traditional or legendary story, usually involving some hero or event, with or without a basis of fact or a natural explanation. It is often concerned with deities and explains some practice, rite, or phenomenon of nature.

Campbell is best known for his work in comparative mythology. He claims that myth originates as observations that interact subconsciously with mental projections and are absorbed without criticism. He says that myths put us in touch with the richest dimensions of our lives, even as our inclination is to interpret them literally. He feels that myths must evolve as the world evolves in order to be relevant to contemporary realities. He claims that myths have four basic functions: the Mystical Function, experiencing the awe of the universe; the Cosmological Function, explaining the shape of the universe; the Sociological Function, supporting and validating social order; and the Pedagogical Function, how to live as humans.[167]

From all indications primitive peoples did not make much of a distinction between observed fact and religious myth. Story telling is how they got their information; there were no newspapers, TV pundits, or fact-checkers. So good stories were what was remembered and passed on. It is often claimed that metaphor originated in mythology.

THE BIBLE AS LITERAL TRUTH

It is common to poke fun at those who take the entire Bible to be literally true. Of course it makes little sense to do so, because much or even most of it is obviously cast in metaphoric language. When the Biblical writers moralize we have to realize that the accepted moral and cultural standards at the time those writers lived were very different from what most of us accept as proper standards today.

Sam Harris reminds us that when the fundamentalist's daughter comes home from yoga class and suggests that some respect ought to be given to the teachings of Krishna, she might be reminded of the Biblical edict from Deuteronomy:[168]:

> If your brother, the son of your father or of your mother, or your son or daughter, or the spouse whom you embrace, or your most intimate friend, tries to secretly seduce you, saying "Let us go and serve other gods" unknown to you or your ancestors before you, gods of the peoples surrounding you, whether near of far away, anywhere throughout the world, you must not consent, you must not listen to him: you must show him no pity, you must not spare him or conceal his guilt. No, you must kill him, your hands must strike the first blow in putting him to death and the hands of the rest of the people following. You must stone him to death, since he tried to divert you from Yahweh your God" (Deuteronomy 13:7-11).

Harris goes on to point out that much or most of what we hold as sacred based on our religious tradition is not sacred for any reason other than it was thought to be sacred *yesterday*[169].

With those caveats, the following from Gurvitz paraphrasing Leviticus are cited for the reader's amusement:[170]:

> Lev.1:9 recommends burning a bull on the altar as a sacrifice, because it creates a pleasing odor for the Lord.
> Lev. 11:6-8 forbids touching the skin of a dead pig because it makes one unclean (think about footballs and baseball mitts and leather upholstery).

A God for Tomorrow 119

>   Lev. 11:10 prohibits working on the Sabbath (and Exodus 35:2. states that those who do should be put to death).
>   Lev. 15: 19-24 disallows contact with a woman while she is in her period of menstrual uncleanness.
>   Lev.19:19 warns against planting two different crops in the same field.
>   Lev.19:27 expressly forbids trimming one's hair around the temples.
>   Lev. 20:14 indicates that people who sleep with in-laws should be burned to death.
>   Lev.21:20 states that one may not approach the altar of God with a defect in one's sight.
>   Lev.25:44 states that one may possess slaves, both male and female, provided they are purchased from neighboring nations.

Not only the Bible but many other ancient texts include statements that now seem strange. Taking such statements as literal guidance for living today seems rather inappropriate.

But metaphor, especially when considered in the light of history and culture, is a different story. The following is an example:

YES VIRGINIA, THERE IS A SANTA CLAUS

On September 21 1987 the New York Sun carried the following now famous piece on its editorial page:

> We take pleasure in answering thus prominently the communication below, expressing at the same time our great gratification that its faithful author is numbered among the friends of The Sun:
>   I am 8 years old. Some of my little friends say there is no Santa Claus. Papa says, "If you see it in The Sun, it's so." Please tell me the truth, is there a Santa Claus?
> *Virginia O'Hanlon*
>
> Virginia, your little friends are wrong. They have been affected by the skepticism of a skeptical age. They do not be-

lieve except what they see. They think that nothing can be which is not comprehensible by their little minds. All minds, Virginia, whether they be men's or children's, are little. In this great universe of ours, man is a mere insect, an ant, in his intellect as compared with the boundless world about him, as measured by the Intelligence capable of grasping the whole of truth and knowledge.

Yes, Virginia, there is a Santa Claus. He exists as certainly as love and generosity and devotion exist, and you know that they abound and give to your life its highest beauty and joy. Alas! how dreary would be the world if there were no Santa Claus! It would be as dreary as if there were no Virginias. There would be no childlike faith then, no poetry, no romance to make tolerable this existence. We should have no enjoyment, except in sense and sight. The external light with which childhood fills the world would be extinguished.

Not believe in Santa Claus! You might as well not believe in fairies. You might get your papa to hire men to watch in all the chimneys on Christmas eve to catch Santa Claus, but even if you did not see Santa Claus coming down, what would that prove? Nobody sees Santa Claus, but that is no sign that there is no Santa Claus. The most real things in the world are those that neither children nor men can see. Did you ever see fairies dancing on the lawn? Of course not, but that's no proof that they are not there. Nobody can conceive or imagine all the wonders there are unseen and unseeable in the world.

You tear apart the baby's rattle and see what makes the noise inside, but there is a veil covering the unseen world which not the strongest man, nor even the united strength of all the strongest men that ever lived, could tear apart. Only faith, poetry, love, romance, can push aside that curtain and view and picture the supernal beauty and glory beyond. Is it all real? Ah, Virginia, in all this world there is nothing else real and abiding.

No Santa Claus? Thank God he lives and lives forever. A thousand years from now, Virginia, nay 10 times 10,000 years from now, he will continue to make glad the heart of childhood. Merry Christmas and a Happy New Year!

Above we have a statement that any reader understands to be metaphor, and no adult would take literally. Indeed there is a Santa Claus, and indeed, in a similar metaphorical way, most people would say there is a God. Making the analogy of God to Santa Claus will seem disrespectful to some readers. I do not mean to disrespect the genuine feelings of those readers, but only to assert that God makes the most sense as a metaphor for something we feel but cannot define.

Spirituality

The traditional definition of spirituality would refer to religious experience. For example Psychologist William James believed that mental events are attributed to a soul, where each person has a soul that exists in a spiritual universe, and leads a person to perform the behaviors they do in the physical world. This was part of what James called *pragmatism*.[171] James defended the right to violate the principle of *evidentialism* (that all belief need be based on evidence, and that faith-based belief is unjustified). He sought to ground justified belief in "hypothesis venturing" as an unwavering principle that would prove most beneficial pragmatically. His doctrine allows one to assume belief in God and prove His existence by what the belief brings to one's life. Justifying belief based on what makes one feel good and makes one's life richer is an interesting argument. It might also be noted that sometimes the truth hurts, so why not engage in pleasurable thoughts?

According to the Dalai Lama[172], a broad definition of spirituality includes a much wider swath of experiences, such as love, compassion, patience, tolerance, forgiveness, contentment, responsibility, harmony, inner peace, and a concern for others. These are aspects of life and human experience that clearly go beyond a purely materialist view of the world, without demanding belief in a supernatural reality or divine being. Spirituality embodies a sense of interdependence of everything and harmony in the universe. Feelings of awe and wonder about where we came from, how we got here, where we are going, what is the purpose of life, etc. can be called spiritual and independent of religion, at least in the sense of belief in any God. It can be said that everyone, atheist or believer, has times of having what can be called a spiritual experience. Spirituality has been associated not only with what is sacred (worthy of veneration) but also with substance abuse (getting high), near-death events, parent-child relationships, and ecological fervor. Meditation, transcendental or otherwise, is said to be spiritual.

Spirituality is a feeling, an experience, which defies explication in literal terms. Spirituality, whether in respect to people or to other aspects of nature, is hard to talk about if the words are intended as denotative (precise specifications with unitary meanings). Mostly by using metaphor we can use words that surely communicate. Doing psychophysics, study of mental experience as a function of the physical properties of external stimuli (like a hearing or vision test), we would not call a spiritual exercise. In contrast, listening to music is clearly spiritual. Many of the great works of music are spiritual, and may be religiously inspired. Who is not thrilled by Beethoven's Ode to Joy or the Hallelujah Chorus, or by the booming organs in the great European cathedrals? One can easily assert that the atheist can just as easily be thrilled by such music. Spirituality corresponds to the enjoyment of nature on almost any physical scale. The more catholic (!) meaning of spirituality is secular.

Seemingly falling in line with our ancient ancestors, people often attribute spiritual qualities to people who are our heroes. Not only Jesus, Moses and Mohammed qualify, but also, depending on who and when, Kennedy, Hitler, Elvis, and Batman qualify. We like kings and queens, and if they don't exist for us in real life we invent them in our literature and in our media. Even in America, founded on the basis that democratic people owe allegiance to no worldly king or dictator, we post photos of our president and other national leaders in the entrances of our public buildings just as do monarchies and communist bureaucracies. Much of the public loved Ronald Reagan, whom many pundits admitted made a better American king than a president. They disliked Jimmy Carter because his appearance and manner did not convey a sense of royalty. In this regard it is worth recalling the amazing outpouring of grief and affection for Diana, Princess of Wales, upon her untimely death. What was it about this woman, born into a wealthy if dysfunctional family, married to a less than exciting English prince, chased by the *paparazzi*, and pictured in all the tabloids, that elicited such a response? Clearly the public of Britain wanted someone they could place on a pedestal who also had the spiritual qualities of beauty and mystery. Spirituality in this sense is natural, but can also be delusory.

Reverence

Reverence is a term usually associated with religion, but it need not be. The ideas of Paul Woodruff (1943-)[173] on reverence are worthy of consideration here. Woodruff defines reverence as a well-developed capacity to have certain feelings (like awe, respect and shame). Reverence, he asserts, begins with a deep understanding of human limitations, and a capacity to be in awe of whatever we believe to be outside our control, to keep us from acting like Gods. Hubris is the opposite of reverence. However reverence is not to be confused with respect per se. The faithful can have much or too little respect. Reverence is capacity to have feelings, not a feeling in itself. Awe is the most reverent of feelings, but awe is inarticulate. Woodruff asserts that it is virtually impossible to act alone in the exercise of reverence; it is inherently a social activity.

Woodruff claims that Thucidides didn't fear Gods, but he feared human arrogance. Socrates asserted that a large component of wisdom is in knowing our own limitations. It was a prevalent Greek idea that reverence grows from acknowledging human weakness. Plato saw reverence as one of the bulwarks of society, and played up the idea of reverence for truth. (Plato may have gone a bit far in a proposed replacing of familial love with community: making all the women wives of all the men.) Protagorus stated that without reverence no group of humans can stand by one another; they will perish. Relative to the ancients Woodruff claims that we have lost not reverence itself, but the idea of reverence.

In ancient Asia Confucius promoted the idea of *li*. The word is translated in a number of different ways. Most often, *li* is described using some form of the word "ritual" but it has also been translated as customs, etiquette, morals, and rules of proper behavior. Reverence is often reinforced by ceremony. Without reverence rituals are said to be empty. To Confucius reverence leads to ceremony and the feelings that make ceremony worthwhile. Unfortunately we are losing many of the ceremonial occasions in which people find ways to be reverent. *Li* does not stand against change, but regulates and orders it. *Li* does not impose hierarchy but makes it harmonious. For Confucius a human being without the feeling of modesty (*ci*) and deference (*rang*) is not human; (this is) the beginning of *li*.

Many of our religious leaders are traditionally called "reverend", implying religious status. Yet Woodruff claims that reverence has more to do with politics and community than it does with religion. He suggests that if you wish to be reverent never claim that God supports your political views. That claim opts you out of the political process. If a religious group thinks it speaks and acts as God commands, that can justify violence, and this is not reverence. According to Woodruff God-fearing is not reverence, since awe is not fear. Religion without reverence is common, though a pity; politics without reverence is catastrophic. What we admire in religions that are not our own tradition is not faith (in that other religion) but the reverence of those believers. Yet, because worship is based on faith, faith can be arrogant, therefore not reverent. Faith-centered religion may place a low value on reverence. When rising doubts cloud the certainty of religious claims, reverence is all the more important. Reverence cannot be expressed in a creed. According to Woodruff its most fundamental expression is said to be music.

Reverence is claimed to defy conversion into rule-based ethics. There are no rules for being courteous or for grieving, for example. Patriotism can be a virtue when a country follows justice. Justice demands reverence, otherwise it can tear people apart. Woodruff suggests that if you desire peace in the world do not pray that everyone share your beliefs. Pray instead that all may be reverent. In fact reverent people may not know what to believe. Wars can be fought by reverent people. Reverence may be true even though beliefs may be false. Humility is not despair and it is not skepticism.

Woodruff points out that in learning communities good teachers listen to their pupils, and in this they are reverent. When teachers are silent it is the student who must speak. Part of good teaching is the ability to discover good things about people, and to show awe at subject matter that cannot be tamed. Without reverence an instructor is not a teacher, a boss is not a leader, and a house is not a home. We know reverence first hand when we are at home, but failures of reverence at home are the most devastating.

Opposing perspectives that seem to converge

The Wall Street Journal in September of 2009 commissioned Oxford historian of religion Karen Armstrong (1944-) and British evolutionist Richard Dawkins to respond independently to the question "Where does evolution leave God?"[174] Armstrong is a well-regarded author of many popular books on the history of religion and a champion of God. Dawkins is probably the most widely read champion of the New Atheism. Neither knew what the other would say. Here are the results. The exchange is quoted in full because in my opinion it shows how close a respected religious apologist and a devout atheist can become.

KAREN ARMSTRONG SAYS WE NEED GOD TO GRASP THE WONDER OF OUR EXISTENCE

Richard Dawkins has been right all along, of course—at least in one important respect. Evolution has indeed dealt a blow to the idea of a benign creator, literally conceived. It tells us that there is no Intelligence controlling the cosmos, and that life itself is the result of a blind process of natural selection, in which innumerable species failed to survive. The fossil record reveals a natural history of pain, death and racial extinction, so if there was a divine plan, it was cruel, callously prodigal and wasteful. Human beings were not the pinnacle of a purposeful creation; like everything else, they evolved by trial and error and God had no direct hand in their making. No wonder so many fundamentalist Christians find their faith shaken to the core.

But Darwin may have done religion—and God—a favor by revealing a flaw in modern Western faith. Despite our scientific and technological brilliance, our understanding of God is often remarkably undeveloped—even primitive. In the past, many of the most influential Jewish, Christian and Muslim thinkers understood that *what we call "God" is merely a symbol that points beyond itself to an indescribable transcendence, whose existence cannot be proved but is only intuited by means of spiritual exercises and a compassionate lifestyle that enables us to cultivate new capacities of mind and heart.*

But by the end of the 17th century, instead of looking through the symbol to "the God beyond God," Christians were transforming it into hard fact. Sir Isaac Newton had claimed that his cosmic system proved beyond doubt the existence of an intelligent, omniscient and omnipotent creator, who was obviously "very well skilled in Mechanicks and Geometry." Enthralled by the prospect of such cast-iron certainty, churchmen started to develop a scientifically-based theology that eventually made Newton's Mechanick, and later William Paley's Intelligent Designer, essential to Western Christianity. But the Great Mechanick was little more than an idol, the kind of human projection that theology, at its best, was supposed to avoid. God had been essential to Newtonian physics but it was not long before other scientists were able to dispense with the God-hypothesis and, finally, Darwin showed that there could be no proof for God's existence. This would not have been a disaster had not Christians become so dependent upon their scientific religion that they had lost the older habits of thought and were left without other resources.

Symbolism was essential to pre-modern religion, because it was only possible to speak about the ultimate reality—God, Tao, Brahman or Nirvana—analogically, since it lay beyond the reach of words. Jews and Christians both developed audaciously innovative and figurative methods of reading the Bible, and every statement of the Quran is called an ayah (parable). Saint Augustine (354-430), a major authority for both Catholics and Protestants, insisted that if a biblical text contradicted reputable science, it must be interpreted allegorically. This remained standard practice in the West until the 17th century, when, in an effort to emulate the exact scientific method, Christians began to read scripture with a literalness that is without parallel in religious history.

Most cultures believed that there were two recognized ways of arriving at truth. The Greeks called them *mythos* and *logos*. Both were essential and neither was superior to the other; they were not in conflict but complementary, each with its own sphere of competence. Logos ("reason") was the pragmatic mode of thought that enabled us to function effectively in the world and had, therefore, to correspond accurately to external reality. But it could not assuage human grief or find ultimate meaning in life's struggle. For that people turned to mythos, stories that made no pretensions to historical accuracy but should rather be seen as an early form of psychology. If translated into ritual or ethical action, *a good myth showed you how to cope with mortality, discover an inner source of strength, and endure pain and sorrow with serenity.*

In the ancient world, a cosmology was not regarded as factual but was primarily therapeutic; it was recited when people needed an infusion of that mysterious power that had somehow brought something out of primal nothingness: at a sickbed, a coronation, or during a political crisis. Some cosmologies taught people how to unlock their own creativity; others made them aware of the struggle required to maintain social and political order. The Genesis creation hymn, written during the Israelites' exile in Babylonia in the 6th century BC, was a gentle polemic against Babylonian religion. Its vision of an ordered universe where everything had its place was probably consoling to a displaced people, though, as we can see in the Bible, some of the exiles preferred a more aggressive cosmology.

There can never be a definitive version of a myth, because it refers to the more imponderable aspects of life. To remain effective, it must respond to contemporary circumstance. In the 16th century, when Jews were being expelled from one region of Europe after another, the mystic Isaac Luria constructed an entirely new creation myth that bore no resemblance to the Genesis story. But instead of being reviled for contradicting the Bible, it inspired a mass-movement among Jews, because it was such a telling description of the arbitrary world they now lived in. Backed up with special rituals, it also helped them face up to their pain and discover a source of strength.

Religion was not supposed to provide explanations that lay within the competence of reason but to help us live creatively with realities for which there are no easy solutions and find an interior haven of peace; today, however, many have opted for unsustainable certainty instead. But can we respond religiously to evolutionary theory? Can we use it to recover a more authentic notion of God?

Darwin made it clear once again that—as Maimonides, Avicenna, Aquinas and Eckhart had already pointed out— we cannot regard God simply as a divine personality, who single-handedly created the world. This could direct our attention away from the idols of certainty and back to the "God beyond God." The best theology is a spiritual exercise, akin to poetry. *Religion is not an exact science but a kind of art form that, like music or painting, introduces us to a mode of knowledge that is different from the purely rational and which cannot easily be put into words.* At its best, it holds us in an attitude of wonder, which is, perhaps, not unlike the awe that Mr. Dawkins experiences—and has helped me to appreciate —when he contemplates the marvels of natural selection.

But what of the pain and waste that Darwin unveiled? All the major traditions insist that the faithful meditate on the ubiquitous suffering that is an inescapable part of life; because, if we do not acknowledge this uncomfortable fact, the compassion that lies at the heart of faith is impossible. The almost unbearable spectacle of the myriad species passing painfully into oblivion is not unlike some classic Buddhist meditations on the First Noble Truth ("Existence is suffering"), the indispensable prerequisite for the transcendent enlightenment that some call Nirvana—and others call God.

RICHARD DAWKINS ARGUES THAT EVOLUTION LEAVES GOD WITH NOTHING TO DO

Before 1859 it would have seemed natural to agree with the Reverend William Paley, in *Natural Theology*, that the creation of life was God's greatest work. Especially (vanity might add) human life. Today we might amend the statement: Evolution is the universe's greatest work. Evolution is the creator of life, and life is arguably the most surprising and most beautiful production that the laws of physics have ever generated. Evolution, to quote a T-shirt sent me by an anonymous well-wisher, is the greatest show on earth, the only game in town.

Indeed, evolution is probably the greatest show in the entire universe. Most scientists' hunch is that there are independently evolved life forms dotted around planetary islands throughout the universe—though sadly too thinly scattered to encounter one another. And if there is life elsewhere, it is something stronger than a hunch to say that it will turn out to be Darwinian life. The argument in favor of alien life's existing at all is weaker than the argument that— if it exists at all—it will be Darwinian life. But it is also possible that we really are alone in the universe, in which case Earth, with its greatest show, is the most remarkable planet in the universe.

What is so special about life? It never violates the laws of physics. Nothing does (if anything did, physicists would just have to formulate new laws—it's happened often enough in the history of science). But although life never violates the laws of physics, it pushes them into unexpected avenues that stagger the imagination. If we didn't know about life we wouldn't believe it was possible—except, of course, that there'd then be nobody around to do the disbelieving!

The laws of physics, before Darwinian evolution bursts out from their midst, can make rocks and sand, gas clouds and stars, whirlpools and waves, whirlpool-shaped galaxies and light that travels as waves while behaving like particles. It is an interesting, fascinating and, in many ways, deeply mysterious universe. But now, enter life. Look, through the eyes of a physicist, at a bounding kangaroo, a swooping bat, a leaping dolphin, a soaring Coast Redwood. There never was a rock that bounded like a kangaroo, never a pebble that crawled like a beetle seeking a mate, never a sand grain that swam like a water flea. Not once do any of these creatures disobey one jot or tittle of the laws of physics. Far from violating the laws of thermodynamics (as is often ignorantly alleged) they are relentlessly driven by them. Far from violating the laws of motion, animals exploit them to their advantage as they walk, run, dodge and jink, leap and fly, pounce on prey or spring to safety.

Never once are the laws of physics violated, yet life emerges into uncharted territory. And how is the trick done? The answer is a process that, although variable in its wondrous detail, is sufficiently uniform to deserve one single name: Darwinian evolution, the nonrandom survival of randomly varying coded information. We know, as certainly as we know anything in science, that this is the process that has generated life on our own planet. And my bet, as I said, is that the same process is in operation wherever life may be found, anywhere in the universe.

What if the greatest show on earth is not the greatest show in the universe? What if there are life forms on other planets that have evolved so far beyond our level of intelligence and creativity that we should regard them as Gods, were we ever so fortunate (or unfortunate?) as to meet them? Would they indeed be Gods? Wouldn't we be tempted to fall on our knees and worship them, as a medieval peasant might if suddenly confronted with such miracles as a Boeing 747, a mobile telephone or Google Earth? But, however God-like the aliens might seem, they would not be Gods, and for one very important reason. They did not create the universe; it created them, just as it created us. Making the universe is the one thing no intelligence, however superhuman, could do, because an intelligence is complex—statistically improbable —and therefore had to emerge, by gradual degrees, from simpler beginnings: from a lifeless universe—the miracle-free zone that is physics.

To midwife such emergence is the singular achievement of Darwinian evolution. It starts with primeval simplicity and fosters, by slow, explicable degrees, the emergence of complexity: seemingly limitless complexity—certainly up to our human level of complexity and very probably way beyond. There may be worlds on which superhuman life thrives, superhuman to a level that our imaginations cannot grasp. But superhuman does not mean supernatural. Darwinian evolution is the only process we know that is ultimately capable of generating anything as complicated as creative intelligences. Once it has done so, of course, those intelligences can create other complex things: works of art and music, advanced technology, computers, the Internet and who knows what in the future? Darwinian evolution may not be the only such generative process in the universe.

There may be other "cranes" (Daniel Dennett's term, which he opposes to "skyhooks") that we have not yet discovered or imagined. But, however wonderful and however different from Darwinian evolution those putative cranes may be, they cannot be magic. They will share with Darwinian evolution the facility to raise up complexity, as an emergent property, out of simplicity, while never violating natural law.

Where does that leave God? The kindest thing to say is that it leaves him with nothing to do, and no achievements that might attract our praise, our worship or our fear. Evolution is God's redundancy notice, his pink slip. But we have to go further. A complex creative intelligence with nothing to do is not just redundant. A divine designer is all but ruled out by the consideration that he must be at least as complex as the entities he was wheeled out to explain. God is not dead. He was never alive in the first place.

Now, there is a certain class of sophisticated modern theologians who will say something like this: "Good heavens, of course we are not so naive or simplistic as to care whether God exists. Existence is such a 19th-century preoccupation! It doesn't matter whether God exists in a scientific sense. What matters is whether he exists for you or for me. If God is real for you, who cares whether science has made him redundant? Such arrogance! Such elitism."

Well, if that's what floats your canoe, you'll be paddling it up a very lonely creek. The mainstream belief of the world's peoples is very clear. They believe in God, and that means they believe he exists in objective reality, just as surely as the Rock of Gibraltar exists. If sophisticated theologians or postmodern relativists think they are rescuing God from the redundancy scrap-heap by downplaying the importance of existence, they should think again. Tell the congregation of a church or mosque that existence is too vulgar an attribute to fasten onto their God, and they will brand you an atheist. They'll be right.

CONVERGENCE?

What so impresses me about this exchange is that Armstrong and Dawkins, which the Wall Street Journal quite naturally assumed would take polar opposite positions, ended up very close to the same place. Armstrong emphasizes that modern science has rendered fundamentalist literalist notions of God as untenable to science and to a rational person, while claiming that science has failed to cope with human consciousness and sense of transcendent reality. She refers to religion as a spiritual exercise, but certain belief as untenable. I believe that this is what Bucky Fuller meant by the quote I put at the beginning of this chapter: "God is a verb".

And Dawkins is certainly correct that "even modern theology, if it looks itself in the mirror, has moved in the atheist direction" to a large extent. Surely modern technology, as viewed by a primitive observer, would surely be attributed to God. But most of the world, modern philosophy notwithstanding, is still mired in that past—and that's our problem.

What is transcendence? Is it another term for "I don't know and I don't understand"?

Does God really have anything useful to do? Is the mythos aspect of Karen Armstrong's argument myth that we can treat the same as we do Santa Claus, or is it some transcendent myth that is a clear guideline for living?

British philosopher Alfred J. Ayer (1910-1989)[175] took a much more cynical view of talking about God as transcendent. He commented that to say that something transcends human understanding is to say that it is unintelligible, and what is unintelligible cannot be significantly described. He claimed that one cannot intelligibly believe in God unless one can give an account of what it means to say God exists.

> If one allows that it is impossible to define God in intelligible terms, then one is allowing that it is impossible for a sentence to be both significant and be about God. To assert that words are inadequate and approximate does not help, for, because words have only the meanings we give them, if we cannot say what we mean, we cannot genuinely claim to mean anything. No sentence which purports to describe the nature of a transcendent God can possess any literal significance.[176].

Contemporary British philosopher of religion Don Cupitt (1934-)[177] allegedly started from a position that human language could never fully express the reality of God. He then evolved to embracing the notion that God is not a Being who exists independently of us, but is instead a product of our language and ideas. This can be restated: God did not create us in God's image; we created God in our image. That is not a new idea, but it is an important one, and I pick up on it later. Cupitt, by the way, sees Jesus as a radical secular humanist,

Can the nature of God be modeled?

This book began with an emphasis on concise, explicit (denotative) models based on observable objects or events. This is the way of science, and it is a proven discipline for thinking, and for making knowledge public. It was also affirmed that connotative language, including myth and metaphor, provide another way of depicting belief. Such belief is surely life enriching, though the reader's interpretation in the latter case is arbitrary, open ended, and not publicly verifiable. One can try to share how one *feels* about something, but the basis for the feeling is ultimately private.

It was stated that when modeling human belief there can be a model of the nature of an object or set of events that people believe to be real, or there can be a model of the reasons or process or mechanism of acquiring and practicing such a belief. Modeling God *per se* is of the first sort. In this case the modeler asks What *is* God, i.e., what is the structure and function of God? How to represent the phenomenon, nature, attributes, or character of God? What can God do, how and under what circumstances?

Can current ideas about the nature of God be evaluated on the basis of the taxonomy of attributes presented earlier: applicability to observables, dimensionality, metricity, robustness, social penetration, and conciseness? Can means of representation briefly mentioned in the chapter on models (verbal, graphic or logical symbolism, including mathematics) be used? How about statistical inference from evidence? Or utility, or decision-making with or without certainty, or information communication and information value, or signal detection, or feedback control—all approaches that are explicated in the Appendix as means to model different aspects of human belief and behavior? In the next section we test the God hypothesis against the attributes of a good model.

TESTING THE GOD HYPOTHESIS AGAINST THE MODEL ATTRIBUTES

Consider now each of the six attributes proposed in Chapter 1, where the assertion was that to the degree that these attributes are present in the fullest sense, we have a model that represents true and useful knowledge. Let's see how well they apply to God.

Attribute 1. Applicability to Observables. If any and all of creation can be called an observable then we are stuck with the question of what is God *not*? There are no data on God, or else the data set includes everything—all of creation. There is nothing that can be observed in any public operational way to distinguish God from anything else. Private transcendental feelings are not operational and so there is nothing to observe.

Attribute 2. Dimensionality. Swinburne asserts that God is the ultimate in simplicity (one dimension—or none). But what exactly is that? Others would claim that God would have to have as least as many dimensions as whatever He creates, which is infinity. That would be impossible to model by any standard of human capability.

Attribute 3. Metricity. In a pantheistic physical universe where God is a being, God would have to comply with criteria of physics and support a cardinal (ratio) metric in every one of the (infinite) dimensions. Again, impossible to model, so we still have no measurable basis for a model.

Attribute 4. Robustness. What is God good for? What can He do? He can make you feel good if you are a believer. And if you believe in revealed truth as in the sacred texts He can serve as a supposed basis for morality and a motivation for good works. He can also serve as a basis for hate and for fighting religious wars that we have witnessed throughout history and which continue to this day. The construct of God is robust for sure, one might say infinitely robust. God is a good rationale for just about everything, many would say rationalization. How do we come to agreement of what use to make of the God idea?

Attribute 5. Social penetration. Here the God construct excels. The concept has penetrated the culture for thousands of years with wide acceptance. No arguments otherwise!

136   What Is God?

Attribute 6. Conciseness. I just wish the theist philosophers who defend the existence of God could be concise in their arguments. I find them circular and very confusing. In contrast there are the oft repeated descriptors: omniscient, omnipotent, and omnibenevolent—concise for sure but hardly constituting an acceptable model beyond the mental model of active imagination. (I can imagine that my pink unicorn has those same attributes.)

Going back to our definition of a model in Chapter 1 and the idea that scientific models are denotative rather than connotative, religious language seems to be entirely connotative, and therefore open to anyone's arbitrary interpretation.

So the God construct flatly flunks the first three criteria (no trace of an observable God, the dimensionality would have to be zero or infinite and therefore unworkable, and no basis for a metric). The God construct surely is robust in the sense that one can try to apply it to anything. However in applicability the minuses seem just as great as the plusses (suffering vs happiness). With regard to robustness in credibility it was mathematician Pierre-Simon Laplace (1749-1927) who famously said "I have no need for that hypothesis" when he was referring to God in relation to celestial mechanics. For social penetration God surely is a winner: the concept has thoroughly pervaded history. Of course the belief that the world was flat had done quite well on the social penetration scale. As to conciseness, if one is happy with "omnipotent, omniscient, and omnibenevolent", that's pretty concise.

In any case God can be said to be a private mental model, something imagined, an idea, however vague the explanation.

So God (and a god) is a robust, pervasive *connotative idea* that can be used by anyone for almost any purpose, and has been for thousands of years. In all other respects there is nothing there to model, certainly not by the standards of modeling in science.

WHAT IS THERE TO MODEL ABOUT GOD?

All of the modeling approaches previously discussed require some input data, something observable to the modeler that can be re-

A God for Tomorrow   137

ported as data. Unfortunately, as readily acknowledged by theist scholars, observables are totally lacking. Philosopher Meister Eckhart (1260-1327)[178] said it many years ago: "God is no thing", meaning nothing tangible. In contrast to God being no thing, God has been said to be everything, infinity, all of creation. Mathematicians and philosophers have been struggling to cope with zero and infinity for a long time.

Modeling infinity is no different from modeling zero with respect to discriminating observables. There is no way to make any distinctions. Zero and infinity are defined as mathematical limits. They are useful concepts in mathematics, fitting into mathematical models mostly as ways of saying what cannot be modeled. By themselves zero and infinity do not constitute models of anything.

Theists agree that God has no space or time dimension. That proscribes any model of physical objects or events by any human being who lives in a world confined to space and time. And that necessarily makes God an idea, a meme, something imagined, a mental model. Of course historically, at least in Abrahamic religions, God has been depicted as an old man sitting on a throne in the sky, surrounded by angels with harps. These *images* have been modeled, for example as pictures on ceilings or on stained glass windows of churches. But today few would accept these images as accurate models of God in the sense the term model has been used here. We can also use objective methods to get people to describe what God means to them and collect data on their verbal or graphical responses, but there would be little consistency. In any case, insofar as God exists for different individuals as private, imagined, mental representations, we are obliged to exclude these from what we have called denotative or scientific models that can be communicated and applied publicly.

However there is one caveat to the above. As earlier noted, ideas of God are generated by the brain (and believed to have been put into our heads by God or the gods, according to the historical recounting by Julian Jaynes). Insofar as God is represented by physical events in the brain, there truly *are* observables potentially available. At the moment they are difficult to measure. Neuroscientists may someday correlate those brain events with other events in the body or the external world. Not much is promising at the moment.

It is fashionable nowadays to say that God is transcendent, but that is a bit difficult to get one's arms around. There is no consensus on the meaning of transcendent. Modeling a transcendent entity seems out of the question, except perhaps by descriptors of God such as power, knowledge, love or beauty—or God as an ultimate hidden and mysterious force behind everything. By themselves those are metaphorical terms, or might be called attributes of a metaphorical model. But such a model does not pass the critical observability criterion of a scientific model.

Getting a person to make a selection as to the most fitting verbal phrase in a questionnaire, as is done by pollsters, does create observables. But because the pollster is the one who constructed the questionnaire, that provides questionable meaning with respect to a scientific model of the individual subject's idea of God. And polling of such data shades into what is discussed in the next section as measuring behavior of people's practice of worship, i.e., modeling the behavior of religious people (in contrast to modeling God *per se*).

Some people have asserted that our relationship to God is similar to an emotional relationship with another person. A religious person loves, honors, and glorifies God, but it is very difficult to model such emotional relationships with scientific modeling, whether we're talking God or human as the recipient of such affection. While emotional relationships are not easy to model using science, metaphorical models do seem fitting. I will not agree that emotion is ultimately beyond science—for many reasons, including the fact that emotion is just experimentally more difficult to reproduce in the laboratory. However the emotional factor is not the main problem in modeling God. The problem is the observability of the target thing to be modeled. A target human being that is loved, honored or glorified is quite observable, as is the behavior of the person doing the loving. A target God is not.

I can only conclude that currently there is no satisfactory way to model such a construct as God, since there is no credible way to specify God as distinguished from anything else. So, on the premise that to be able to model is to have knowledge, and vice versa, *public* knowledge about God appears to be impossible, at least for now.

Where God *per se* is not modelable, that is not true of human behavior in the practice of religion.

Can religious practice be modeled?

Modeling religious practice is an example of the second type of belief model: in this case how and why people acquire belief in God and carry out their worship behavior. The object of modeling here would be to characterize the behavior of people with respect to religious belief and participation. One can distinguish models of people, how they acquire belief and practice religion, as contrasted to modeling the nature of the God concept per se. The distinction is subtle and some might assert that there can be no God that exists other than how people actively express what they believe and how they behave with respect to that belief—model dependent reality again.

With regard to the attributes and to the properties of the models cited earlier, religious practice is a very different story from the concept or nature of God *per se*. Religious practice surely can be modeled by science and has been. To be sure there is already a significant literature on the topic. However I would claim that scientific probes of why people believe what they say they believe, and how they practice that belief, has been timid and not as penetrating as is justified by the importance of the subject in our society.

USING SCIENCE TO STUDY RELIGION THE SAME AS WE WOULD STUDY ANYTHING ELSE

As previously mentioned Daniel Dennett sees religious practice as a natural phenomenon that can be studied by science much as any other aspect of human behavior.[179] It is probably true that some people take offense at such a notion, in the same way that they did with the Kinsey report, the scientific study of human sexuality. Religion, like sex, is regarded by some as personal and private. One of Dennett's research challenges is to use his theory of memes to trace how religious tendencies and ideas spread from person to person, and even seek to maximize their own spread. For example, computer-based social networks are amenable to making such measurements; they are already being used to evaluate the spread of consumer preference, political commentary, etc.

Religion is already being subjected to certain kinds of scientific investigation. Demographic poll-taking about beliefs is part of that. Journals like *Skeptical Inquirer* publish investigations of reported near-death experiences of "seeing God", the efficacy of prayer, "religious miracles" and so on. The proposed modeling criteria can normally be satisfied, the same as is true any other social science, given that there is some specific behavioral event to measure so as to provide objective data.

It is true that many of the dependent measures will be subjective data, which probably means that researchers will have to use categorical data, and can aspire to order metrics at the most. The robustness of the models will be evaluated in terms of effectiveness in saying how religious practices help or hinder feelings, mental health, economics, government or corporate policy, or international relations. Social penetration of any model would have to wait for the science to be done. My point is not that such studies have not been done, but that studies and models have not been done nearly to the extent that is warranted, considering how religion plays such an important role in many people's lives.

Not everyone agrees with Dennett. "The problem with studying religion scientifically is that you do violence to the phenomenon by reducing it to basic elements that can be quantified, and that makes for bad science and bad religion," said Dr. Richard Sloan, a professor of behavioral medicine at Columbia and author of the book, "Blind Faith: The Unholy Alliance of Religion and Medicine."[180] To me this seems like a lame rationalization to shy away from critical thinking. As has been affirmed throughout this book, religion cannot be reduced to mathematics, but it would seem that metricity at the low end (nominal categorization and ordering) *can* be applied. We can certainly measure human time and energy and dollars spent on religious activities—these are objective data with cardinal metrics. And we can be systematic in using subjective scales and other psychometrics of belief and preference that are at the current frontier of economic and psychological modeling.

So, with regard to the six attributes, all can be applied, depending on the aspect of religious practice being studied. There are plenty of observables: what people say and what they do in and out of religious services. Observables can include physiological measures

A God for Tomorrow 141

of feeling and words that are associated in conjunction with brain scans. There is room for single as well as multidimensional studies such as factor analysis and correlation. Many measures would be categorical or ordered preference, but time and money measures do provide ample opportunity for cardinal metricity. Robustness and social penetration (acceptance) will depend on models yet to be developed; that future is hard to judge since so few models are out there. There is sure to be controversy since modeling in this arena tampers with strong feelings. In any case models can be as concise as any other models in social science and anthropology.

I can imagine any and all of the models mentioned in Chapter 1 (and later provided as examples in the Appendix) being applied to religious practice. For example logic trees are already being applied to what are called *belief networks*: how belief in one thing is likely (statistically) to lead to some other belief, the end result being a model of how belief states relate to one another with numbers on likelihood of association. Similarly, the Bayesian mathematics model (see Appendix) can predict how convergence of belief in alternative causes results from a person's experience with a series of events and their past associations of those events with the alternative causes.

Religious practice entails many decisions about how to spend time and money under certainty and uncertainty and the contingent value associations, so all the decision models to be described in the Appendix would seem to apply. There are game situations that impinge on morality, as will be more fully described in the Appendix for the competitive game model. There are also threshold signal detection and feedback control mechanisms involved in health aspects of religion.

In the next five subsections some obvious questions about religious practice are posed, ones that seem quite amenable to scientific investigation and modeling.

MODELING THE ACQUISITION OF DIFFERENT KINDS OF BELIEF

A Jesuit priest name Gian-Carlo Colombo, who was the *advoca-*

tus dei (advocate for God) for the Voltaire Society, a student philosophy discussion society at Oxford University in the 1950s, distinguished several meanings of the word *belief*.[181] He proposed the most straightforward meaning to be "belief that….", meaning belief that a particular proposition is true. Such a belief can be measured by a simple question such as: Do you believe God exists? Or do you believe God can perform what we call miracles? If there is an expectation that the person questioned is telling the truth the questioner must accept the answer.

A different meaning of belief Colombo proposed to be "belief in…", for example: Do you believe in the Bible? Do you believe in Capitalism? Do you believe in Obama? In this case there is no question about whether these entities exist. The implied questions have to do with whether the person questioned agrees with and/or would follow the recommendations of the document, theory or person. Colombo asserts that this is a stronger form of belief than "belief that…" about some proposition. The best way to test the "belief in…" is to gather evidence of how the person behaves— whether behavior is consistent with what he/she says. For example, Bayesian updating (Appendix) might be used here. The previously described computer *estimation model* that updates itself by interacting with the world and then is used as a basis for taking action is analogous to acquisition of "Belief in…". When that model is applied to a human its internal (mental) belief model can be said to drive the human's behavior.

Colombo had a third category of belief he called *faith*, that in his paper obviously has to do with faith in God, a belief allegedly so strong that it becomes the driving force of one's life. He asserts that faith in God needs no justification, for if it did there would not be faith. He refers to it as based on "interior experience", rather than external perception, and argues against Kierkegaard as to whether it is necessarily subjective. Colombo states that faith in God, as he characterizes it, is conviction with objective certainty. Here is where I would have to disagree. Especially since there is no observable, it must be subjective, namely belief in an idea. That one behaves *as though* an idea has a basis in reality does not make the idea real.

PRAYER: DOES IT WORK?

Looking back in history there are good reasons why certain religious practices such as prayer developed as they did. Ancient peoples built altars on which they sacrificed living creatures including children because they honestly thought that would win them favor with the gods.

Prayer is a prominent component of essentially all religious practice. Asking favors of God or the gods though prayer has been standard for thousands of years. Intercessory prayer, praying for others, is admirable caring. But a salient question is whether intercessory prayer really works, whether those prayed for become better off. Various scientific studies have been conducted ever since Francis Galton first addressed it in 1872.[182] But little credible evidence has become available that shows that prayer influences the probability that the request will come true.

C.S. Lewis (1898-1963), writing on the efficacy of prayer[183], comments disparagingly about

> ....those artificially contrived experiences which we call experiments. Could this be done about prayer? I will pass over the objection that no Christian could take part in such a project, because He has been forbidden it: You must not try experiments on God, your Master.

Lewis goes on to suggest that people praying in an experiment would not really be praying but only mouthing the words. Quoting Hamlet, he asserts that "Words without thoughts never to heaven go".

Actually many experimental studies on prayer have already been done. The great majority show no significant effect. One can find on the internet reports of double blind experiments that purport to show with statistical significance that medical patients have better outcomes if patients are prayed for. However most of these are supported by religious organizations and are therefore suspect as being biased. If patients are informed or otherwise get wind of the fact that they are being prayed for there is an obvious opportunity for a placebo effect, well established in behavioral science. So let someone know you are praying for them, and an effect cannot be disputed.

Eric Stockton[184], agreeing with Lewis that experiments are not possible (but with a different perspective!) comments: "Of course, there is a question whether a true test of prayer is even possible." He points out in a letter to the editor of *Skeptical Inquirer*[185] that

> If prayer works because of God's intervention, and God is the omniscient deity of Christianity (or most any major religion), then He knows He is being tested. As such, He could accept or reject whatever prayer is offered, and either choose to give or not give evidence that it works. It would be impossible to properly blind such an experiment if it's the deity we're talking about. If it is supposed to be the prayer itself that heals, rather than God intervening, then we don't have that issue, but we instead have to wonder how it might be that such prayer might work, if we ever get a decent study that shows it does, that is.

In many religions, including Christianity, one purpose of prayer is not to ask for things to happen, but to praise and honor God, and develop a personal relation. This in turn raises the question of what that means if God is transcendent and intangible. Since that God must be imagined (there can be no other way of making contact) is that any different from one obtaining satisfaction from identifying with any other personal hero, say a famous movie personality or athletic superstar? And then if that is what is going on, and the person obtains satisfaction from such a personal relationship, is there anything unusual in that? We all enjoy our heroes, whether in business, sports, personal relations or religion.

WHY DO PEOPLE AFFILIATE WITH ONLY ONE TRIBE?

People tend to regard religious institutions in much the same way as they do athletic teams: they tend to become fans of one team or another. One is expected to identify a religious preference one way or another. When this author did his service during the Korean war his dog tags had to say Catholic, Protestant of Jew. There was no alternative. The following makes the point. It is an exchange between a young Indian boy and his parents in Yann Martel's novel *Life of Pi*.[186]

>"But I want to pray to Allah. I want to be a Christian."
>"You can't be both. You must be one or the other."
>"Why can't I be both?"
>"They're separate religions. They have nothing in common."
>"That's not what they say! They both claim Abraham as theirs. Muslims say the God of the Hebrews and the Christians is the same as the God of the Muslims. They recognize David, Moses and Jesus as prophets."
>"What does this have to do with us, Piscine? We're Indians."
>"There have been Christians and Muslims in India for centuries. Some people say Jesus is buried in Kashmir."
>He said nothing, only looked at me, his brow furrowed. Suddenly business called.
>"Talk to Mother about it."
>"Mother"
>"Father and I find your religious zeal a bit of a mystery."
>"It is a mystery."
>"Hmmmm. I don't mean it that way. Listen, my darling, if you're going to be religious, you must be either a Hindu, a Christian or a Muslim. You heard what they said on the esplanade."
>"I don't see why I can't be all three."

Society tends to force us to choose between religions, to join one tribe or another. Why should not each person consider them all and synthesize his or her own religion? Actually some religious institutions do try to do this. One is the Bahai faith, that explicitly seeks to combine the best from Christianity, Islam, and Buddhism. Another is the Unitarian Universalist Society, which welcomes atheists as well as all shades of believers.

DOES RELIGIOUS PRACTICE ENHANCE HEALTH?

There is growing evidence from epidemiological data, clinical trials and cross-sectional studies of a positive correlation between religious practice and health. These studies appear in peer-reviewed journals, have been reported by different research groups, and have been replicated for persons of all ages, races and socioeconomic strata. For example the Women's Health Initiative, through surveys and an annual review of medical records, found that women over 50 were 20% less likely to die in any given year if they attended religious services weekly (15% reduction if they attended less than weekly) compared to those that never attend religious services.[187] This analysis was controlled for age, ethnicity, income level and (most importantly) current health status. However concern remains that perhaps religious people are either more likely to be mentally healthy in the first place (based on personality or genetic influences) or that uncontrolled factors are responsible for these associations.

These findings raise the interesting question of whether it is rational for people to practice religion and express belief in God because that makes them feel good. Is belief in any untruth ever justified, for example if it generates happiness? The answer would seem to be yes, provisionally. If no one is harmed and belief (in a hypothetical untruth) makes the believer happy it is hard to assert that such a person should be denied that good feeling. Of course believers might contend that God really does help them, that it is more than a psychological effect of their effort to believe, their commitment in belief. (I remind the reader that, as discussed earlier, effort to believe in a technologically-produced virtual environment does make it seem more real, even though it is contrived).

It can be said that no current understanding of anything is completely true (science is continually refining the truth). I think that many professed believers justify their belief this way. I can only suggest that there is satisfaction if one aspires to be intellectually honest and actively seek truth.

DO RELIGIOUS INSTITUTIONS DO MORE GOOD THAN HARM?

I find this a very difficult question to answer. Globally we see that the clash between the values of Western Christianity and Middle Eastern Islam, played out in the media and in international politics, are precipitating global conflict. The ancient rivalries based on who should have succeeded the prophet Mohammed many centuries ago, or who is responsible for killing Jesus, appear infantile. And it is the innocent people who suffer.

On the very local level, however, within small communities where tribal values are held in common, we see that religious institutions perform many good deeds. They comfort the sick and lonely, and promote good causes. African American churches were clearly instrumental in the civil rights movement in the U.S. Religious institutions provide a sense of community that government agencies are incompetent to do. The sense of community is mostly a good thing, but sometimes it manifests peer pressure and tribal reinforcement for people to take up causes that are not very admirable. So a question that emerges is: Can institutions that revolve around commitment but are not religious produce similar benefits without the costs?

DO CHURCH-GOERS SAY WHAT THEY REALLY BELIEVE?

Having sat with a very small sample of churchgoers in discussions about God over a period of several years, this writer's opinion is that it is very uncomfortable for most people to talk about God openly. Of course my sample may be biased; it probably is biased in one way or another. The subject of God is intellectually intimidating for many. At least in Western cultures many folks are just not comfortable sharing their true religious beliefs, because often those beliefs are not well articulated in people's own minds (mentally modeled). Most folks who were brought up to attend church, or say they profess one faith or another, will continue to follow their habits and traditions, "believing in believing" as Dennett so aptly puts it, and do not want to rock the boat. For this reason getting directly at religious belief through scientific methods is a tricky but challenging pursuit.

Readers may remember that just before Christmas in 2012 there was a horrific massacre of twenty first grade children and seven teachers in Newtown, New York. This was but one of hundreds of handgun killings by deranged youth in the U.S. in recent years. My wife and I watched the moving memorial service on TV. Clergy from many faith traditions, including Roman Catholic, Jewish, Muslim, Bahai, and multiple flavors of Protestant Christians offered prayers in a wonderful display of togetherness. President Obama spoke and also emphasized the coming together. The Muslim commented on the "artificial divisions" between faith traditions. (I agree, why do we perpetuate, even celebrate these divisions?) One of the clergy commented that the victims are now in a "better place". (Better place? If death is better then why the sadness?) The service was moving precisely because of the human mutual caring, not because God contributed very much. He appeared to be absent as the children were being murdered. But believers persist in affirming God's love and feeling that somehow such heinous crimes are part of His plan.

RELIGIOUS PRACTICES ARE CULTURE, AND CHANGING CULTURE IS NOT EASY FOR THE BRAIN

Understanding religion in a scientific way is hardly a new idea, and it is totally naïve to think that it can be done easily. Religion is deeply embedded in human culture. But that is no excuse for not putting effort into new thinking and new models.

In an interview at the Berkeley Institute of International Studies in 2000 a late friend of mine, professor and neurologist Lawrence Stark, had some interesting comments about mental models and God:[188]

> So much of our interaction is within our own brains, and the contact we have with other people and with the outside world is very sparse. People can have a model in their head and that model subsumes their thinking process, and it's almost impossible to change that model. So one can have a model of a gray-haired God up in the sky, and if you believe

that, then everything that happens is a result of that person watching over you and doing this and doing that. Once you have that model, it's very hard to shake the model. Each brain cell in our cortex has about 20,000 connections; 10,000 to other cells, and 10,000 from other cells. And of those 10,000 inputs and outputs to each cell in the cerebral cortex, only one of them goes to the outside world, for example to move a muscle. Only one of them, on average, comes from the outside world, for example, to carry a vision signal, or a temperature signal. These billions of neurons are all talking to each other through all these connections, and they're only getting sparse information from the outside. So the generation of models in people's heads and the functioning of those models are what drives them. I think that's one of the real problems in humanity, that people can't really interact, and the way they form their models is shaped by very primitive forces in our culture, and in every culture. I think people who want to change the world are going to have to change the models.

Redefining God

CREATING GOD IN OUR OWN IMAGE?

Abrahamic religions promote the idea that humans are "created by God in His own image", at least that's what Genesis says about Adam and Eve. Of course this statement applies to meanings of "image" that are not restricted to a visual image: love, forgiveness, etc. In any case the "image" of today's human that God is said to have created is not so admirable. Most folks are more hateful, ignorant, fatter, and less than ideal in many other ways: is that the image of God they want to present?

What seems more obvious is what Don Cupitt and others have said: that we humans create God in our own image. For many it's an old man in the sky looking down and smiling on all of us, or ready to punish us if we don't toe the line. Usually it's some kind of anthropomorphic entity capable of caring about each and every one of us, including all animals, bacteria, plants and living cells (and all subatomic particles in the universe?!). God is regarded as an ideal person: all loving, all knowing, all powerful. The trouble is, there is nothing we can observe, so no real "image" available.

A LIBERAL JEWISH "PLAUSIBLE GOD"

The philosopher Mitchell Silver analyzes the theology of three contemporary Jewish philosophers, Mordechai Kaplan, Michael Lerner and Arthur Green in terms of what he posits as a dichotomy between an "Old supernatural God" and a "New God."[189] The New God is seemingly aligned with Spinoza's "one substance" God, comprising the entirety of nature, and having no separate parts and no personal attributes such as will, interest or desires.

Silver characterizes the New God as potential energy for goodness and self-consciousness, a "value motivator", and "whatever there is in nature that makes good things possible." He claims that the New God is also a name for wonder. Theism from this new perspective is equivalent to optimism, while atheism equates to pessimism. Where purely natural laws operate without judge or judgment, the New God perspective is seen as a basis for a world that returns good for good, and evil for evil.

The New God, Silver claims, is more a celebration of life and self than the Pauline denial of this world. The New God's divinity is more like beauty than truth, and joy in the mysteries of existence than the traditional characterization of God as a supernatural omnipotent omniscient person. Religious truth is thus an aesthetic claim, and "does not speak to the factual nature of reality". The job of God language then is not to produce belief, but rather to motivate "so as to produce affect and effect".

Where the terms *secular* and *humanism* are commonly used together, Silver makes a distinction, noting that pure secularism denies any kind of God. Secularism is naturalism plus atheism, whereas humanism can accommodate the New God. He speaks of God as a heuristic for prayer, and defines contemplative prayer as reverential active appreciation of life and of our universe. This is not contemplation of propositions regarding truth, but rather is contemplation of images that create experiential value. He quotes Green as asserting that God only exists where He is imagined, and so serves to name the mystical experience and its cause.

Because Silver's New God is expressed in terms of imagination, mysticism, aesthetics, optimism and human values, it can be said to be the epitome of connotation. It is not much closer to an entity that can be modeled denotatively than the supernatural Old God. However, it is decidedly closer to a message of this book, that respectful humanism is what is important. I believe the goal can be called secular humanism, embodying the kind of reverence so nicely expressed earlier in this book according to Paul Woodruff. It also seems to me there is no need for calling Silver's New God orientation God. I prefer to assign the God term to all of what remains a mystery about life and the universe—which amounts to just about everything.

A BETTER DEFINITION OF GOD (REVISITING GOD-OF-THE-GAPS)

Recall Joseph Campbell's definition that "God is a metaphor for a mystery that absolutely transcends all human categories of thought". And recall the notion of *God-of-the-gaps*, filling holes in our lack of knowledge with a supernatural agent. The God-of-the-gaps term has been used historically as a pejorative term against those who do not believe fully.

But let us reconsider whether filling those holes in our knowledge and understanding with a supernatural entity is appropriate. Why not fill the holes with honest admission that we don't know and don't understand so much of what we experience. Most such gaps we will never be able to fill. We can easily go along with Campbell and retain the word God, as traditionally used, in the metaphor category. Indeed, why not encourage *use of the term God to refer to all that is mystery—without any connotation of a supernatural God*? I rather think that many modern churchgoers, when they stop to think about it, place their belief squarely there, but are reluctant to admit that.

Scientists can seem arrogant, as many critics of the new atheism are fond to point out. Science does not have all the answers. Indeed, built into the scientific methodology is robust effort to disprove whatever "facts" currently prevail. Unfortunately the public typically does not appreciate this point.

There is so much we do not know and understand. Humility is healthy in this regard, and we need more when it comes to the big questions about who we are and where we came from. But that certainly does not mean that we abandon intellectual honesty and rationality by substituting the easy answer that God did it. The universe is full of wonders, mysteries we do not and surely will not ever understand. God can happily serve as shorthand for respect and awe for those aspects of life that are clearly beyond our grasp. That in no way accedes to supernaturalism. Let's be honest with ourselves.

Evolve the church into a secular community organization

What is the proper role for church organizations? Church organizations are marvelous vehicles for encouraging mutual caring within their congregations as well as outside. Caring for one another in the local community as well as the world community is not inconsistent with tenets of all the world religions. There is no need to reject organizations serving that very important need that local and state governments do not and cannot provide.

To accomplish these objectives why do we need the supernatural religion component? We call the religious institutions faith communities, but is the faith (presumably faith in a supernatural God and faith in the sacred texts) really necessary to the community part? Is the purpose of the religious component to engender fear— that if we do not love our neighbors God will send us to hell? If we do not believe is there a chance that we are forever condemned, so that according to Pascal's wager it would be wiser to believe and not risk even a small chance of eternal damnation? If we do not at least act like we believe will we be ostracized from the tribe? I suspect some people really do accept those justifications for "belief" (however insincere).

There are other motives to question religion. Religion as a basis for morality is being questioned in the public square as never before, e.g. by Sam Harris.[190] With regard to faith, how about faith in morality derived from pragmatic experience? Instead of religious faith how about engendering faith in one another? A community organization devoted to building faith in one another and spreading that into the community and into the world would seem to be a good thing.

It is easy to imagine the kind of secular congregation meeting I'm talking about. We need not dispense with a choir and music, even traditional sacred music. Sacred music is part of our culture and is common in many otherwise secular music venues. In the revised "churches" there could be talks by folks selected by a governance committee, or panel discussions. There could be organizational activities of various kinds, committee reports, activities for children—pretty much all the same activities as at present with the exception of liturgy. Prayer to God could be replaced by contemplative exercises designed to enhance appreciation for the beauty and the wonders that surround us. Religious education could be replaced by moral/ethical education. No problem meeting in the (former) church buildings.

Actually some church congregations have been moving in these directions for years. Probably the Unitarian Universalist Society is farthest along. Then there are groups such as the Bahai, who selectively draw inspiration from just about all the world's religions. Unfortunately both groups are marginalized by "true believers" in the standard religions.

Of course much of what I applaud in the above paragraphs is already being pushed by organizations that call themselves secular humanists. There exist various organizations that promote secular humanism. They have also been known as just humanists, freethinkers, ethical culturists, and "brights" (Dennett's proposed term[191], which this writer finds repugnant). Auguste Comte (1798-1857), the founder of positivist philosophy, attempted to produce a religion of humanity in France in 1851. A humanist manifesto was created at the University of Chicago in 1933. The International Humanist and Ethical Union was founded in 1952, when a gathering of world humanists met under the leadership of Julian Huxley. The American Humanist Association, founded in 1941, has many associated groups such as the Council for Secular Humanism. The International Humanist and Ethical Union (IHEU) is the world union of more than one hundred humanist, rationalist, irreligious, atheist, ethical culture and freethought organizations in more than 40 countries. So the idea of secular humanism is certainly not new.

I suspect that those whose health is currently sustained by attending religious services would fare just as well in meetings of the secular humanist organization. The togetherness and the mutual caring and the good works would still be there.

5

CONCLUSIONS

This book has reviewed the nature of science and scientific modeling as well as that of religious belief, including ancient and modern arguments for God. The contrast in the language and considerations of science with those of religion reveals a stark difference in modes of thinking. This is a difference long recognized but continuing to puzzle and alienate people on both sides of the divide.

Most people would agree that there are ways of knowing that are not scientific modeling or any form of science (although one philosophical perspective insists that reality can only be known through models). But if and when we can model something, then we feel that we know that something, or at least can affirm our beliefs about it and are comfortable communicating it to others unambiguously. Scientific modeling is also important because the effort to model forces us to think about what we really believe. For those reasons we have asserted that religion should not be immune from being tested by efforts at scientific modeling.

History shows that primitive peoples utilized myths to explain to themselves things that were totally mysterious. Those myths were their models, but such myths do not have the desirable denotative attributes of scientific models that have been outlined here. Early peoples worshipped the sun, which was somewhat rational since the sun is our known source of energy and sustainer of life. Since then mankind has regressed to worship of anthropomorphic entities and political figures characterized, for example, by divine revelation and virgin birth.

Modern critical thinkers about cosmology and the origins of life, including theologians, scientists and other laity, are rapidly abandoning traditional perspectives in favor of a reverent sense of mystery and an appreciation of evolution. However, in a sense we are right back to the attitude of our primitive ancestors. The theologians ask us to believe in a transcendent God as a means to cope with the mystery. But by definition a transcendent entity is not amenable to expression in tractable human language.

In the secular world we have a record of accomplishment through use of conscious imagination, scientific experimentation, analysis and modeling. However most of current society has not evolved very far from clinging to those old beliefs of an omnipotent, omniscient supernatural God up there who loves us and hears our prayers. There is evidence that for some people belief in a supernatural God provides happiness and sustains health. Others are content and fare just fine with daily lives in a secular society that respects rationality as a basis for thinking and action. Surely everyone is entitled to his or her own beliefs, whether logical or illogical. However religion does appear to support a double value standard when contrasted to daily intellectual pursuits in the otherwise secular world.

The mystery aspect of ultimate reality need not be discouraging. As the old saying goes, the more you know the more you know what you don't know. And that is a non-converging process. We don't know and don't have models for almost everything.

We conclude that we cannot apply science to model the nature of a supernatural God *per se*, as there is nothing there to model that humans are capable of understanding or talking about. Words used by theists like *transcendent* are not amenable to human understanding, since by their very meaning they are beyond ordinary human experience. I would make the comparison to the concept of *infinity*, which is defined as a mathematical limit, beyond comprehension.

However we can and have modeled human beings in their religious practices. Efforts at such modeling deserve to penetrate further into why people believe and what (they say) they believe. This will help us examine ourselves and our culture more clearly.

Religious institutions should at least move toward distinguishing and accepting the disparate essential roles in life of *logos* and *mythos*, reasoned discourse in denotative modeling and legitimate subjective feelings expressed through metaphor. Primitive peoples made little distinction between these ways of thinking. Modern religious institutions do much the same. In any discourse it should be made more clear which is being assumed.

It would be healthy to admit that the religious tradition of saying man is made in the image of God is to say nothing sensible because God cannot be modeled and there is no clear and understandable image as to God's constitution or function. Clearly God is really conceived, at least to a great extent, in the image of man: just the reverse of the standard phrase.

"God" could become a useful metaphor for what we don't know and don't understand. God would be conceived not as a supernatural reality to be worshipped but rather as a truth about uncertainty to be respected, a truth about ourselves in relation to the universe. Then God could be "believed" in that sense. Such an orientation would discourage hubris and promote reverence and awe for the wonder and beauty of the natural world. It would encourage people to take responsibility for shaping life rather than depending upon God to do it.

With this perspective the new "believer" can still (metaphorically) "know God" in his heart, and "know God" in the beauty of nature, in the faces of children and in the good deeds that people do for other people. Reverence, as described earlier, which has nothing necessarily to do with religion and belief in something supernatural, is highly relevant in this respect.

An evolution of the concept of God, plus an evolution of religious institutions to become secular institutions serving many of the same secular objectives as they now serve, would be constructive and consistent with evidence-based science. Such an evolution will take time, since cultures change slowly.

Intellectual honesty is best served by abandoning belief in the supernatural while embracing metaphor and recognition of the subjective factors in life that are so difficult (but not necessarily impossible) to fit into a scientific framework.

Indeed we need new models. *We need to remodel God to be what we don't understand about our natural surround, a new kind of God that demands our utmost respect for the unknown and for our own limitations.* We need to remodel our religious institutions to promote secular reverence for those things in life here and now that are most worthy, wonderful, and beautiful. We need new models of community participation to promote caring and faith in one another that can be spread to the whole world. These models are worthy of our celebration, in faith and trust. These can be logical scientific models. But that in no way diminishes the role of metaphor for communicating and engaging participation. Bring on the metaphor, and let God be a metaphor for mystery. But hold the supernatural.

APPENDIX:

EXAMPLES OF OBJECTIVE MODELS THAT CHARACTERIZE BELIEF

> All the evolution we know proceeds from the vague to the definite.
> —Charles Sanders Peirce, Collected papers, 1958

> In our description of nature the purpose is not to disclose the real essence of the phenomenon but only to track down, insofar as it is possible, relations between meaningful aspects of our experience.
> —Niels Bohr, 1934

Objective models come in many flavors, as appropriate to the context and what is intended to be communicated. In Chapter 1 there was mention of various kinds of models to exemplify different languages for modeling: words, graphics, logic of time and causality, and mathematics. Most scientific models are expressed by combining all three of these languages, using words to explain the purpose and identify the variables, using graphics and mathematics to represent structure and relationships.

This Appendix describes various models used to characterize human interaction with the world. Included are some types of models that I have taught, have used in research, or have had a hand in developing. The explanations of these models follow those I have presented in several books.[192]

Of course there exist hundreds of models of every type of human endeavor from (all disciplines of) science and technology to business and industry to economics and politics to health and medicine to whatever. All have to do with belief—what the humans who developed the models and those who have come to accept and use the models believe to be acceptably true and useful for some small slice of reality.

As implied by the Peirce quote above, modeling (and science in general) regarding any phenomenon starts from a qualitative description and tends, with some luck, toward quantitative and/or symbolic prediction. As implied by the Popper quote at the beginning of Chapter 1, older models are continually refined by refutation and replacement.

One rationale for including human behavioral models here is that these are models that apply to human psychology of belief. We are concerned here not simply with what humans believe but also with the psychology of belief, how external stimuli as well as our senses, perceptions, memories and decision capabilities work to result in belief.

After stating the gist of each model I very briefly suggest a way that model might apply to some aspect of religious belief or practice. But keep in mind that these models were never designed at the outset to apply to religion. By gaining a better idea of what scientific modeling is all about one presumably would be in a position to formulate new models to apply to any particular hypothesis or aspect of religious belief or practice.

Examples of models that use different forms of language

VERBAL MODELS

Many models are expressed in words only. Historians, philosophers, theologians, newspaper columnists, sportswriters, all use words in print media to express their beliefs about how some things or events are structured or relate to other things or events. In the most general case novelists, poets, and lyricists are verbal connotative modelers, but we choose to exclude those models because they do not intend to denotate the explicit truth.

Below, for example, are Charles Darwin's own words in *On the Origin of Species*[193] that I have taken to be a summary explanation of his theory of natural selection, more commonly known as the theory of evolution. Of course he wrote many more words of explanation in that famous work. But these words do exemplify what could be called a verbal model.

> Evolution by natural selection is a process that is inferred from three facts about populations: 1) more offspring are produced than can possibly survive, 2) traits vary among individuals, leading to differential rates of survival and reproduction, and 3) trait differences are heritable. Thus, when members of a population die they are replaced by the progeny of parents that were better adapted to survive and reproduce in the environment in which natural selection took place. This process creates and preserves traits that are seemingly fitted for the functional roles they perform.

Darwin's theory is often stated as "survival of the fittest." That phrase is clearly *not* an adequate verbal model since it says nothing about the mechanism by which traits are passed on to the later generations of the same species. Any model must have sufficient explanatory detail.

Words can be used to help explain quantitative relationships. Figure A1 provides a simple example[194] allegedly used to explain a computation process to school children.

Essentially all scientific models in their presentation in scientific papers have to be augmented by words, necessary to explain what the model is all about, state the limitations, and help the reader navigate the graph, diagram or math. That does not necessarily make such papers verbal models.

Representations of God by philosophers and theologians have almost always used verbal models, though such models cannot be called scientific models as I have defined them as they are lacking in certain of the previously discussed six attributes. Most importantly they lack any basis in observables.

162   Appendix

You buy 3 boxes of cereal at $3.25 each and one gallon of milk for $2.30. To find how much the groceries will cost, you can use a verbal model to write and evaluate an expression.

$$\boxed{\text{Total cost of groceries}} = \boxed{\text{Number of boxes of cereal}} \times \boxed{\text{Cost per box}} + \boxed{\text{Cost of milk}}$$

$= 3 \times 3.25 + 2.30$ Substitute values.

$= 9.75 + 2.30$ Multiply first.

$= 12.05$ Then add.

Answer: The cost of the groceries is $12.05.

Figure A1. Computation process example for evaluating the cost of groceries.

GRAPHS, MAPS AND SCHEMATIC DIAGRAMS

Many models render their message mostly in terms of graphics, usually accompanied by a few words to identify the variables and assist with the explanations. The graphics can be line graphs, charts, diagrams, maps, tables, or photos. Some pictures really are worth a thousand words, and need little additional explanation. Some kinds of explanations are very difficult or impossible to convey in words, and a graphic is essential. Below are several examples. These are all models that tell the user about quantitative relationships in the given context.

Plots of data fitted by mathematical functions are a common form of model. For example, consider the well-known bell curve, also known as the Gaussian probability density function (Figure A2). For whatever context this image is used it usually tells the

Appendix   163

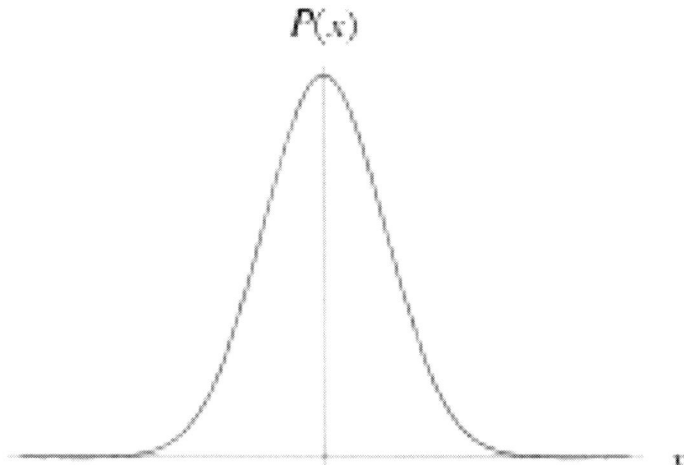

Figure A2. Gaussian probability density function.

viewer that, given some value on the x-axis, the value shown on the y-axis is (or is an estimate of) its probability (likelihood of occurrence relative to other values). This curve is commonly used as a model because of its attractive mathematical properties, namely that there is a precise mathematical function relating probability P to x. Observed data may or may not fit the model, and never will fit exactly.

There are many different mathematical functions that are used for fitting empirical data. If one is lucky enough to find a good fit, that mathematical function becomes an easy way of generalizing the data. But there is nothing magical about any particular form of abstraction (the math) as related to the reality (the data). Whatever mathematical function fits the data is as good as any other, except that some may be simpler to use.

A related example is shown in Figure A3 along with some actual data[195]. It is somewhat more difficult to understand because of how the axes are structured, but it results in a simple straight line model of the data. The horizontal axis in this case is the cumulative fraction of test subject teams that responded within the time shown in the vertical axis, with the vertical axis scaled logarithmically. Each data point represents the time taken by a team of experienced nuclear power plant operators to successfully perform a critical safety operation. This author, having been one of the experimenters, and having known that a particular distribution known as a log normal has been known to fit human response time data (the dots) in simple experiments, tried that mathematical function. *Voila*, it luckily produced a pretty good fit. So in this case the straight line (on this particular set of axes) is the model.

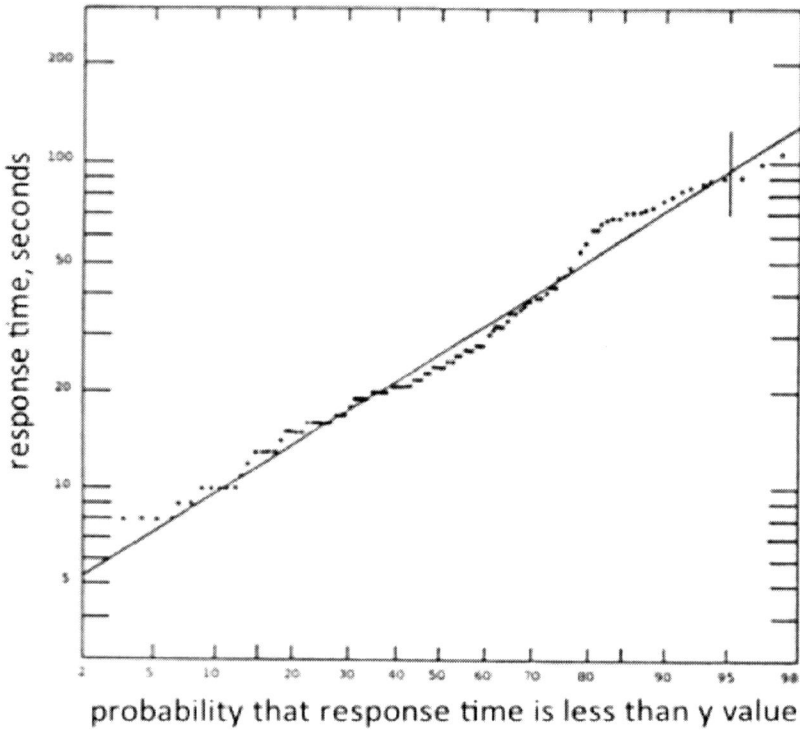

Figure A3. Response times of nuclear plant operator teams to properly respond to a major accident alarm. For the particular mathematical function used (log normal), using specialized graph paper (logarithm on y axis, Gaussian percentiles on x axis) reduces that function to a straight line. The 95th percentile mark is seen to be roughly 100 seconds.

Appendix   165

Sometimes a relationship between two or more functional plots is what comprises the model. Figure A4 shows the generic form of supply-demand curves that are basic to economics. As the selling price of a given product goes down there will be more demand by buyers (demand curve). From the producer's perspective, as the price increases there is greater profit and therefore greater willingness to produce (supply curve). At the crossover point there is an equilibrium that determines what will tend to occur in practice.

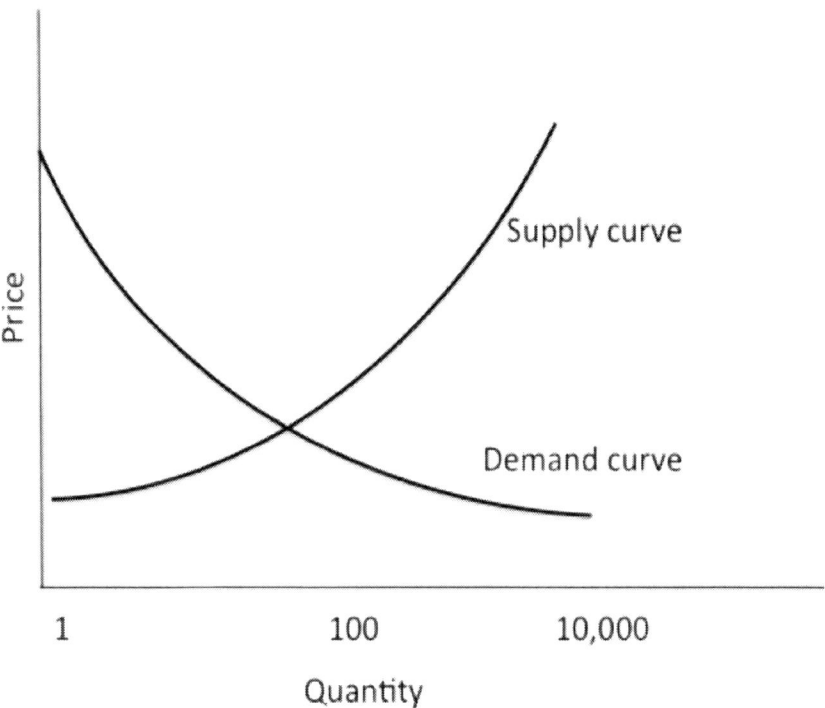

Figure A4. Hypothetical supply-demand curves.

166   Appendix

A map is another kind of graphic model that normally needs words only to identify locations on the map. The main message is the spatial layout, the quantitative relation of the mapped entities to one another. Figure A5 is an example

Figure A5. Map of the United States.

The reader is surely familiar with Michelangelo's Creation of Adam representation on the ceiling of the Sistine Chapel in Vatican City (Figure A6). It surely can be said to be an example of a graphic *metaphorical* model of God based on the Genesis story. There is no observable with respect to which such a model is isomorphic to God. It is based on the painter's imagination. Thus it is not a scientific model.

Figure A6. Creation of Adam by Michelangelo.

Appendix   167

LOGIC DIAGRAMS

Logic tree models display component elements and tell the user a relationship between the elements in causation sequence. For example Figure A7 depicts a *forward chaining tree*, commonly also called an *event tree*, where events are labeled by letters A, B, C, etc. It shows that following some *initiating event* (arrows indicate time sequence) either A or B can happen.

Typically transition probabilities are assigned to the lines connecting the initiating event I to A and B or any other pair of letters (P_{BE} is shown for the B to E transition). For example assume the probability from initiation to A is $P_{IA}=0.7$, and from initiation to B is $P_{IB}=0.3$. The two numbers must add to one since the model implies that there are no other possibilities. Now C is shown to happen because of either A or B. And given that B happens C, D or E can happen with some transition probabilities (that again must add to

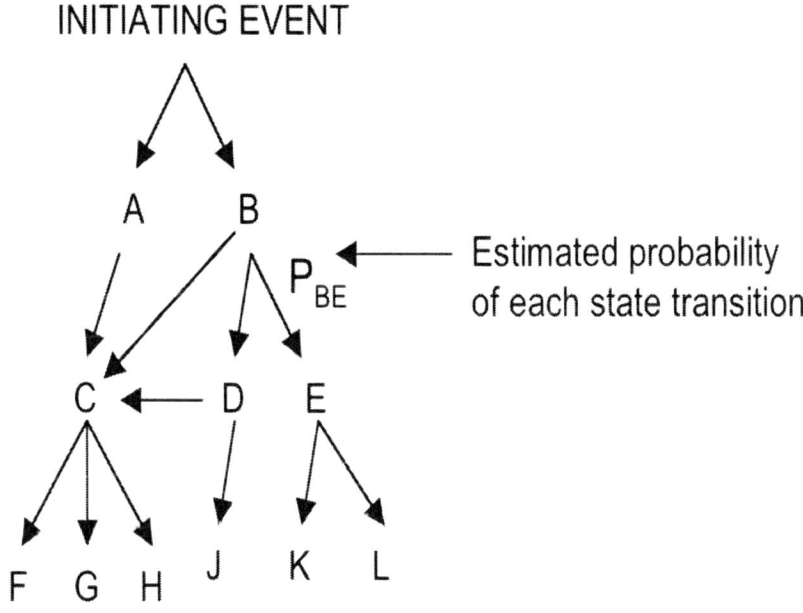

Figure A7. Forward chaining tree.

one). The probability of any event occurring is equal to the probability of the previous event multiplied by the transition probability to the new event (e.g., the probability of E occurring is P_{BE} times 0.3. Working our way down the graph one can calculate the probabilities of occurrence of each final state F, G, H, J, K or L.

This model is useful for representing the behavior of any complex system, including people or teams of people. Where do the probability numbers come from? They are derived from recorded frequencies of events that actually happened. With enough frequency data one has a pretty good estimate of the transition probabilities. Event tree models are particularly useful in analyzing the ways that various accidents can happen.

Another type of causality may be represented in what is often called a *backward chaining* tree (Figure A8). This type of network model combines the logic of necessity and that of sufficiency. It is often used by safety analysts in representing the chain of causation in accidents, and hence is referred to as a *fault tree*. It is probably the most reasonable single technique to use in modeling accident causation. The logical relationships are indicated through symbols of AND and OR logic, where the ANDing of two or more events means that both those events are necessary for an indicated result to occur, while the ORing of two or more events means that either event is sufficient for the next event to occur. One starts from the top event and considers what possible events or combinations of events might cause that event to occur. The diagram indicates that either A or B is judged sufficient to have caused the top event. Both C and D are modeled as necessary to cause A, while any of F, G and H are sufficient to cause B. Both J and K are modeled as necessary to cause H. Developing this type of model is tedious, but is especially useful as a discipline of thinking about what causes what, including what is necessary and what is sufficient. It is commonly used in analyzing causality chains in accidents or spread of diseases.

Appendix 169

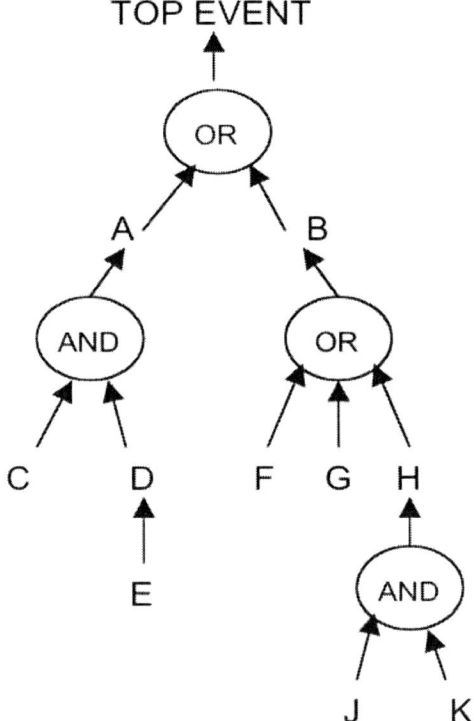

Figure A8. Backward chaining tree, where AND indicates necessity, OR indicates sufficiency.

One can use either the forward or the backward chaining logic tree to represent chaining of beliefs. With the forward chaining tree a model might take as initiating event a belief in God, which might be assumed to cause (moving down), with a certain probability, a belief in heaven. That in turn might be assumed to cause with some probability a belief in one's going to heaven, etc. For the backward chaining tree, attendance at a certain church might be modeled to have been necessarily caused by a spouse's wealthy father who went to that church, which may be caused by several sufficient reasons assumed in the model (e.g., the church having a lot of affluent members, proximity to the father's home) and so on (downward in the chain).

170 Appendix

Graphical models can get very elegant. The physicist Richard Feynman developed what are called Feynman diagrams to portray on a space-versus- time plot the interactions of subatomic physical particles.[196] They will not be described here because they entail significant understanding of particle physics. For entertainment a reader interested in graphic *complexity* might look up the term *complexity* in a web search and find a truly stunning array of graphical images.

FUZZY LOGIC

Fuzzy logic allows for evaluating particular objects or events (e.g., college basketball players) to be represented by the degree to which any fuzzy variable (e.g., particular words for height such as tall or short, or words for intelligence such as brilliant or average) are relevant to that individual thing. Rules can then be exercised based on combinations of multiple verbal phrases interconnected by logical AND and OR. Fuzzy logic contrasts with the more conventional *crisp logic* where each object or event is represented in very specific objective terms (e.g., a basketball player having numerical height of 6 feet six inches and a grade point average of C). Evaluation by crisp logic is difficult because crisp logic rules are lacking for evaluation against many other individuals with differing combinations of the same attributes.

The advantage of fuzzy logic is that it is closer to the way real people think and do evaluations, whereas rules for comparing many items where each item is identified by specific objective identifiers are difficult for people to concoct. For the reader interested in the math, below is an example of how fuzzy logic works. In his book *Fuzzy Thinking*[197] Bart Kosco provides an excellent review of the ideas. Interestingly, he takes up the relation between fuzzy logic and God, and other imponderables of philosophy. He uses the Kanizsa square illusion (Figure A9) to suggest that God is like the square that isn't there. Nice metaphor, but no scientific model there!

Appendix   171

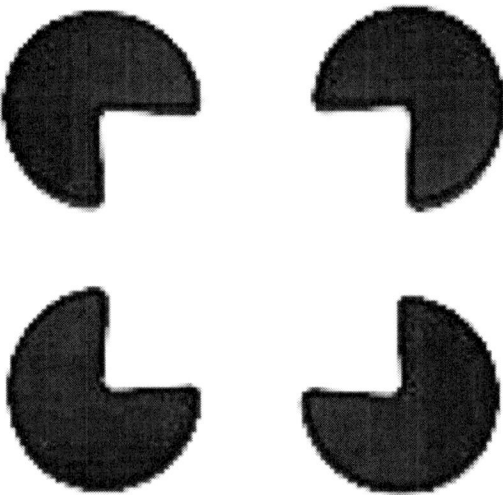

Figure A9. Kanizsa square illusion.

An essential point is that words like tall and short, fast and slow, fat and skinny (and many other descriptors) correspond to and map upon physical variables, depending on context. Those physical variables as well as the corresponding words presumably can be used to characterize the observable objects or events of interest. However many other words such as love and hate, admiration and envy, indeed just about all words that express feelings, do not map upon physical variables very well, and there is no easy observable for the emotional words per se. Clearly a facial expression in a photo or a drawing conveys an emotional state; one can relate emotional words to the curvature of the mouth, or eyebrows, etc. but these I would categorize as metaphorical relations. Fuzzy logic works with rules couched in ordinary words that are associated with physical observables; it does not work with metaphor.

Appendix

MATHEMATICS OF FUZZY LOGIC

In fuzzy logic a descriptive word (such as *tall* or *short* or *fast* or *clever*) has a numerical degree of truthfulness or applicability as applied to some person or thing. The truthfulness or relevance number is called *membership*, and it ranges from 0 to 1 (see Figure A10). In the context of a college basketball player, his six foot six inch height may be 0.8 for the fuzzy term *very tall* and 0.3 for the term *moderately tall* on a hypothetical relevance scale. Grades may be a second consideration for his coach when selecting the team, who might want to distinguish *brilliant* players from those who are just *average*. The subject player might have mediocre C grades, and so have a 0.1 for *brilliant* and a 0.9 for *average*. Figure A10 shows a plot of the hypothetical membership functions for the four fuzzy variables labeled, which can applied to our subject basketball player.

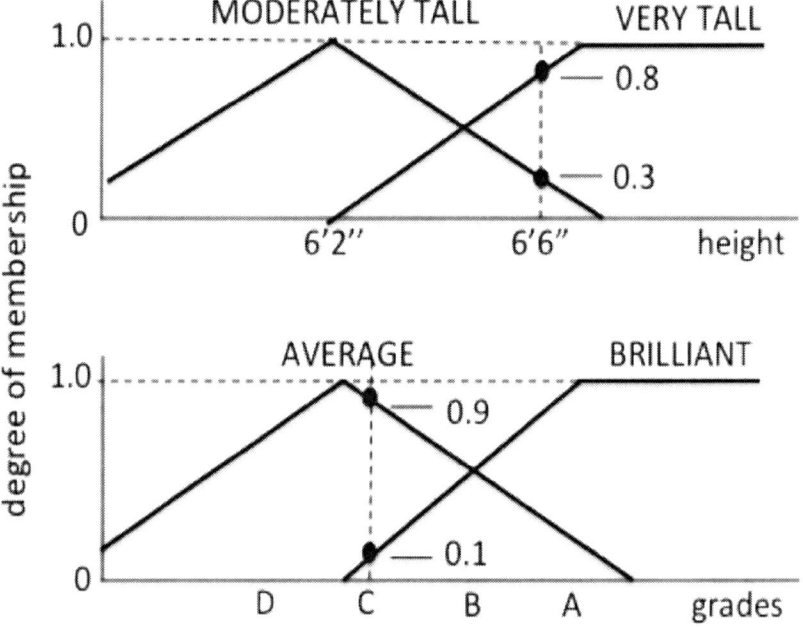

Figure A10. Hypothetical fuzzy membership functions for basketball players.

So the coach may decide in his mind on a selection rule for who gets chosen for the team: "Select if a player is *moderately tall* AND *brilliant*, OR *very tall* AND *average intelligence*", the ANDs and ORs representing logical operations. For each candidate player and their fuzzy membership values the rule is parsed and then evaluated, yielding a single relative rating number. The coach would then select the players with the highest ratings. The evaluation involves parsing the rule into component comparisons and then assigning the individual's membership numbers to the fuzzy terms in the rule. Next this requires taking the minimum of any two terms connected by AND, and the maximum of any two term connected by OR.

Applying the rule and parsing we get a player who is (0.3 AND 0.1) for the first part of the rule, and (0.8 AND 0.9) for the second part. The convention is to take the minimum for AND and the maximum for OR. Thus, considering only what is in the parenthetical components in the first sentence of this paragraph, we get (0.1) OR (0.8) for the full rule in quotes above. Then taking account of the OR between parentheses we get a final score of 0.8 as a fuzzy ranking for this player. That would be compared to a similar scoring process for all other players. Then players with the highest scores would be selected.

The reader may find more complete discussion of fuzzy logic in Kosko[198] and a web tutorial at www.seattlerobotics.org/encoder/mar98/fuz/flindex.html.

STATISTICAL INFERENCE FROM EVIDENCE

The most widely accepted normative model for weighting evidence is probably the theorem nominally attributed to an English clergyman, Rev. Thomas Bayes (1701-1761). It is called Bayes' theorem, and it results from simple algebra concerning probabilities of hypotheses, probabilities of associated evidence (data), and probabilities of contingencies between hypotheses and data. It is pure logic with the only assumption being that the hypotheses are mutually exclusive (only one is true) and collectively exhaustive (all possibilities are accounted for) and that the contingent probabilities are correct. The math for deriving and applying Bayes' theorem is given in below.

The evidence from behavioral decision experiments is that people look for evidence to confirm already held subjective probability ratios and do not weight available evidence according to the logic of Bayes' theorem. Bayesian models converge on one hypothesis or the other much faster than most people are willing to accept. In fact many kinds of data disconfirming various stated beliefs and assertions are often available but are disregarded. Experiments also show that people tend to accept only the evidence that agrees with their prior hypotheses (*confirmation bias*). Another pitfall in thinking revealed in Bayesian decision experiments is the tendency to use several very specific alternative hypotheses that are readily imagined plus a single "everything else" hypothesis, which does meet the requirement that the total set of hypotheses be mutually exclusive and collectively exhaustive. Often, however, insufficient consideration is given to those other hypotheses and kinds of evidence.

With respect to religion, Bayes' theorem could conceivably be applied to deduce the probability of someone being a believer based on the probabilities of various biographical (racial, educational, socioeconomic) facts about them in comparison to belief or disbelief in the general population.

MATHEMATICS OF STATISTICAL INFERENCE FROM EVIDENCE

The relative truth of any two hypotheses $H(A)$ and $H(B)$ can be derived and continually updated for new evidence D_i by using Bayes' theorem. This is done in conjunction with contingent probabilities. From basic combinatorics we know that

$$p(A|B)\, p(B) = p(B|A)\, p(A) = p(A,B),$$

where A and B can be any two events. The vertical bar means "given what follows", so $p(A|B)$ means probability of A given that B is known to be true. $p(A,B)$ means the probability of A and B occuring jointly.

Appendix   175

In its simplest form Bayes' theorem is derived directly from the first two terms above, namely

p(A|B) = p(B|A) p(A) / p(B)

If we substitute H for A and D for B, where H represents "hypothesis" or "underlying truth" or "cause" and D represents "data observed" or "apparent symptoms" or "effect," we have

p(H|D) = p(D|H) p(H) / p(D)

This means that once some data (evidence) is available for a case of known H, after knowing D we can refine any prior estimate of probability of H, p(H). This is done by multiplying p(H) by p(D|H) and dividing by p(D) (the Bayes equation above). P(D|H) is what we know from a prior experience, i.e. where we knew H to be true and then we observed D. p(D) is the probability of that data being observed in general, independent of other circumstances.

Now suppose we observe some specific event D_1 and use the above equation to refine our prior knowledge p(H) to get

p(H |D_1) = [p(D_1|H) p(H) / p(D_1)].

Then we observe D_2. It is now possible to use the above equation again to determine the new expectation of H,

p(H| D_1 and D_2), by substituting p(H |D_1) as the current prior knowledge of H. That is

p(H| D_1 and D_2) = p(D_2|H) [p(D_1|H) p(H) / p(D_1)] / p(D_2)

where the term in square brackets is p(H |D_1).

Suppose from the beginning we had two independent hypotheses, H_1 and H_2 and went through the above process. Then we could take a ratio of the two equations and would find that p(D_1) and p(D_2) would drop out since they are common to both equations, leaving

$$\frac{p(H_1 \mid D_1 D_2)}{p(H_2 \mid D_1 D_2)} = \frac{p(D_2 \mid H_1)}{p(D_2 \mid H_2)} \cdot \frac{p(D_1 \mid H_1)}{p(D_1 \mid H_2)} \cdot \frac{p(H_1)}{p(H_2)}$$

The first term is called the *posterior odds ratio*. The last term is the *prior odds ratio*. The two terms in between are called *likelihood ratios* for D_2 and D_1 respectively. This process can be extended to any number of likelihood ratios (they don't have to be independent of one another) to find a posterior odds ratio. In general the posterior odds ratio is the product of all available likelihood ratios for all salient data, times the prior odds ratio.

Obviously the above formulation does not care about the order in which the data (evidence) are observed. It assumes the process statistics are stationary (don't change with time). Old data counts just as much as new data. If desirable, since the world is not always stationary, a Bayesian updating process can be adjusted to discount data the older it is.

Further exposition of Bayesian decision making is found in www.cs.haifa.ac.il/~rita/ml_course/lectures/Tutorial_bayesian-Risk.pdf.

Examples of models of human cognition

Below are mentioned nine models that are widely employed to characterize how people perceive stimuli in the world, assign value to what they perceive, and make decisions and act upon those decisions. In each case I say what is being modeled and give the qualitative gist of how the model works. I then comment very briefly on how that model might relate to issues of religious belief. The mathematical substance of the models in all but the first case is provided for the reader who might be interested.

Many of the models have some mathematics behind them, which tends to make them normative models, and where the particular mathematical logic provides a convenient baseline against which to compare empirical data. As noted earlier, there is no reason the real world is compelled to fit the mathematics. The reader

Appendix   177

can skip the math if the intention is to glean the general idea of what the model is about. I hope at least reading what follows here will convey the idea that models offer details from a narrow but well-defined perspective on the segment of reality they treat. References are given for the reader who wishes to go deeper.

A QUALITATIVE MODEL OF LEVELS OF COGNITION AND ACTION

Human cognition processes are complex and can hardly be explained by one simple model. The diagram in Figure A11 has become popular in the field called *cognitive engineering*, where engineers and psychologists attempt to understand human behavior in performing well defined tasks such as baking a cake, piloting an aircraft or operating a nuclear power plant. Although it is purely qualitative it distinguishes three different levels of cognition that resonate with researchers in the field. At the lowest level is *skill-based behavior*, those stimulus-response activities that are well learned and are performed automatically with little or no conscious attention. Steering a car would be an example.

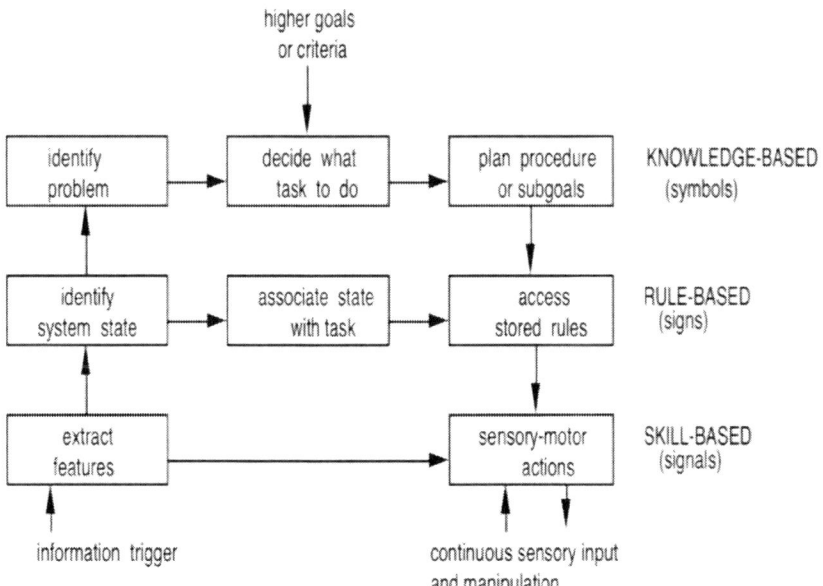

Figure A11. The skill-rule-knowledge cognitive hierarchy (after Rasmussen.[199])

In the middle is *rule-based behavior,* meaning stimulus-response behavior that is mostly but not entirely conscious, where a stimulus provokes a remembered set of responses. An example would be reading a recipe and baking a cake accordingly.

At the highest level is *knowledge-based behavior,* meaning thinking original thoughts based on past knowledge. Here the stimulus poses the challenge and the constraints, and the problem must be solved or a plan of action developed from scratch. The implication according to the upward-pointing arrows on the left is that, when possible, information from the outside world leads to a response at the same level, but otherwise is "kicked upstairs" to the next higher level to be dealt with (arrows on the right). The skill-rule-knowledge model is useful in helping the analyst think about how different components of behavior relate to one another.

This qualitative model serves to suggest how higher level thinking subsumes lower level rule-following and still lower level skills. With respect to religion the model might be used, for example, to connect commitment to a religious belief (top level) to rule-following for attending church (middle level) in turn to habitual gestures or prayers within the church service (bottom level).

CORRELATIONAL MODEL OF HUMAN PERCEPTION

Another cognitive model represents the way in which a person makes judgments among alternatives based on a succession of correlations: first in the process of raw sensing of physical entities, then at the level of perceiving differences, and finally in making judgments.

Anyone who has taken a statistics course knows that correlation between two sets of items does not necessarily mean causality (since two correlated things can be caused by a third thing). However correlation is strongly suggestive of causality if there is a close time order between them, and we then tend to make the reasonable assumptions of some causal connection.

When a person makes judgments about some environmental state or property, there are three transformations that occur. First, some observable cues or physical evidence is likely to occur and

Appendix   179

lend more believability to one truth about the world rather than another. Second, the human must see, hear, or touch the cues and weight their relevance to the discrimination to be made, the process we call perception. And third, the human must be able to make use of the accessed and weighted cues to render a specific judgment. Figure A12 conveys the idea using the metaphor of an optical lens, the concept being a contribution by the psychologist Brunswik (1956).[200]

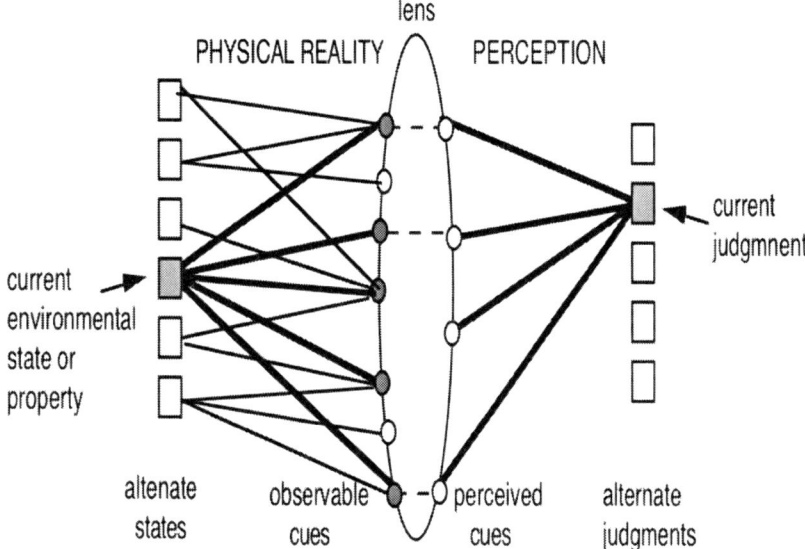

Figure A12. Interpretation of Brunswik Lens Model.

The idea is that physical reality (at left) is seen through a "lens", and the effects (rays, heavy lines at left) of the present physical state or property of interest generate a set of cues (small dark circles on the left side of the lens) that are potentially observable. Other states may generate cues also, some of them the same, some diffcrent from the left-side dark-circles. (This is the first transformation.) All cues from the dark circles are not necessarily perceived or properly weighted as relevant by the human (circles on the right side of the lens), so that some cues are mistakenly perceived or weighted (circles not connected by dashed lines). In any case the human ends up focusing on a set of perceived cues on the right side of the lens.

(This is the second transformation) The final transformation is the human using the perceived cues to make a judgment. (The correlation between states on the left and judgments on the right is the overall performance of the information- acquisition-plus-judgment.

With respect to religion, I could imagine this model being used to characterize how worshipers in a church service pick up cues (or not) and perceive what they are expected to think and do. Or how bits of information they observe in the media or about others form their eventual judgments on religious issues.

MATHEMATICS OF MODEL OF HUMAN PERCEPTION

This model considers how well humans judge the truth of some environmental state. Mathematically the correlation between judgment and state is

$$R = R_1 G R_2 + C(1 - R_1)^{0.5}(1-R_2)^{0.5}$$

R_1 is the state-to-observables correlation at left in Figure A12. R_2 is the perceived cues -to-judgment correlation at right. G is the correlation between the cue weighting generated by the environment and the cue weighting corresponding to the judgment. The first term is the linear additive correlation from state to judgment. The second term is another correction factor, where C is the positive or negative correlation between the residuals of the human and environment models.

C is in the range (-1, +1). Usually C is found to be essentially zero, indicating that linear-additive models are sufficient to describe judgment. But there are cases in the literature where C is significant (say 0.4 or 0.5) indicating that humans can sometimes make use of more complex (e.g., curvilinear) patterns in the relationship between the environment cues and a state.

The advantage of this model is that it combines characterization of the environment with characterization of the human. Measures other than correlation may also be utilized to do this. For example, given the conditional probabilities of various cues for various states, Bayesian updating (as explained above) can be employed to assess the relative probabilities of alternative states.

The reader is referred to Kirlik[201] for more on this model, and its application to human experiments.

HUMAN JUDGMENT OF UTILITY (RELATIVE WORTH)

To most people *utility* means "usefulness" in a very general sense. But in economics it means relative subjective worth. Relative worth is different from money. If you are a rich person the utility of the next dollar is less than if you are a starving person, though the dollars are the same in either case. If you have just eaten a large bowl of ice cream the utility of another bowl is less than the utility of the first bowl, even though the dollar cost of the next bowl is the same as that of the first.

But how to define and measure utility? This problem of relative worth and fairness in economic welfare plagued philosophers such as Jeremy Bentham (1748-1832)[202] and John Stuart Mill (1806-1873)[203] for 100 years. However John Von Neumann (1903-1957) in 1944 defined utility by an axiom and an experimental procedure.

The procedure is straightforward and requires the experimental subject (whose utility or relative worth is being determined) to make comparative relative worth judgments between three things (objects or events). One thing is initially assumed to have high value, one has a low value, and the third has a value somewhere in between. The procedure results in locating where the value of that third thing lies on the utility scale. From repeated trials one can derive a utility function for a large set of things, starting from the given high and low limits, and mapping the relative worth against the physical variable.

In economics and engineering one is often seeking *multi-attribute utility functions*, mathematical equations that define relative goodness in terms of different weightings on a number of salient attributes of the thing being chosen. For example, the goodness of a teacher might have to do with intelligence, preparation and personality, to name only a few attributes. Cars have attributes of passenger capacity, fuel economy, comfort and style. For any choice one can keep thinking of additional attributes that might be relevant. But keeping the attributes to a tolerable number, by collecting all the weights every individual assigns to each of the set of attributes, one might hope to reach a consensus set of weights. There is a whole sub-field making efforts to do this, but there are numerous methodological issues, such as what is included in the set of attributes, how they are stated, are the attributes really independent, and more difficult, is goodness really simply a linear sum of weighted attributes or some more complex function. The interested reader is referred to Sheridan and Ferrell[204].

Utility models are invaluable in deciding on how different people, representing different demographic backgrounds (interests, educational, cultural or economic) assign *different* relative worth to different beliefs, public policies, etc. Such models are widely used in management, marketing, policy planning, and system engineering.

In the religion domain utility models might be applied to how people value religious practices that consume time and dollars relative to other ways they spend their time and money. Such models might also be applied to evaluating the relative importance of reasons for religious belief.

MATHEMATICS OF HUMAN JUDGMENT OF UTILITY

We start with measuring utility in its simplest form, and for a single variable that we are subjecting to the utility measure (we can assume dollars for now). The Von Neumann axiom specifies the utility U of an object or event C, occurring with certainty, in terms of a *lottery* of two other objects or events and their known utilities. We define

$$U(C) = p\, U(A) + (1-p)\, U(B)$$

where utility U is measured in some abstract dimension, call it *utiles*. We shall see that this equation has its meaning only in relative terms, where p and (1− p) are probabilities of mutually exclusive and collectively exhaustive events A and B.

The simplest way to use this idea is to let A and B be extremes of the range of the attribute on which we wish to scale utility, say A = 100,000 dollars and B = 0 dollars. Define A to have utility one and B to have utility zero. If we were to let p = 0.5, then, according to the

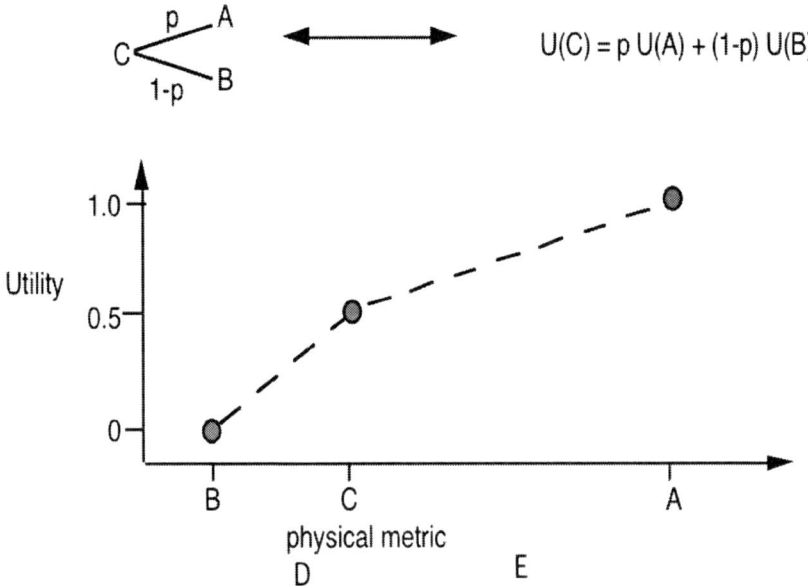

Figure A13. The definition and experimental elicitation of a person's utility.

definition of utility, $U(C) = 0.5$. In terms of Von Neumann's axiom that means we would be indifferent between having C for sure and a 50-50 lottery (chance) of $0 and $100,000, as represented by the upper part of Figure A13.

The question is: what is the corresponding C, i.e. where does it lie on the dollar scale? Implementing an indifference judgment experiment, most of us would select a point along the horizontal physical metric axis in Figure A13 significantly less than $50,000, as shown. We would not want to risk gaining nothing, assuming we are only given this one opportunity. From this we note that the utility curve would not likely be a straight line.

Such a concave downward curve means the decision-maker is *risk averse*, opting for something less than expected value in order not to risk gaining nothing. Risk aversion is why we purchase insurance, paying the insurance company a relatively small amount to avoid the risk of a very large consequence. The insurance company, by insuring many clients, can afford to play on an expected value basis. The individual risk-taker cannot afford that luxury.

This same procedure as above can then be repeated to determine other points on the utility curve. To determine the location of a point D that represents a utility of 0.25 between B and C (see Figure A13). The definition and experimental elicitation of a person's utility indifference judgment experiment is repeated. Now C and U(C) are taken to represent the maximum of the range on each axis respectively, with B and U(B) the zero point, and a subjective judgment is made of where D would lie for the judge to be indifferent. To determine the location of a point E between C and A representing U=0.75, C and U(C) are taken to represent the minimum of the range, with A and U(A) at the maximum, and another 50-50 indifference judgment is made. Theoretically one can continue in this manner, but because of experimental error only several points are usually sufficient between 0 and 1 for any attribute that a reasonable curve can be drawn.

It should be noted that the procedure as summarized above assumes smooth monotonicity between the anchor points initially assumed (B and A in this example). But consider for some attribute there is a known maximum utility in between the anchor points, say at F. This could occur, for example, if one is determining a utility function for desired height or weight or the size of a hamburger, where an intermediate value at F is preferred to either extreme. In this case two utility functions should be determined, one between B and F, the second between F and A.

DECISIONS UNDER CONDITIONS OF CERTAINTY

Now we look at models of how people make other kinds of choice decisions. Decision under certainty means everything is known and available; there are no probabilities to contend with, only the selection among available alternatives. Which cereal on the supermarket shelf to buy? Which car in the showroom to purchase? Which girlfriend to propose to?

The answer presumably is to select the alternative with the greatest utility. But, as indicated above, this demands selection among alternatives that differ in many ways—a problem of multi-attribute utility, as mentioned above. So the need is to envision the alternatives in juxtaposition with respect to their attributes as well as their relative utilities. This will help determine which alternatives can be cast aside and which come close to having the same utility. Sometimes gut feelings come into play that are not accounted for in the initial utility judgments, and may dictate modifications in the utility picture. The considerations in making such decisions are further described in a quantitative example below.

With regard to application to religion, decisions under certainty could include deciding which church to attend, which prayer to pray, or whether to go to church or watch television.

MATHEMATICS OF DECISIONS UNDER CERTAINTY

Consider Figure A14. This depicts what is called a decision space, in this case with points (letters) representing choice alternatives. For example let us assume a decision-maker is deciding between used trucks, any of which might do the job.

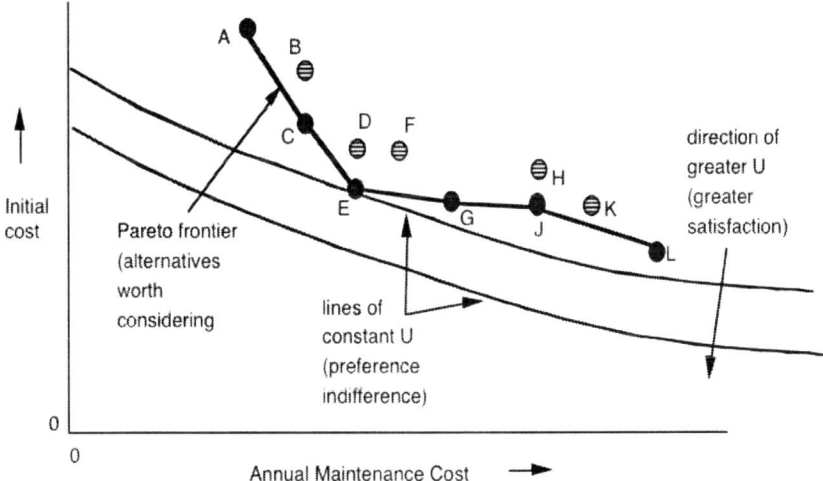

Figure A14. Pareto frontier and utility curve intersection determines optimal choice.

To make the example simple, only two attributes are shown, maintenance cost and initial cost, assuming the decision-maker is mostly concerned with cost. We also assume that cost is defined as utility, as discussed above, since there may be considerations of how much to keep in the bank, time to get repairs done, etc. which are taken into account when establishing the two cost axes. In general there are more than two attributes of any decision so a decision space is a multi-dimensional, which cannot be represented here in a simple graph. Assume in this example that only a finite number of trucks is available, so the decision maker must decide among those combinations shown by the dots.

Notice that some choices *dominate* other choices, i.e., for the same maintenance cost truck C has lower initial cost than truck B. A rational decision-maker would always prefer C over B. Truck E similarly dominates D. J dominates H for initial cost and also K based in this latter case on maintenance cost, where initial cost is the same. A, G and L are not dominated, assuming G has slightly higher initial cost than J. Together with C, E, and J these trucks comprise a set of non-dominated alternatives which trade-off initial cost and maintenance cost. No purpose is served by considering the other alternatives, since the total cost for them is still greater than any of the others that are just as good in other respects.

The example assumes the decision-maker can get lower initial cost only at higher maintenance cost. The points on the heavy line are said to form a *Pareto frontier*, named after an Italian economist Vilfredo Pareto (1848-1923). The rational decision-maker rejects whatever is up and to the right of this line, and wants to be down and to the left. Unfortunately there is no low initial cost AND low maintenance truck. The Pareto frontier defines the best that can be had, the set of alternatives from which to choose, but still leaves the decision-maker having to decide among the points on this line.

How to decide? The rational choice is to select the alternative with the greatest utility as defined in the last section. Assume that the two light lines are hypothetical constant utility curves, determined, for example, by the Von Neumann procedure described above. Each is a line of utility *indifference*, defining a tradeoff between the two cost attributes. For a set of such lines "better" is down and to the left, since the attributes are costs. Therefore the best choice is the point of intersection of the Pareto curve with the indifference curve of best utility, in this case point E. Of course one need not draw the Pareto curve explicitly, since one could evaluate U of each truck on the Pareto curve and go right to the alternative with greatest utility. But when there is a large number of alternatives, or a continuous space, it is helpful for the decision-maker to consider the Pareto frontier explicitly.

Note that there are two kinds of tradeoff curves in decisions under certainty: (1) the Pareto frontier, which rejects dominated alternatives and represents a trade between alternatives based only on the direction of better or worse, but has nothing to do with the subjective utility trade between attributes; and (2) the utility indifference curves, which represent the subjective utility trade between attributes, but say nothing about available alternatives.

DECISIONS UNDER UNCERTAINTY

When the states of the world and consequences of each decision are known only by probabilities that are less than one (the decision must be made without knowing for sure what will happen), then we are talking about *decision under uncertainty*. Under uncertainty any decision option has attached to it two or more consequences, each of which has a probability.

Now the decision maker is stuck with having to weigh the relative value (or utility) of the consequences of each decision alternative *if those consequences occur* along with the probability that they *will* occur. How to do this? One must decide on whether to (1) be very conservative and look only at the worst that can happen, or (2) to consider the consequences, good or bad, in direct proportion to their probabilities, or (3) something in between. The details of the model are provided below.

With respect to religion, decision under uncertainty is the type of decision model that might be applied to the religious skeptic who considers the downside consequences of not believing. Especially of concern is the *Pascal wager* after French scientist/philosopher Blaise Pascal (1623-1662) mentioned earlier. Recall the gist: if God exists (with whatever probability) and you don't believe, then hell awaits you forever (depending on the probability of God's condemnation), whereas if there is no God then it does not matter so much what you believe. So on balance it's better to believe just for that reason, since hell for eternity is a high enough cost that you can skip the probabilities. There are of course some other considerations about the Pascal wager, and these were discussed earlier.

As in daily life, choices about religious preference and church attendance have consequences, and those consequences have probabilities (how much money I am expected to give, how I balance giving to church versus giving to other charities, what kinds of people I will mix with, how I will like the church service, whether God will favor what I decide, and whether He/She even cares). Insofar as probabilities can be assessed, most decisions can be treated as decisions under uncertainty and do have rational solutions.

MATHEMATICS OF DECISIONS UNDER UNCERTAINTY

The decision under uncertainty is represented in Figure A15, sometimes called a *payoff matrix*. In this example there are three decision options shown, A, B and C, and two independent contingencies (not under the decision-maker's control), X which is known to occur with probability 0.3, and Y, which is known to occur with probability 0.7. The numbers in the cells are the payoffs for each combination of contingency and decision. Payoffs can be stated in dollars, or in terms of other quantities such as time or effort, or in utility, as described above.

Normally, especially if one expects to make repetitive decisions in the same environment of contingencies and payoffs, one selects that decision which has the highest expected payoff (see first column at the right in Figure A15). This would be decision C, where expected value is $(0.7 \times 6) + (0.3 \times 3) = 5.1$.

However there are other criteria that may apply, as indicated by the max and min columns to the right. A risk-taker may be attracted to a selection based on what will yield the maximum possible payoff, and choose B hoping for a payoff of 7. More likely, and particularly if this is a unique decision not to be repeated, the decision-maker may choose A which is the best of the worsts, the

CONTINGENCIES

	X p(x) =0.7	Y p(y) =0.3	expected value	max	min
A	5	5	5.0	5	5
B	7	0	4.9	7	0
C	6	3	5.1	6	3

DECISIONS

Figure A15. Sample payoff matrix for decisions under probabilistic contingencies.

most conservative decision, the one that minimizes the downside risk. This called a *minimax* decision.

Buying insurance is an example of an everyday minimax type of decision. The insurance buyer pays a small premium of money to avoid the risk of a great loss, even though on an expected value basis he would get a greater payoff. The insurance company, by repeating many insurance transactions and settlements, operates on expected value and makes money in doing so.

INFORMATION COMMUNICATION

Information, in terms of the meaning of any given message, is essentially not possible to model, since it is totally dependent on context and the prior knowledge of the persons or systems sending or receiving the information. However another definition of information was first developed by Claude Shannon (1916-2001)[205] in 1949, originally intended for use in telephone technology, but today broadly applicable.

The idea is simple, yet profound. The measure of information in a message is simply how unexpected the message content is, i.e., the degree of uncertainty or possible variety about the message before it is sent. After the message is received, if the message is known with certainty, then the uncertainty or surprise is reduced to zero. That difference in level of surprise (based on probability) determines the information transmitted from sender to receiver.

Below is the math to make the calculation of information transmitted as well as related quantities called input information, output information, noise and equivocation. The reader interested in applications of these concepts to human systems is referred to Sheridan and Ferrell (1974)[206].

There is another definition of information, often used as a measure of complexity of something. In essence it is the length of a string of 1 or 0 symbols required to completely describe the thing. It is called *Kolmogorov complexity*, after the Russian mathematician A.N. Kolmogorov.[207]

How might information models apply to religious belief? One could apply a Shannon information metric to measure the surprise content of a sermon or religious tract or statement of belief relative to what one expected. If the outcome was exactly as expected there would be no information communicated, nothing learned. The message would have been completely predictable. I hope that is not the case with this book!

MATHEMATICS OF INFORMATION COMMUNICATION

Shannon's information metric is simply the logarithm base 2 of the inverse probability, assuming that after the message is sent its probability of expectation is 1 (log base 2 of one is zero, i.e., no uncertainty). Thus if one of two equally likely messages is sent and received (a one bit reduction of uncertainty) there is less surprise than if one of 16 equally likely messages is transmitted. (The latter is a four-bit reduction of uncertainty, where number of transmitted bits is $\log_2(16) = 4$ in this case.) Think of the game "20 questions" where the answer can be only yes or no. Assuming the questioner is good at framing questions so as to divide the possibilities into two equally likely categories, she can ask "Is the answer (one of the two categories)?" By successively narrowing categories the answer can always be obtained. The number of yes-no questions is the equivalent number of bits of information.

Actually transmitted information is but one of the useful measures of a message communication process. Information communication can be somewhat more complex, where information (variety) is lost or added in the process. Thus one can distinguish between *input information* (uncertainly before the message is sent), *equivocation* (the potential uncertainty reduction that is never transmitted, i.e., variety that is lost in process), *transmitted information* (intended variety that would be reduced were it not for *noise* (uncertainly or variety added in the sending process), and *output information* (the uncertainty that would still need to be brought to zero after the message is received, because of corruption along the way due to equivocation or noise). The diagram in Figure A16 shows these relations, where transmitted information equals input minus equivocation, or output information minus noise, the latter meaning output equals transmitted information plus noise.

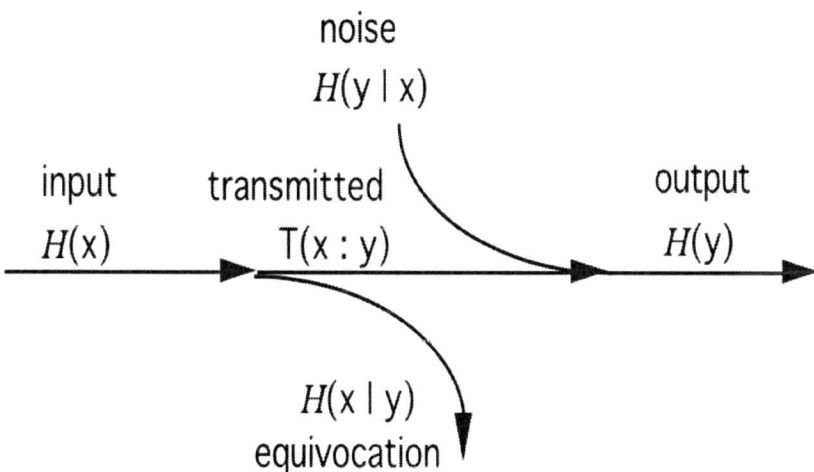

Figure A16. Information relationships.

192   Appendix

The following are the key definitions concerning the information communication process diagrammed in Figure A16, where subscript i refers to various inputs and subscript j refers to various outputs:

Input information
$H(x) = \text{Sum over } i \text{ of } p(x_i) \log_2[1/p(x_i)]$
Output information
$H(y) = \text{Sum over } j \text{ of } p(y_j) \log_2[1/p(y_j)]$
Noise
$H(y \mid x) = \text{Sum over } i \text{ and } j \text{ of } p(x_i, y_j) \log_2[1/p(y_j \mid x_i)]$
Equivocation
$H(x \mid y) = \text{Sum over } i \text{ and } j \text{ of } p(x_i, y_j) \log_2[1/p(x_i \mid y_j)]$
Transmitted information
$H(x:y) = \text{Sum over } i \text{ and } j \text{ of } p(x_i, y_j) \log_2[p(x_i \mid y_j)/p(x_i)]$

Information transmitted = input – equivocation = output – noise
$H(x:y) = H(x) - H(x \mid y) = H(y) - H(y \mid x)$
A more extensive treatment of the problem, along with discussion of how this can be applied to human behavior, is found in Sheridan and Ferrell[208].

INFORMATION VALUE

Information value is based on a particular decision problem explicated by Raiffa and Schlaifer (1961)[209] and later elaborated by Howard (1966)[210] and others. It refers to a situation where the future is currently known only in terms of the probabilities of its possible states, but where research yet to be done would (ideally) reveal the future state with certainty. It also assumes that for any given future state the payoff for any action decision is known.

The question is: what is it worth to commit now (still only knowing the probabilities of alternative future states) to do the research and so know the future state in time to make a wise response to it? So information value is defined as the difference in what one can gain by the ability to know the exact future state (based on perfect research), compared to having to commit to action ahead of time knowing only the probabilities of alternative future states. Being ready to make spot investments or policy changes as events unfold is big business, and is also the basis for spending money on research. Without such readiness (or "insider information" on what is about to happen) a decision must be made that is not likely to be optimal as the future unfolds. An example is provided below.

One application of this model is here and now: Reading this book takes time and effort, especially to overcome boredom that is understandably correlated with all this stuff about models. Is it worth your effort? Will whatever insights you would gain about future realities improve your ability to cope over and above not having those insights, and is the utility of that difference sufficient to overcome the time and effort costs of further reading? This of course is at issue for any educational effort, including that in religion or philosophy. Under what circumstances does education pay off? Presumably it does give a clearer picture of the future, narrowing down the probabilities through better understanding. Education researchers are struggling to attach probabilities and values (utilities) based on observable evidence gleaned from case histories.

MATHEMATICS OF INFORMATION VALUE

Consider a simplest numerical example: Let the future be X with probability 0.5, and Y also with probability 0.5. Assume that we know that if X occurs the payoff for action A is 4 and for action B is 7. If Y occurs the payoff for action A is 6 and for action B is 3. If one could adjust the action to fit the future X or Y event, whatever the research points to, one commits to action B for X (yielding 7) and action A for Y (yielding 6). So before the research is done (to say which of X or Y will occur) we know that the result of the research would yield if an expected payoff $(0.5 \times 7) + (0.5 \times 6) = 6.5$. But without the research one can only expect payoff for selecting $A = (0.5 \times 4) + (0.5 \times 6) = 5.0$, and payoff for selecting $B = (0.5 \times 7) + (0.5 \times 3) = 5.0$ also. Thus before even knowing whether X or Y will occur we know that it is worth $6.5 - 5.0 = 1.5$ to do the research, so 1.5 is the information value.

The following generalizes the information value problem: Assume future states x have known probabilities of occurrence. Let $V(u_j | x_i)$ be the gain or reward for taking action u_j when a future x is in state i, where V can be money or time or energy or any measure of value. Ideally a decision-maker would adjust u_j (select j) to maximize V for whatever x_i occurs, yielding $\max_j V(u_j | x_i)$. In this case the average reward over a set of x_i can be predicted to be

V_{avg} = Sum over i of $p(x_i)\{\max_j$ of $V(u_j | x_i)\}$.

If the decision-maker must select u_j ahead of time with no opportunity to select the ideal for whatever x_i that may occur, knowing x only as a probability density, $p(x_i)$, then the best a rational decision-maker can do is to select u_j (ahead of time) to be the greatest expected value in consideration of the whole density function $p(x_i)$. In this case the average reward over a set of x_i is

V'_{avg} = $\max_j$ of {Sum over i of $p(x_i) V(u_j | x_i)$}

Information value, then, is the difference between the gain in taking the best action given whatever specific x_i occurs, and the gain in taking the best action in ignorance of any specific x_i, i.e., knowing only $p(x_i)$. This difference is

$V^*_{avg} = V_{avg} - V'_{avg}$

There is usually a cost to get the information or to do the requisite research. That should also be subtracted from V^*.

If God existed the payoff for knowing that might be enormous, over and above the payoff for making decisions in the absence of that information. However we would get very different answers for information value depending on what probabilities and payoffs are assumed. The Pascal wager assumptions are one approach, but not the only one. A more mundane use of information value might apply to expenditure of funds and time to educate Americans on theistic and anti-theistic assumptions with regard to evidence and models—what this book is about.

Appendix   195

COMPETITIVE DECISIONS: GAME MODELS

Game models occur for decision-making in a competitive environment — sports, business, war, or personal competition. They model a situation where each competitor (normally two) must make a decision not knowing what the other competitor will decide, but where the outcome for each (same or different) depends on the combination of the two decisions. The game model is described mathematically in the next section below.

If both parties decide on war they will see battle. If one decides on war and the other decides on peace, the former will conquer the latter. If they both decide on peace, both sides will benefit, but not as much as a winner getting the spoils of war. What strategy should each play? One can imagine that the moves made in repeated plays depend very much on the outcome of immediate past plays and the trust or lack thereof that develops.

Religious institutions compete, and their competition can be modeled as a game. Religions always profess peace and love. But their history belies this ideology. If an expression of belief by one person or demographic group is not in accord with the dogma of some other one, that is often taken as a basis for hate and even murder. Examples abound, from the mediaeval crusades (blessed by Pope Urban II) to the current Sunni-Shiite wars, to the hate demonstrations of the Westboro Baptist Church against those who disagree with their idea of Biblical teachings, and so on. Both sides in the game have their ideals, and act according to what they perceive will net them the greatest payoff. But often they do not take into account how the payoffs change after repeated plays — due to changes in opinion by the players or forces from the outside.

On a happier front one can model how consistent acts of kindness by one party can over time convert some other party (say an urban gang member) from taking every selfish advantage to reciprocating with love and cooperation.

MATHEMATICS OF GAME MODELS

Consider the two payoff matrices of Figure A17, and assume that, instead of given X and Y probabilities, the X and Y contingencies are determined by an intelligent opponent. The first number in each cell is the corresponding payoff (or penalty) to one's self and the second number is the payoff to the opponent. Each player is trying to maximize his payoff. In these examples we mention only two interesting classes of game situations. Both examples are for *zero-sum* games, where one party's gain is the other party's loss. (This need not be the case; the numbers could take different values.)

Typically a *minimax* strategy is employed in zero-sum situations, choosing the option with the least downside risk, the most conservative strategy. For the matrix at left above one's own minimax is A, since it is the best of the worst outcomes, depending on what the opponent does. (If one's own decision is A the worst of –3 and –1 is –3. If one's own decision is B the worst of –4 and –5 is –5, so the best of –3 and –5 is –3, pointing to A as the minimax. The opponent's minimax is X; (the worst of 3 and 4 is 3 for X, the worst of 1 and 5 is 1 for Y, so the best of these is 3, pointing to X).

With these particular (arbitrarily chosen) numbers A happens to be a *dominating* own strategy, since A is better than B for both X and Y moves of the opponent. The opponent, however, has no dominating strategy, since, while X is better for him when you choose A, Y is better for him if you choose B.

A game situation with an interesting history and moral lessons in called *prisoner's dilemma*. This game, at the right in Figure A17,

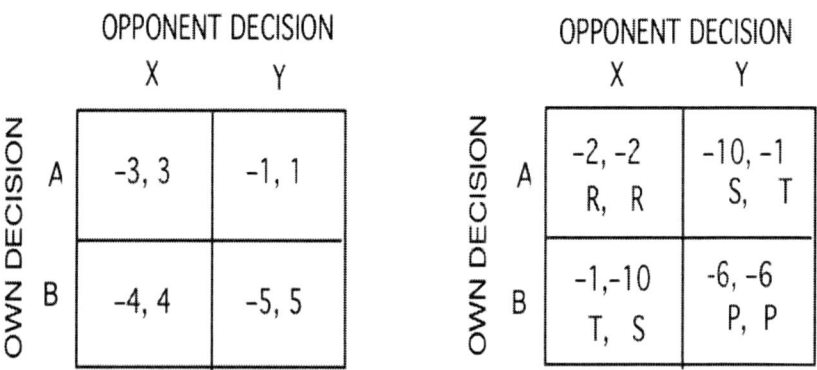

Figure A17. Dominating and non-dominating strategies (at left) and prisoner's dilemma (right).

is named for the dilemma a prisoner has in deciding whether to keep silent about his fellow prisoner (cooperate) or provide harmful testimony about him and gain a lighter sentence (defect). In the matrix at right, the upper left cell is mutual cooperation, both keeping quiet about the crime (both rewarded R with a light sentence). The lower right cell is mutual defection, testifying against the other (both punished with P). The other two cells are where one testifies T against the other and wins a light sentence, while the other tries to cooperate but becomes a sucker S with a heavy sentence. Thus if you defect (choose B) while your colleague tries to cooperate (chooses X) you lose little and he suffers great loss. If you both cooperate (A,X) you both suffer only a moderate loss, while mutual defection (B, Y) results in moderate punishment. Notice that both players have minimax and dominating strategies (B,Y) — mutual defection. Yet paradoxically this conservative minimax result (–6 for both players) is significantly worse than the more risky mutual cooperation result (-2 for both). A prisoner's dilemma situation is defined by the constraints T>R>P>S and R > 0.5 x (S+T).

This paradoxical situation is not unlike many situations in politics, business and personal life where each party's effort to get the advantage over another party can result in greater cost to both parties than if they cooperate to mutual advantage. But the temptation to defect is so rational! There seems to be a great moral lesson in this simple game, which many researchers have studied and writers have commented upon.[211] Religions teach love, which is risky, but mutual love pays off. Hate is often justified as more rational.

SIGNAL DETECTION

The signal detection model characterizes how people or electronic systems succeed or fail in detecting signals when the signals are corrupted by noise or are otherwise faint (near the threshold of seeing, hearing or touching). The "noise" can be visual, auditory or tactile, or can be some form of mental distraction. In computer or other complex systems noise can take various other forms of signal corruption. While this model was originally developed for radar applications, it has been a key model for analyzing and reporting experiments in human psychophysics of sensing and perception.[212]

The model includes a factor that accounts for whether one is conservative (avoiding risk) or liberal (accepting risk). One interesting result of many experiments is that people change their tendency to make detections (indicate what they "truly" see or hear) according to how much they are rewarded, even for very basic judgments like hearing a tone or seeing a light near the threshold of hearing or seeing. The mathematics to specify the decision criterion (whether to decide signal or noise) as a function of probabilities, rewards and costs, is given below.

The signal detection model might be applied to experimental investigations of the efficacy of prayer, or to reports of faith healing, so-called miracles or other types of religious experience. Or it might be applied to something mundane like how well the sermon came across given the bad acoustics in the church hall.

MATHEMATICS OF SIGNAL DETECTION

Consider a truth table such as that shown in Figure A18. This depicts a situation where the truth can take two forms, a signal mixed with noise (SN) or noise alone (N). The decision-maker must respond with a best guess as to what the signal was. As shown, there are rewards (R) and costs (C) depending on whether the judgment was correct or incorrect. There can be prior subjective expectations (probabilities) of SN or N occurring.

The model assumes that the decision-maker seeks to maximize the rewards minus costs, in light of what signal evidence e is experienced. The normative signal detection model assumes that the observer's brain conjures up two bell curves (Gaussian probability density functions) as shown in Figure A19. The two mental curves are assumed to be displaced from one another by distance d' along an evidence axis e, where the curves (vertical axis) indicate the probability (strength of evidence) for SN or N given a particular level of evidence e* that would balance rewards minus costs, and thus serves as a criterion. The distance d' is a function of the signal-to-noise ratio. TN means true negative and TP means true positive; MS means miss and FA means false alarm. So, according to the model, in consideration of both the perception and the relative re-

Appendix   199

| | TRUTH | |
	SN	N
DECISION SN	R TP true positive	C FA false alarm
N	C MS miss	R TN true negative

Figure A18. Payoff matrix for signal detection.

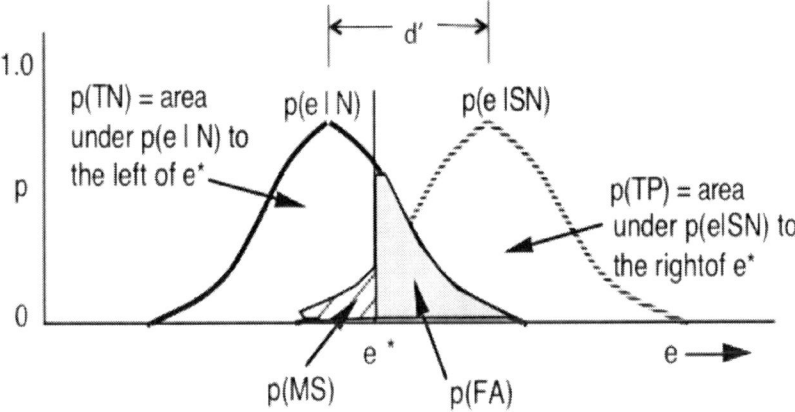

Figure A19. Probability densities for evidence in signal detection.

wards and costs, the decision-maker will decide SN if the perceived e is greater than c* and decide N if e is less than e*. Clearly if the reward for a true positive were very large and all other rewards and costs very small the decision-maker would have to move the criterion e* leftward, toward saying SN most of the time (fewer misses, but many more false alarms). The math specifies how the balance between prior probabilities, strength of evidence e in signal perception, rewards and costs is ideally made.

Appendix

The results of such an experiment can be summarized in what is called a relative operating characteristic, or ROC curve. It is a cross plot of probability of true positive on the Y axis and that of false alarm on the X axis. These are the only independent variables since p(TP) is 1-p(MS) and p(FA)= 1-p(TN). Normative mathematical analysis states that an ideal decision-maker will operate with a criterion at some point (e*) on one of the concave downward ROC curves shown in Figure A20. Ideally one would like to operate at the upper left corner, always (p=1) deciding SN when the signal was a true SN (true positive) and never (p=0) deciding SN when N is true (false alarm). Unfortunately that is not possible because of the overlap in the perception curves in Figure A19. Operating anywhere along the diagonal straight line indicates indifference (no signal discrimination ability, the two bell curves completely overlap. The ROC curves move toward the upper left as the signal-to-noise ratio (d') increases. So the decision-maker is stuck with operating along some one ROC curve. Where he puts the criterion e* along the ROC curve is a function of the tradeoff among the rewards and costs in consideration of prior probabilities.

Here is a mathematical derivation of the decision criterion (see Figures A19 and A20): Let p(SN) be the prior probability of a SN and p(N) be the prior probability of N. p(N) = 1–p(SN) since the two events are mutually exclusive and collectively exhaustive. To maximize expected reward one should decide <u>SN</u> when the expected

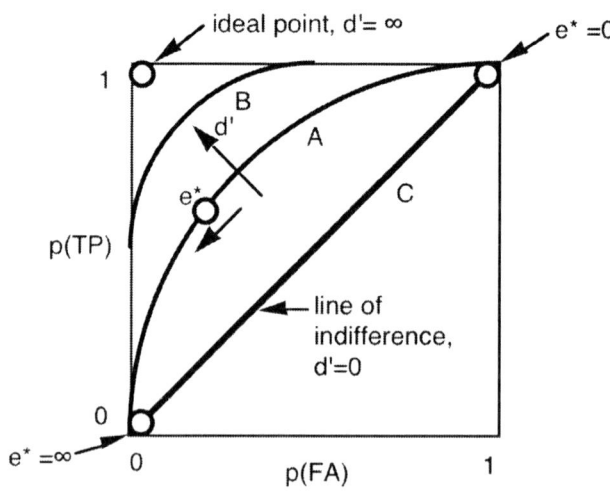

Figure A20. Relative operating characteristic (ROC).

Appendix

value of doing that is greater than the expected value of deciding $\underline{N}$. We use the underlined $\underline{SN}$ and $\underline{N}$ to represent the human decision and non-underlined SN or N to represent the actual condition, the truth. The expected value criterion is met when the expected value (EV) of deciding $\underline{SN}$ exceeds the expected value of deciding $\underline{N}$, namely $EV(\underline{SN}) > EV(\underline{N})$, or when

$$p(SN) R_{TP} + p(N) C_{FA} > p(N) R_{TN} + p(SN) C_{MS}$$

(which assumes the cost values C are negative numbers), or when

$$p(SN) (R_{TP} - C_{MS}) > p(N) (R_{TN} - C_{FA})$$

In a more useful form, decide $\underline{SN}$ when

$$\frac{p(SN)}{p(N)} > \frac{(R_{IN} - C_{FA})}{(R_{TP} - C_{MS})}$$

Now remember that p(SN) and p(N) are prior probabilities before one gets additional evidence e from whatever source. After that bit of new evidence we have better estimates, p(SN | e) and p(N | e). Thus the after-evidence criterion to optimally decide $\underline{SN}$ is when

$$\frac{p(SN \mid e)}{p(N \mid e)} > \frac{(R_{TN} - C_{FA})}{(R_{TP} - C_{MS})}$$

Since p(SN | e) p(e) = p(e | SN) p(SN) and p(N | e) p(e) = p(e | N) p(N) according to Bayes' rule, when the two expressions are set in a ratio the p(e) term drops out, and we have

$$\frac{p(SN \mid e)}{p(N \mid e)} = \frac{p(e \mid SN) \, p(SN)}{p(e \mid N) \, p(N)}$$

With substitution and rearrangement of terms with only p(e | SN) / p(c | N) on the left side of the inequality we get the decision criterion in a most useful form: decide $\underline{SN}$ if

Appendix

$$\frac{p(e \mid SN)}{p(e \mid N)} > \frac{p(N)}{p(SN)} \frac{(R_{IN} - C_{FA})}{(R_{TP} - C_{MS})}$$

The left side of the above equation) is a so-called *likelihood ratio* for any evidence e, while the right side is an *apriori* constant generally called *Beta* in signal detection theory. More on this topic is found in Green and Swets[213].

FEEDBACK CONTROL

Feedback control occurs where a sensed error in performing a task precipitates a corrective movement, much as the driver of a car continually senses error relative the course he/she wishes to follow and makes corrective movements on the steering wheel. Feedback control has a rich history. It has been apparent since antiquity that self-correction is inherent in nature. Especially since the Enlightenment we have discovered self-correcting mechanisms in animals that focus the eyes, move the limbs, etc.

Self-correcting mechanisms are now common in everyday life. Thermostats regulate the temperature in our home heating systems. Float valves control the water level on our toilets after we flush. Automatic elevators take us to the desired floor. Autopilots steer our ships and aircraft. Robots are set to perform all sorts of tasks in in our factories. A well-developed engineering theory of automatic control implemented in computers enables great sophistication in today's automation. The mathematics section below summarizes the basic ideas of the feedback control model.

Feedback control models have mostly been applied to physical systems, but more recently they have seen application to economics, marketing and management, where what is being controlled is something less tangible. One application that comes to mind in the religion domain is church leader control of behavior through persuasion and coercion — to get congregants to follow a particular course of belief or worship. Control actions can take the form of verbal motivation from the pulpit or through religious documents). Alternatively, the model might be used to analyze the effects of feedback from churchgoers to church leaders, to get them to stop some objectionable behavior.

MATHEMATICS OF FEEDBACK CONTROL

In the history of technology the flyball governor on a steam engine was designed to control the engine speed to a preset value. In Figure A21 at the left, as the engine shaft spins (1) centrifugal force forces the weight balls out (2) and the collar (3) slides up against a spring. The collar is connected to the steam valve (not shown) and this movement throttles down the steam, which slows the engine until there is a balance against the spring. Scottish physicist James Clerk Maxwell (1831-1879) is credited with the first mathematical analysis of the flyball governor in 1868. This is a typical case in the history of technology where a practical mechanism was developed by intuition and the theoretical analysis followed later.

The water level control in a toilet tank (at the right in the figure) offers another example of a very simple and historic feedback controller found in most homes. After the toilet is flushed by opening the main valve seat (1) the water in the tank exits into the bowl and the float ball goes down permitting intake water under pressure (2) to fill the tank. Meanwhile the increased pressure on the main valve seat (1) forces it to close, cutting off the flush. Eventually the level in the tank is high enough that the float ball lever (3) cuts off the water intake (4). In this way the water level is regulated to a particular depth in the tank.

Another form of automatic feedback control is the home thermostat that everyone is familiar with. If measured temperature is

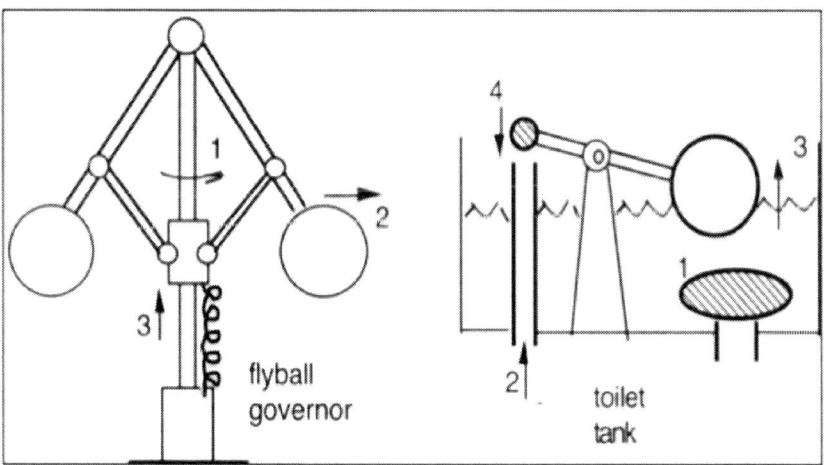

Figure A21. Flyball steam engine governor and toilet tank water level control.

lower than some adjusted reference setting a simple device turns the heat on, and if it is higher it turns the heat off. A several degree "dead-zone" is built into the mechanism to keep the thermostat from stuttering right at the set point.

By the time of World War II, the art of feedback control systems was well developed in the form of gun aiming systems, aerial bombardments systems, etc. Among the early contributors was Norbert Wiener (1894-1864)[214], who coined the term *cybernetics*, referring the control in both animal and machine.

The classical diagram for feedback control is shown in Figure A22, with the labels in this case relevant to a human operator as providing the control logic. The blocks represent input-output functional transformations of the circulating signals, and the circles with the Greek sigma represent simple summation (subtraction when there is a minus sign on the input).

Think of the driver of a car. If there is any error (e) or discrepancy between a desired reference state r (the direction where one intends to go) and the visually observed actual direction y, the human operator adjusts the steering wheel to make a correction u. The car (in general a controlled process) responds accordingly, heading in direction x, which is measured visually, indicating a new direction y. If there is any continuing error the driver makes another

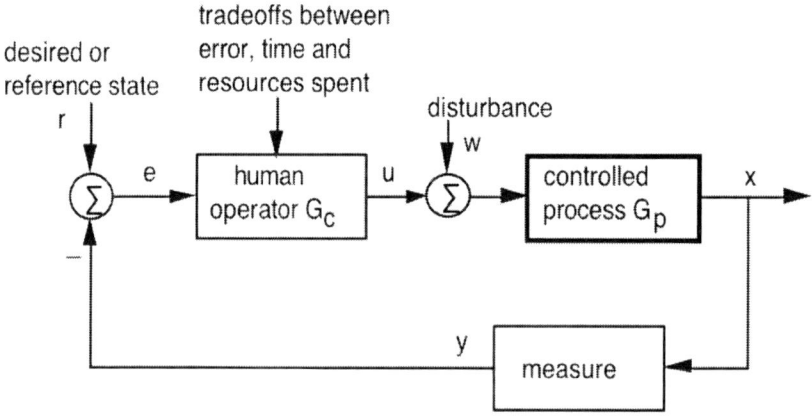

Figure A22. Classical feedback control diagram.

correction. Because of twists and turns of the road (a continually changing r) as well as wind disturbance (w), or imperfection in steering or vision, the driver must make further corrections, continually trying to drive the error to zero. This is how any feedback control system works.

In general, the controlled process is some complex dynamic electromechanical system best represented by a differential equation. The general control problem is to make system output state x match desired state r in spite of disturbances w (weather, electrical or mechanical interference, etc., depending on context). The objective is to get a smooth response to any changes in r, and prevent instability. A system faces instability when the time lags that occur around the control loop add up to one half cycle at any frequency (sine wave) component in the signals circulating around the loop. When this occurs, what is meant to be negative feedback, that is intended to reduce error, becomes positive feedback, so that the error increases, potentially without bound. Thus the controller, be it human or electromechanical, must compensate to prevent instability.

Feedback control by human operators has an interesting history. During the 1950s the government began a major effort to determine the equations characterizing human operators in the above type of system. The reason was that in high performance aircraft the pilot's control characteristic must be made compatible with the aircraft dynamic equation, since it is the whole loop that determines control performance and stability. What became evident was that within bounds the human tends to compensate for the controlled process dynamics so as to make the entire loop behave properly. This is well specified in mathematics (McRuer and Jex, 1967[215]; Sheridan and Ferrell, 1974 [216]), and was one of the first instances where engineers and psychologists came together to provide a sophisticated scientific solution to matching humans to machines. However as aviation technology developed, except for light private aircraft, there was less need for humans to be direct–in-the-loop controllers. All bigger aircraft now have autopilots, and the human pilots more and more control aircraft by supervising the autopilots.

Referring to Figure A22 the following algebraic calculations will make some essential points about how feedback control works. Each of the G terms is an input-output functional relationship

Appendix

(transfer function) couched in differential equations. G_c represents the *controller* (e.g., driver or pilot or mechanical controller) and G_p represents the controlled *process*, the car or airplane. The diagram in Figure A22 implies that

$$x = G_p(u+w) = G_p G_c(r-x) + G_p w$$

assuming y is a perfect measurement of x. Collecting terms and re-arranging gives the transfer functions for output x in terms of goal input r and disturbance w,

$$x = [(G_c G_p)/(1+G_c G_p)] r + [(G_p)/(1+G_c G_p)] w$$

In a simple case the controller G_c is an output/intput ratio or *gain coefficient* K and the controlled process G_p is an integrator (e.g., a fixed steering wheel input makes the car direction change at a fixed rate) represented algebraically as (1/s),

$$x = [(K/s)/(1+K/s)] r + [(1/s)/(1+K/s)] w$$

which, when numerators and denominators are multiplied by s yields

$$x = [K/(s+K)] r + [1/(s+K)] w$$

Note that as the controller gain K gets large the closed loop transfer function x/r approaches 1, (which means, for example, the car follows the twists and turns of the road perfectly), while x/w approaches zero, (which means the disturbance is completely cancelled).

Thus the simple solution to automation might seem to be negative feedback with as great a gain as possible, to be as sensitive as possible to any error between r(t) and x (t). Unfortunately it is not quite so easy, as gain that is too great will lead to instability. That requires further considerations that we will not detail further here.

The reader is referred to wikipedia.org/wiki/Control theory for a more extensive treatment of feedback control.

REFERENCES AND NOTES

[1] Hawking, S. and L. Mlodinow, *A Brief History of Time*, NY: Bantam Books, 2010.
[2] Foucault, M., *The Order of Things: An Archaeology of Human Sciences*, NY: Pantheon, 1980, P.77.
[3] Luhrmann, T.M., *New York Times* Op-Ed, 30 May, 2013.
[4] *Behavioral Modeling and Simulation from Individuals to Societies*, Washington DC, National Academy Press, 2008. See also *A Guide to Models in Governmental Planning and Operations*, Washington DC, US Environmental Protection Agency, 1974.
[5] Gruber, T., Toward Principles for the Design of Ontologies Used for Knowledge Sharing, *International Journal Human-Computer Studies,* Vol. 43, Issues 5-6, November 1995, p.907-928.
[6] Macionis, J. J., *Sociology 14th Edition*, Boston: Pearson, 2012. p. 11.
[7] Wikipedia.org/wiki/Max_Weber.
[8] *Routledge Encyclopedia of Philosophy*, NY: Routledge, 1998.
[9] Chomsky, N., *Syntactic Structures*, The Hague: de Guyter, 1957.
[10] Domjan, M. (Ed.), *The Principles of Learning and Behaviour*, Fifth Edition, Belmont, CA: Thomson/Wadsworth, 2002.
[11] *Stanford Encyclopedia of Philosophy*. Palo Alto, CA: Stanford University, 2014.
[12] Ibid.
[13] *www.aaas.org/spp/sfrl/projects/testim/mftest.htm.*
[14] Kuhn, T., *The Structure of Scientific Revolutions, Chicago, IL,* University of Chicago Press,1962.
[15] Examples are from Wikipedia, after looking up the respective categories.
[16] Cress, D., *Rene Descartes (Meditations)*, Indianapolis, IN: Hackett, 1979.
[17] *Stanford Encyclopedia of Philosophy*, Ibid.
[18] Christianson, G., University of Chicago Press, 1995.
[19] *Stanford Encyclopedia of Philosophy*, Ibid.
[21] Ibid.

[22] Nickerson, R.S., Confirmation bias: A ubiquitous phenomenon in many guises, *Review of General Psychology*, Vol.2, No.2, 175-220, 1998. See also Kahneman, D., *Thinking Fast and Slow*, NY: Farrar, Straus and Giroux, 2014.

[23] Campbell, J., *The Hero with a Thousand Faces*, Novato, CA: New World Library, 1949.

[24] Bridgeman, P., *The Logic of Modern Physics*. NY: MacMillan, 1927.

[25] Stevens, S.S., *Handbook of Experimental Psychology*, NY: John Wiley, 1951 (see chapter 1).

[26] Hawking, S., *The Theory of Everything*, Mumbai, India: Jaico Publishing House, 2006.

[27] Moray, N., Models of models of mental models, Chapter 22 in T. Sheridan and A. Van Lunteran (Eds.), *Perspectives on the Human Controller*, Mahwah NJ: Lawrence Erlbaum, 1997.

[28] Ockham's razor is attributed to his discussion in Book II of Ockham's *Commentary on the Sentences of Peter Lombard*, the latter being a Biblical commentary (1495).

[29] McRuer, D. and H. Jex, A review of quasi-linear pilot models, *Transactions on Human Factors in Electronics*, Institute of Electrical and Electronics Engineers, HFE8-3, 231-249, 1967.

[30] Anderson, J. R., *The Adaptive Character of Thought*, Hillsdale, NJ: Erlbaum, 1990.

[31] Salvucci, D. D., Modeling driver behavior in a cognitive architecture, *Human Factors, 48*, 2000, pp. 362-380.

[32] Wiener, N., *God and Golem Inc.: A Comment on Certain Points where Cybernetics Impinges on Religion*, Cambridge, MA: MIT Press, 1964.

[33] Wikipedia/ Arrow impossibility theorem.

[34] US Government, *Code of Federal Regulations*, Washington DC: US Government Printing Office.

[35] Zadeh, L., Fuzzy Sets, *Information and Control*, Vol. 8, pp. 338-353, 1965.

[36] *Journal of Trust Research*, NY: Routledge (Taylor and Francis).

[37] Lee, J. and K. See, Trust in automation: designing for appropriate reliance, *Human Factors*, 48(1), pp. 50-80, 2004.

[38] Hume, D., *Treatise on Human Nature* (1739).

[39] Shafer, G., *A Mathematical Theory of Evidence*. Princeton, NJ: Princeton University Press, 1976.

[40] See pp. 346-353 of Sheridan, T., *Telerobotics, Automation and Human Supervisory Control*, MIT Press, 1992 for a discussion on trust of computers.

[41] Dennett, D., *Breaking the Spell: Religion as a Natural Phenomenon*. NY: Penguin, 2006.

[42] Sheridan, T.B. and D. Zeltzer, Virtual Reality—Really? Ch. 6 in Agre,

P.E. and D. Schuler, *Reinventing Technology, Rediscovering Community*, Greenwich, CT: Ablex, 1997.

[43] Sheridan, T., *Telerobotics, Automation and Human Supervisory Control*, Cambridge, MA: MIT Press, 1992.

[44] The DaVinci surgical robot, by Intuitivesurgery.com, Sunnyvale, CA is now in many US hospitals.

[45] Sheridan, T. and D. Zeltzer, Ibid.

[46] This topic is discussed extensively in the MIT Press journal *Presence: Teleoperators and Virtual Environments*.

[47] The author and a colleague encountered an interesting situation when the Archdiocese of Boston complained that the proposed title of a scientific journal we were launching, "Presence" was too close to their own publication. We had to add a colon and the words "Teleoperators and Virtual Environments" to satisfy the church as well as copyright rules.

[48] Rene Descartes in *Stanford Encyclopedia of Philosophy*, Palo Alto, CA: Stanford University.

[49] Ibid.

[50] Zahorik, P. and R.L. Jenison, Presence as being-in-the-world, *Presence: Teleoperators and Virtual Environments*. 7, 1998, pp.78-89.

[51] Gibson, J.J.,*The Ecological Approach to Visual Perception,* Boston, MA: Houghton Mifflin, 1979.

[52] Jaynes, J. *The Origin of Consciousness in the Breakdown of the Bicameral Mind*, Boston, MA: Houghton Mifflin, 1976.

[53] Various scholars have documented the change from oral communication, especially including poetry, to communication in written form. Among them is Eric Havelock of Harvard. See his Preface to *Plato*, Cambridge, MA: Harvard University Press, 1963 and *The Muse Learns to Write,* New Haven, CT: Yale University Press, 1986.

[54] Sher, C., Neuroimaging, auditory hallucinations, and the bicameral mind, *Journal of Psychiatry and Neurology*, 25(3), pp. 239-240, May 2000.

[55] Kalman, R.E., A new approach to linear filtering and prediction problems, Journal of *Basic Engineering,* Trans. ASME 82D, pp. 33-45, 1960.

[56] Martin, M., *Atheism, Morality, and Meaning*, Buffalo, NY: Prometheus Books, 2002.

[57] see Deism.com in Wikipedia.

[58] Martin, M. ibid.

[59] Egyptian gods (From www.ancientegypt.co.uk).

[60] Ibid.

[61] www.pantheon.org/ *Encyclopedia Mythica.*

[62] Ibid.

[63] *Stanford Encyclopedia of Philosophy*, Ibid.

[64] Ibid.
[65] Ibid.
[66] Urban Dictionary.com.
[67] Aslan, R.. *Zealot: The Life and Times of Jesus of Nazareth,* NY: *Random House,* 2013.
[68] www.philosophyforum.net/Religion/Nicene Creed.
[69] *Stanford Encyclopedia of Philosophy,* Ibid.
[70] Ibid.
[71] Ibid.
[72] www.pbs.org/wgbh/pages/frontline/shows/religion/story/mark.
[74] *Stanford Encyclopedia of Philosophy,* Ibid.
[75] Ibid.
[75] www.pbs.org/empires/islam/profilesmuhammed.
[76] www.wikipedia.org/wiki/Shia–Sunni.
[77] http://gbgm-umc.org/umw/bible/crusades.stm.
[78] www.jewishvirtuallibrary.org/jsource/biography/Moses.html.
[79] *Stanford Encyclopedia of Philosophy,* Ibid.
[80] wikipedia.org/wiki/Isaac_Luria.
[81] wikipedia.org/wiki/Martin_Luther.
[82] wikipedia.org/wiki/John_Calvin.
[83] *Stanford Encyclopedia of Philosophy,* Ibid.
[84] wikipedia.org/wiki/Blaise_Pascal.
[85] Spinoza, B., in *Stanford Encyclopedia of Philosophy,* Palo Alto, CA: Stanford University.
[86] wikipedia.org/wiki/Isaac_Newton's_religious_views.
[87] Cosgrove, M.R., *The Review of Metaphysics,* Vol. 27, No. 3, A Commemorative Issue: Thomas Aquinas, 1224-1274, Mar., 1974, pp. 513-530.
[88] Locke, J. and B. Spinoza, in *Stanford Encyclopedia of Philosophy,* Ibid.
[89] More, H., Ibid.
[90] Hume, D., Ibid.
[91] Kant, I., *Critique of Pure Reason,* (1781) Nabu/Amazon Press, 2012.
[92] Diderot, D., *Internet Encyclopedia of Philosophy.*
[93] Fuerbach, L., in *Stanford Encyclopedia of Philosophy,* Ibid.
[95] Palmer, P., *The Question of God,* NY, Routledge, 2001. This book reviews the arguments in detail.
[96] Anselm, Ibid.
[97] wikipedia.org/wiki/Cosmological_argument.
[98] wikipedia.org/wiki/Samuel_Clarke.
[99] wikipedia.org/wiki/Watchmaker_analogy.
[100] Harris, S., The *Moral Landscape*: *How Science Can Determine Human Values,* NY: Free Press, 2010.
[101] Pascal, B., in *Stanford Encyclopedia of Philosophy,* Ibid.

102 wikipedia.org/wiki/Russell's teapot.
103 Wittgenstein, L., *Tractatus Logico-Philosophicus,* Internet Encyclopedia of Philosophy.
104 Craig, W., and Q. Smith, *Theism, Atheism and Big Bang Cosmology,* NY: Oxford Clarendon, 1993.
105 www.infidels.org/library/modern/gabe_czobel/swinburne.
106 Stenger,V.J., *God: The Failed Hypothesis,* Amherst, NY: Prometheus, 2007.
107 Plantinga , A., *Where the Conflict Really Lies,* NY: Oxford, 2012.
108 wikipedia.org/wiki/Occam's_razor.
109 wikipedia.org/wiki/Robert_McKenzie_Beverley.
110 LeCompte du Noug, P., *Human Destiny,* NY: Arden Library, 1981.
111 wikipedia.org/wiki/Paul_Tillich.
112 Reese, M., *Just Six Numbers: The Deep Forces that Shape the Universe.* NY: Basic Books, 2000.
113 Alexander, E., *Proof of Heaven.* NY: Simon and Schuster, 2012.
114 Dawkins, R., *The God Delusion,* Boston, MA: Houghton Mifflin, 2006.
115 Dennett, D., *Breaking the Spell,* NY: Penguin, 2006.
116 Harris, S., *The End of Faith,* NY: Norton, 2004.
117 Hitchens, C., *God is not Great,* NY: Hatchette Books, 2007.
118 Stenger, V.J., *The New Atheism,* Amherst NY: Prometheus, 2009.
119 Kurtz, P., *Science and Religion,* Amherst NY: Prometheus, 2003.
120 Martin, M., *Cambridge Companion to Atheism,* NY: Cambridge University Press, 2007.
121 Darwin, C., *The Origin of Species,* London: John Murray, 1859.
122 www.Wikipedia: Alfred_Russel_Wallace.
123 Dawkins, R., *The Blind Watchmaker: Why the Evidence of Evolution Reveals a Universe without Design.* NY: Norton, 1941.
124 Dawkins, R., *The God Delusion,* Boston, MA: Houghton Mifflin, 2006.
125 Plantinga , A., *Where the Conflict Really Lies,* NY: Oxford, 2012.
126 Collins, F., *The Language of God,* NY: Free Press, 2006.
127 Martin, M., *Morality and Meaning,* Amherst NY: Prometheus, 2002.
128 Harris, S., *The End of Faith,* NY: Norton, 2004.
129 Harris, S., *Letter to a Christian Nation,* NY: Knopf, 2006.
130 Harris, S., *The Moral Landscape,* NY: Free Press, 2010.
131 *Science, Evolution and Creationism,* Washington, DC: National Academy of Sciences Press, 2008.
132 Drummond, H., *Ascent of Man,* Lowell Lectures, 1894.
133 Dennett, D., *Breaking the Spell,* NY: Penguin, 2006.
134 Dawkins, R., *The Selfish Gene.* NY: Oxford, 1976.
135 nytimes.com/2006/02/19/books/review/wieseltier.
136 Wilson, E. O., *Consilience,* NY: Knopf, 1998.
137 Hamer, D., *The God Gene: How Faith is Hardwired into our Genes,* New York: Doubleday, 2004.

[138] wikipedia.org/wiki/God_gene.
[139] Stenger, V.J., *God the Failed Hypothesis,* Amherst NY: Prometheus, 2007.
[140] Stenger, V.J., *The New Atheism,* Amherst NY: Prometheus, 2009, p 12.
[141] wikipedia.org/wiki/Edwin_Hubble.
[142] *Scientific American* article on The Multiverse, January 2010.
[143] Ibid.
[144] Mazlish, B., *The Fourth Discontinuity.* New Haven, CT: Yale University Press, 1967.
[145] Gould, S. J., *The Rock of Ages,* NY: Norton, 1981.
[146] wikipedia.org/wiki/Non-overlapping_magisteria.
[147] Ibid.
[148] Shermer, M., *The Believing Brain*, NY: Henry Holt, 2011.
[149] Associated Press-GFK poll conducted by GfK Roper Public Affairs & Corporate Communications. Dec, 2011.
[150] www.americanreligionsurvey-aris.org.
[151] *www.huffingtonpost.com/2012/.../americans-believe-in-creationism.*
[152] *The Huffington Post* 06/26/2012.
[153] religion.blogs.cnn.com/.../pew-survey-doubt-of-god-growing-quickly.
[154] www. Pew Forum. Org.
[155] Mattei, D., *Religious Beliefs in Europe: Factors of Accelerated Decline.* See wikipedia.org/wiki/Religion_in_Europe.
[156] www.trincoll.edu/lingua/Ricci_Eurobarometer_2005.
[157] www.ipsos-mori.com: *Polls & Publications, Research Archive.*
[158] *Science and Creationism*: A View from the National Academy of *Sciences.* Washington, DC: National Academies Press, 1999.
[159] *Science, Evolution and Creationism,* Washington DC, National Academies Press, 2008.]
[160] www.britannica.com/EBchecked/topic/9356/agnosticism.
[161] *www.* commons.wikimedia.org/wiki/File:Theological_positions.png.
[162] *www.*oxforddictionaries.com/us/definition/american_english/Manichaeism.
[163] www.reasons.org/blogs/.../exploring-manichaeism-st.-augustine-part-3.
[164] Soskice, J.M., *Metaphor and Religious Language.* Oxford UK: Clarendon, 2002.
[165] Ibid.
[166] Ellwood, R., *The Politics of Myth: A Study of C.G. Jung, Mircea Eliade and Joseph Campbell,* Albany NY, State University of NY, 1999.
[167] Campbell, J., *Creative Mythology*, NY: Penguin, 1968.
[168] Harris, S. *The End of Faith,* NY: Norton, 2004, p.18
[169] Ibid.
[170] Gurvitz, I., *Deconstructing God*, self published, 2011.

[171] James, W., *Pragmatism*. Amherst, NY: Prometheus 1991.
[172] Dalai Lama, *Ethics for the New Millennium*, New York: Riverhead Books, 1999.
[173] Woodruff, P., *Reverence*, NY: Oxford, 2001.
[174] *Wall Street Journal*, September 9, 2009. See also worldnewstrust.com/richard-dawkins-and-karen-armstrong.
[175] wikipedia.org/wiki/A.J. Ayer.
[176] Soskice, J. M., Ibid.
[177] www.doncupitt.com/non-realism.
[178] *www.wikipedia.org/wiki/Meister_Eckhart*.
[179] Dennett, D., Ibid.
[180] www.books.google.com, *Medical Ethics*.
[181] Colombo, G.C.. An Analysis of Belief, *Downside Review*, Vol. 77, No. 247, Winter, 1958.
[182] Galton, F., C.S. Lewis, *Fortnightly Review*, vol. 12, pp. 125-35, 1872.
[183] C.S. Lewis, *The Efficacy of Prayer*, Google eBooks.
[184] www.Straight Dope.com.
[185] *Skeptical Enquirer*, July/August 2000.
[186] Martel, Y., *Life of Pi*, NY: Harcourt, 2001, page 72.
[187] healthland.time.com/2011/.../study-religious-folks-have-a-sunnier-outlook...Nov 11, 2011.
[188] http://scan.berkeley.edu/larry/.
[189] Silver, M., *A Plausible God: Secular Refllections on Liberal Jewish Theology*, NY: Fordham University Press, 2006.
[190] Harris, S., *The Moral Landscape*, NY: Free Press, 2010.
[191] Dennett, D., *Breaking the Spell*, NY: Penguin, 2006.
[192] Sheridan, T. and W. Ferrell, *Man-Machine Systems*. Cambridge, MA: MIT Press, 1974. See also Sheridan, T., *Humans and Automation*. NY: Wiley, 1992.
[193] Darwin, C. (1859), *On The Origin of Species*, chapter 14, p.503..ISBN-0-8014-1319-2.
[194] From Wikipedia / "verbal model".
[195] Kozinski, E. et al, Performance measurement system for training simulators. Report NP-2719. Atlanta, GA: Electric Power Research Institute, 1982.
[196] *wikipedia.org/wiki/Feynman_diagram*.
[197] Kosko. B., *Fuzzy Thinking*, NY: Hyperion, See Chapter 15 "Man and God".
[198] Ibid.
[199] Rasmussen, J., A.M. Pejtersen and L.P. Goodstein, *Cognitive Systems Engineering*, NY: Wiley, 1994.
[200] Hammond, K.R. and T.R. Stewart, (Eds).*The essential Brunswik: Beginnings, explications, applications.* NY: Oxford University Press. (2001).

[201] Kirlik, A., *Methods and Models of Human-Technology Interaction*, NY: Oxford, 2006.
[202] Bentham, J. and J.S. Mill, *The Utilitarians*. NY: Doubleday, 1986.
[203] Ibid.
[204] Sheridan, T. and W. Ferrell, Ibid.
[205] C. Shannon and W. Weaver, *The Mathematical Theory of Communication*, Champaign, IL, University of Illinois Press, 1998.
[206] Sheridan, T. and W. Ferrell, Ibid.
[207] Li, M. and P.M.B. Vitanyi, *An Introduction to Kolmogorov Complexity and Its Applications*, Medford, MA: Springer 2010.
[208] Sheridan, T. and W. Ferrell, Ibid. See also Sheridan, T., Ibid.
[209] Raiffa, H. and R. Shlaifer, *Applied Statistical Decision Theory*, Cambridge, MA: Harvard University School of Business Administration, 1961.
[210] Howard, R., Information value theory. *IEEE Transactions on System Science and Cybernetics*, SSC-2, 22-26.
[211] www.prisoners-dilemma.com.
[212] Green, D. and J. Swets, *Signal Detection Theory amd Psychophysics*, NY: Wiley, 1966.
[213] Ibid
[214] Wiener, N., *Cybernetcs, the Control and Communication in the Animal and the Machine*. Cambridge, MA: MIT Press, 1948.
[215] McRuer, D.T., and H.R. Jex, A review of quasi-linear pilot models, *Ibid*.
[216] Sheridan, T. and W. Ferrell, Ibid.

BIBLIOGRAPHY

Angeles, Peter. *Critiques of God*. Amherst NY: Prometheus, 1997.
Armstrong, Karen. *The Great Transformation*. NY: Knopf, 2006.
Armstrong, Karen. *A History of God*. NY: Random House, 1993.
Armstrong, Karen. *The Case for God*. NY: Knopf, 2009.
Armstrong, Karen. *The Battle for God*. NY: Ballantine, 2000.
Barth, Karl. *God Here and Now*. London: Routledge, 1964.
Bering, Jesse. *The Belief Instinct*. NY: Norton, 2011.
Bilington, Ray. *Religion without God*. Oxford: Routledge, 2002.
Cahn, Steven and David Shatz. *Questions about God*. NY: Oxford, 2002.
Campbell, Joseph. *Creative Mythology*. NY: Penguin, 1968.
Campbell, Joseph. *The Inner Reaches of Outer Space*. Novato, CA: New World Library, 2001.
Campbell, Joseph. *The Power of Myth*. NY: Random House, 1991.
Campbell, Joseph. *Thou Art That*. Novato, CA: New World Library, 2001.
Cox, Harvey. *The Future of Faith*. NY: Harper Collins, 2009.
Cox, Harvey. *When Jesus Came to Harvard*. NY: Houghton Mifflin, 2004.
Craig, William and Chad Meister. *God is Great, God is Good*. Downers Grove IL: Intervarsity Press, 2009.
Craig, William and Q. Smith. *Theism, Atheism and Big Bang Cosmology*. Oxford UK: Clarendon, 1993.
Comte-Sponville, Andre. *The Little Book of Atheist Spirituality*. NY: Viking, 2006.
Collins, Francis. *The Language of God*. NY: Free Press, 2006.
Cunningham, George. *Decoding the Language of God*. NY: Prometheus, 2010.
Dawkins, Richard. *The God Delusion*. Boston MA: Houghton Mifflin, 2006.
Dembski, William (Ed.). *Mere Creation*. Downers Grove IL: Intervarsity Press, 1998.
Dennett, Daniel. *Breaking the Spell*. NY: Penguin, 2006.
Ellwood, Robert. *The Politics of Myth*. Albany NY: State University of NY Press, 1999.

Fromm, Erich. *Escape from Freedom*. NY: Holt, 1941.
Fromm, Erich. *Man for Himself*. NY: Holt, 1990.
Flew, Anthony. *There is a God*. NY: Harper Collins, 2007.
Gibson, Arthur. God and the Universe. NY: Routledge, 2000.
Gould, Steven Jay. *The Mismeasure of Man*. NY: Norton, 1981.
Greenblatt, Stephen. *The Swerve*. NY: Norton, 2011.
Greene, Brian. *Fabric of the Cosmos*. NY: Knopf, 2004.
Greene, Garrett. *Imagining God*. San Francisco: Harper and Row, 1989.
Gurvitz, Ian. *Deconstructing God*. Self published, 2011.
Hagerty, Barbara. *Fingerprints of God*. NY: Penguin, 2009.
Hamer, Dean. *The God Gene*. NY: Random House, 2005.
Harris, Sam. *Free Will*. NY: Simon and Schuster, 2012.
Harris, Sam. *Letter to a Christian Nation*. NY: Knopf, 2006.
Harris, Sam. *The End of Faith*. NY: Norton, 2004.
Harris, Sam. *The Moral Landscape*. NY: Free Press, 2010.
Hart, George. *A Dictionary of Egyptian Gods and Goddesses*. London: Routledge, 1986.
Hawkins, Stephen and L. Mlodinow. *The Grand Design*. NY: Random House, 2010.
Hedges, Chris. *I Don't Believe in Atheists*. NY: Free Press, 2008.
Hitchens, Christopher. *God is Not Great*. NY: Hatchette Books, 2007.
Hitchens, Christopher. *The Portable Atheist*. Cambridge, MA: DaCapo Press, 2007.
Kahneman, D. *Thinking Fast and Slow*. NY: Farrar, Straus and Giroux, 2014.
Kardong, Kenneth. *Beyond God*. Amherst, NY: Humanity Books, 2010.
Kuhn, Thomas. *The Structure of Scientific Revolutions*. Chicago: University of Chicago Press, 2nd edition, 1970.
Kurtz, Paul. *Science and Religion*. Amherst NY: Prometheus, 2003.
Lewis, Clive S. *The Question of God*. NY: Free Press, 2002.
Luhrmann, T.M. *When God Talks Back*. NY: Random House, 2012.
Martin, Michael. *Cambridge Companion to Atheism*. Cambridge University Press, 2007.
Martin, Michael. *Morality and Meaning*. Amhest NY: Prometheus, 2002.
Plantinga , Alvin. *Where the Conflict Really Lies*. NY: Oxford, 2012.
Popper, Karl. *The Logic of Scientific Discovery*. London: Routledge, 1934.
Preus, J. Samuel. *Explaining Religion*, New Haven: Yale University Press, 1987.
Proctor, Robert and E.J. Capaldi (Eds.). *Psychology of Science, Implicit and Explicit Reasoning*. NY: Oxford, 2012.
Raymo, Chet. *Skeptics and True Believers*. NY: Walker, 1998.
Robinson, John A.T.. *Honest to God*. Louisville, KY: Westminster John Knox Press, 2002.

Russell, Bertrand. *Why I am Not a Christian*. NY: Simon and Schuster, 1957.
Shermer, Michael. *How We Believe*. NY: Freeman, 1999.
Shermer, Michael. *The Believing Brain*. NY: Holt, 2009.
Silver, Mitchell. *A Plausible God: Secular Reflections on Liberal Jewish Theology*. Fordham University Press, 2006.
Soskice, Janet. *Metaphor and Religious Language*. London: Oxford, 2002
Stenger, Victor. *The New Atheism*. Amherst NY: Prometheus, 2009.
Stenger, Victor. *God the Failed Hypothesis*. Amherst NY: Prometheus, 2007.
Swinburne, Richard. *Epistemic Justification*. London: Oxford, 2001.
Weiner, Norbert. *God and Golem Incorporated*. Cambridge, MA: MIT Press, 1964.
Wilbur, Kenneth. *The Marriage of Sense and Soul*. NY: Random House, 1998.
Wilson, Edward O. *Consilience*. NY: Knopf, 1998.
Woodruff, Paul. *Reverence*. NY: Oxford, 2001.
Wright, Robert. *The Evolution of God*. NY: Little Brown, 2009.

INDEX

abduction 21
ACT-R cognition model 42
advocacy 25
agnostic 113, 114, 115, 116
analogy 62
Anselm of Canterbury 25, 82, 83, 85, 86, 90
anthropic principle 95
applicability to observables 32
Aquinas, Thomas 11, 24, 81, 83, 86, 128
argument from design 86
argument from morality 87
argument from mystical experience 87
Aristarchus 102
Aristotle 24, 73, 78, 86
Armstrong, Karen 95, 125, 132, 133
Arrow, Kenneth 43
Ashby, Ross 23
Ashkenazi, Isaac Luria 82
Augustine of Hippo 80, 81, 115, 126
Ayer, Alfred J. 133

backward chaining tree 168, 169
Bacon, Francis 18
Bahai 145, 148, 153
Bayes' theorem 50, 173, 174, 175, 206

Belatthaputta, Sanjaya 114
belief models 6, 47, 50
belief network 141
beliefs about God 71
believing in believing 147
Bentham, Jeremy 186
Berkeley, George 3, 148
Berra, Yogi 15
Beverley, Robert MacKenzie 93
Bhagavad Gita 63
bias 19, 25, 40
Bible 118
bicameral 48, 60, 62, 63, 64
big bang 95, 102, 103
Blind Watchmaker 97
Bohr, Niels 159
Brunswik, Egon 182
Buddha (Siddhartha Gautama) 79
Buddhism 145

Calvin, John 82
Campbell, Joseph 26, 117, 151
changing culture 148
Chomsky, Noam 16
Christianity 80, 83, 84, 115, 126, 144, 145, 147
church-goers 147
Clark, Samuel 86
Collins, Francis 98
competitive decisions 200

Comte, Auguste 11, 153
conciseness 37, 136
conditioned stimulus 16
confirmation bias 25, 174
Confucius 123, 124
connotation 1, 2, 6, 9, 12, 13, 27, 29, 31, 134, 136, 151
consciousness 24, 60, 107, 132
control engineering 64, 68
Copernicus 105
cosmological argument 86
cosmological parameters 95
Council for Secular Humanism 154
Craig, William Lane 91
creationism 99, 113, 114
Cupitt, Don 133, 149
cybernetics 23, 42, 204

Dalai Lama 121
Darwin, Charles 23, 93, 97, 98, 105, 126, 128, 161
Dawkins, Richard 96, 97, 100, 107, 125, 128, 129, 132
decision under certainty 189, 190
decision under uncertainty 192, 193
deduction 21
definition of a model 28, 151
demographics 111
Demosthenes 47
Dennett, Daniel 52, 64, 96, 100, 131, 139, 140, 147, 153
denotation 1, 2, 3, 5, 9, 10, 12, 28, 29, 30, 37, 122, 134, 136, 137, 151, 156
Descartes, Rene 22, 24, 59, 82, 83
descriptive model 44
deterministic model 45
Diana, Princess of Wales 123
Diderot, Denis 84
difficulties of discourse 72

dimensionality 33, 135
Diogenes Laertius 71
disproving God's existence 88
DNA evidence 107
Doppler effect 103
doubt 22
Drummond, Henry 99
dynamic model 45

Eckhart, Meister 128
Egyptian religious practice 74, 75
Einstein, Albert 15, 18, 95, 103
epistemology 12, 85
estimation theory 64, 65
Euclid 102
Eurobarometer poll 113
evidence 23, 92, 173, 174
evidentialism 121
evolution 15, 16, 23, 43, 93, 97, 98, 99, 105, 107, 113, 114, 125, 129, 130, 131, 156, 157, 159, 161
examples of objective models 159
expansion of space 95, 103

faith 51
feedback control 202, 203
fifth discontinuity 104
Firth, Roderick 98
forward chaining tree 167, 169
Freud, Sigmund 105, 109
Fuller, R. Buckminster 109, 132
fuzzy logic 46, 170, 172

Gallup poll 111
Galton, Francis 143
game models 200
Genesis 127, 128, 149, 166
Gilgamesh Epic 64
gnostic 114
God and Golem, Inc. 42
God-of-the-gaps 99, 151
Gould, Stephen Jay 106, 107, 114

graphical model 162
Greek gods 29, 49, 62, 73, 76, 77, 79, 81, 123, 204
ground of being 94
Gurvitz, Ian 118

Hamer, Dean 101
Harris, Sam 87, 96, 99, 101, 107, 118, 153
Hawking, Stephen 2
health 146
Hebrew Bible 61, 62, 64, 78, 87, 115
Heidegger, Martin 59, 60, 69
Heisenberg, Werner 12
Hindu gods 78, 79, 112
Hitchins, Christopher 96
Homer 61
Hubble telescope 23, 103
human cognition 30, 179
human operator 41, 55, 57, 204, 205
human perception 181
Hume, David 49, 83, 86
Huxley, Thomas 15, 114, 154

image of God 149
immersion 54, 56, 58
induction 21
infinity 135, 137, 156
information communication 194, 195
information value 197, 198
internal model 66, 67
interval scale 35, 36
Ipsos Research Institute 113
Islam 72, 80, 81, 145, 147

Jaynes, Julian 60, 61, 62, 63, 64, 87, 137
Jesus 2, 78, 79, 80, 81, 96, 107, 122, 133, 145, 147
Jung, Carl Gustav 71

Kalman, Rudolf 65
Kanizsa square 170, 171
Kant, Immanuel 83, 84, 94
Kierkegaard, Soren 142
Kirlik, Alex 186
knowledge 2, 8, 10, 11, 12, 15, 16, 19, 42, 43, 46, 60, 71, 73, 81, 84, 85, 120, 128, 134, 135, 138, 151, 175, 181, 194
knowledge-based behavior 181
Kolmogorov complexity 195
Kosco, Bart 170
Kuhn, Thomas 19
Kurtz, Paul 96

ladder of beliefs 7
language games 13
Laplace, Pierre Simon 98, 136
level of cognition 180
lens model 182
Leviticus 118
Lewis, C.S. 143, 144
li 123, 124
Life of Pi 145
likelihood ratio 179, 202
logic diagram 167
logical reasoning 20
logos 73, 127, 156
Luria, Isaac 82, 128
Luther, Martin 82

Maimonides 81, 128
Manichaeism 115
map model 162
Martel, Yann 145
Martin, Michael 59, 73, 82, 95, 96, 98
Maxwell, James Clerk 203
Mazlish, Bruce 105
McRuer-Jex control model 41, 205
mental model 17, 19, 20, 22, 25, 36, 38, 41, 43, 55, 59, 66, 67, 136, 137, 148

metaphor 1, 5, 12, 13, 26, 27, 29, 32, 61, 116, 117, 119, 121, 122, 134, 151, 156, 157, 158, 170, 171, 182
metaphysics 24
metricity 34, 135
Mill, John Stuart 186
mind-body dilemma 90
mind-body dualism 58, 91
minimax 194, 201 202
model attributes 31, 134
modeling belief acquisition 141
Moore, G.E. 49
morality 98
More, Henry 83
Muhammad 2, 80, 81
multiverse 95, 102, 104
mystery 13, 77, 81, 83, 117, 123, 145, 151, 156, 158
myth 1, 5, 6, 9, 27, 28, 75, 83, 100, 116, 117, 127, 128, 133, 134
mythos 127, 133, 156

National Academy of Sciences 99, 113, 114
nature of God 1, 5, 6, 73, 81, 134, 139
near-death experience 96
negative atheism 73
new atheism 101, 125
Newton, Isaac 36, 38, 63, 83, 126
Nickerson, Raymond 25
Nietzsche, Freidrich Wilhelm 71, 84, 116
nominal scale 35
normative model 44

objective model 8, 159
objectivity 26
observation process 68
Ockham, William of 37, 92
ontology 10, 85
operant conditioning 16

Oracle of Delphi 63
ordinal scale 35
Origin of Species 97, 161

Paley, William 87, 97, 126, 129
Pareto frontier 190, 191, 192
Pascal, Blaise 82, 88, 152, 192, 193, 199
Pavlovian conditioning 16
payoff matrix 193, 194
Peirce, Charles Sanders 22, 49, 159, 160
Persian gods 77, 78
Pew Research Center 111, 112
philosophical perspective 11
physicalism 90
Plantinga, Alvin 92, 97, 98
Plato 79, 123
plausible God 150
poetry 63
Polkinghorne, John 101
Popper, Karl 15, 19, 160
positive atheism 73
pragmatism 121
preference intransitivity 43
prescriptive model 44
presence 58
private knowledge 22
probabilistic model 45
Protagorus 114 123
public knowledge 22
Pythagorus 78

Quran 80, 109, 126

Ra, the sun god 75, 76
ratio scale 34, 35, 36
recent theistic arguments 90
redefining God 149
Rees, Martin 95
religious language 116, 136
religious practice 3, 32, 58, 75, 100, 139, 140, 141, 143, 187

Index   223

religious traditions 80
reverence 123, 124, 157
robustness 36, 135, 141
ROC curve 205
Roman gods 76, 77, 78, 83, 85, 115, 148
rule-based behavior 181
Russell, Bertrand 88, 89

Santa Claus 119, 120, 121, 133
schematic diagram 162
schizophrenia 63
Scientific American 104
scientific method 17, 18
scientific modeling 2, 3, 5, 10, 138, 155
second law of thermodynamics 93
secular church 152
semiotics 28, 29
Shannon, Claude 194, 195
Shermer, Michael 109, 110
Shia 80, 81
signal detection 202, 203
Silver, Mitchell 150, 151
simile 26
simulation 9, 54, 56, 58
Sistine Chapel 62, 166
Skeptical Inquirer 140, 144
skepticism 4, 22, 74, 83, 119, 124
Skeptics Society 109
Sloan, Richard 140
social penetration 36, 135, 140
Socrates 78, 79, 123
Soskice, Janet 116
Spinoza, Baruch 82, 150
spirituality 32, 73, 101, 121, 122, 123
Stark, Lawrence 148
static model 45
statistical inference 173
Stenger, Victor 91, 96, 101
Stevens, S.S. 34

Stockton, Eric 144
subjective model 1, 8, 12, 13, 43, 50, 56, 59, 62, 82, 116, 140, 142, 156, 157, 174, 186, 189, 192, 203
Sunni 81
supernatural 1, 58, 86, 99, 100, 110, 131, 150, 151, 152, 156, 157, 158
supply-demand curves 165
suppression of disbelief 58
Supreme Court 26
Swinburne, Richard 91, 92, 93, 135

taxonomy of model attributes 31, 39
telemanipulation 55, 56, 57
teleology 24
theos 73
Thucidides 123
Tilich, Paul 94
transmitted information 196
Trojan Wars 62
trust 51
Trust Research 48

unconditioned stimulus 16
Unitarian 97, 145, 153
unk-unk 34, 50
utility 186, 187

Vedic Hinduism 114
verbal model 160
virtual reality 52, 53
Von-Neumann axiom 187

Wall Street Journal 125, 132
Wallace, Alfred Russel 97
Weber, Max 12
Whitehead, Alfred North 47
Wiener, Norbert 22, 42, 204
Wieseltier, Leon 100
Wilson, Edward O. 100
Wittgenstein, Ludwig 13, 90
Woodruff, Paul 123, 124, 151

Yahweh 62, 63, 78, 118
Yankelovich survey 111

Zoroaster 77, 78

CPSIA information can be obtained at www.ICGtesting.com
Printed in the USA
BVOW04s1334071014

369759BV00002B/7/P